Case Studies in Effective Schools Research

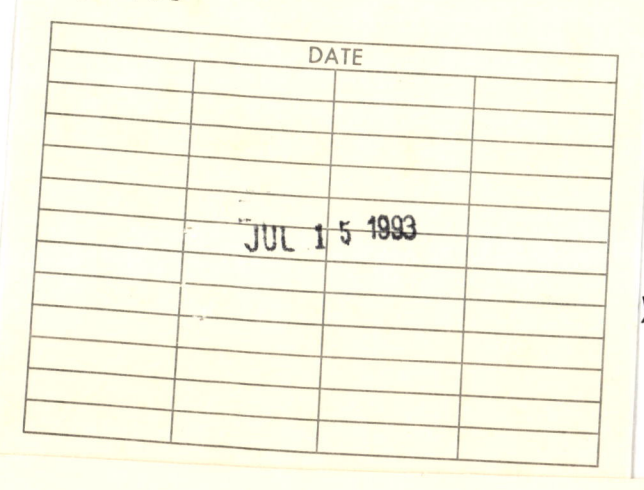

...ioners in School Districts
...emented Successfully
...ent Programs based on
...Schools Research

...Taylor, Ph.D., Editor

...y Lawrence W. Lezotte, Ph.D.

/HUNT PUBLISHING COMPANY
...ulevard P.O. Box 539 Dubuque, Iowa 52004-0539

Copyright © 1990 by National Center for Effective Schools Research
and Development, a unit of Wisconsin Center for Education Research
at the University of Wisconsin–Madison

Library of Congress: 90–60010

ISBN 0–8403–5804–0

All rights reserved. No part of this publication may be reproduced,
stored in a retrieval system, or transmitted, in any form or by any
means, electronic, mechanical, photocopying, recording, or otherwise,
without the prior written permission of the copyright owner.

Printed in the United States of America
10 9 8 7 6 5 4 3 2 1

Contents

Acknowledgments, **v**
Definition of Effective Schools Model or Process, **vii**

Introduction, **1**
Barbara O. Taylor

The Language of Practice, **9**
Barbara O. Taylor

Reaching for Excellence and Equity in Prince George's County Public Schools, **13**
John A. Murphy, Louise F. Waynant

A Case for Equity and Quality: How One Team Is Making it Happen in Norfolk, VA, **39**
Dr. Gene R. Carter, Ann B. Madison, Eddie D. Hall, Dr. Thomas B. Lockamy

Alma Public Schools, **51**
William R. McKinstry, George R. Gibbs

"Every Anoka-Hennepin Student Will Learn", **63**
Claudia Risnes

School Effectiveness at the Secondary Level: The Glendale Union Model, **75**
Marc S. Becker, Janet N. Barry

School Improvement in Geary County Schools, **89**
Dr. Max O. Heim, Dr. David Flowers, Patricia Anderson

The Effective Schools Program in the East Detroit Public Schools, **99**
Joan Buffone, Emil Ciccoretti

Mishawaka Moves to Improve, **109**
R. Steven Mills

San Pasqual Union School District: Working Towards School Effectiveness, **127**
Janet Chrispeels, Mary Beall

Effective Schools Do Make a Difference in Jackson, Mississippi, **143**
Carol R. Adams, Henriette L. Allen, Robert N. Fortenberry

Implementing Effective Schools Research in Spencerport, New York, **155**
Robert E. Sudlow

Middle Cities in Michigan, **183**
Lynn Benore

Lessons Learned by Lawrence W. Lezotte, **195**

Glossary, **201**
Appendices, **207**

Acknowledgments

The National Center wishes to thank Sally B. Pratt, Ph.D., for her help in editing the case studies, and Lucille Lewsader, who typed the manuscripts during the editing process. The collection of case studies, *Introduction,* and *Lessons Learned* were read and reviewed by Daniel U. Levine, professor of educational administration, Center for the Study of Metropolitan Problems in Education, School of Education, University of Missouri, Kansas City; and Kent D. Peterson, associate professor of educational administration, School of Education, University of Wisconsin—Madison, and director, The National Center for Effective Schools Research and Development. They report that the case studies reflect their own extensive experience as consultants and researchers in the public schools across the country. They believe the publication can be used well as a supplementary resource for graduate teacher education, and for graduate courses in Educational Administration, or Leadership courses of instruction.

We also wish to acknowledge the good work of Beverly A. Bancroft, Ph.D., formerly associate director of the National Center for Effective Schools (1986–88) who conceptualized this investigation and created the original case study questionnaire, which was sent to the districts in the spring of 1988.

Barbara O. Taylor, Ph.D.

Definition of the Effective Schools^{SM} Model or Process

The Effective Schools model or process is a framework for school reform which is based on evolving research from both empirical investigations and case studies of schools across the country that have been successful in teaching the intended curriculum of basic skills to *all* their students. (Basic skills may include comprehensive reading skills, oral and written communication skills, computing skills, problem solving, higher order thinking skills, and social skills).

In this model the individual school is viewed as the targeted unit of improvement. Each school, through a faculty-administrator team-planning approach, utilizes the concepts and elements of the Effective Schools process to develop and implement a long-range improvement plan. In addition, the model promotes district-wide restructuring for improvement, and to become effective requires that the district be committed to the program for at least three to five years.

Two criteria for measuring effectiveness have evolved: quality and equity. Having a quality standard assures that the level of achievement in a school is high. Having an equity standard assures that the high achievement does not vary significantly across the subsets of the school's student population. Not only are these standards critical to the definition of "Effective Schools," they are fundamental when planning and implementing the Effective Schools process for school improvement.

Two elements are key to the success of the model. First, the school must develop and state a school mission. Second, the school must be willing to accept the "Effective Schools" program as a *comprehensive* plan. Developing a school improvement plan on a piecemeal basis and focusing on only two or three of the characteristics ("correlates") which define an Effective School destroys the cohesiveness of the program and decreases the chance for significant and lasting improvement at the school.

The five or seven characteristics of Effective Schools (see "correlates" in the Glossary) which define the educational programs at these schools tend to work together to foster both the organizational dynamics and the context of shared values which promote a school climate or culture conducive to teaching for learning for all. The model is driven by shared decision-making at the school site, which is based largely on data collected by school-wide and district-wide monitoring systems.

The National Center for Effective Schools Research and Development uses the capitalized phrases "Effective Schools Research" and "Effective Schools model or process" to denote the comprehensive model espoused by the National Center and founded upon the research literature. "Effective Schools" is a service mark (SM) of the National Center for Effective Schools Research & Development.

Introduction

Barbara O. Taylor, Ph.D.

The National Center for Effective Schools Research and Development takes pride in presenting these case studies of school improvement. Each report stands on its own and is written in the language of the authors as they report their story of school improvement based on the Effective Schools Research model. The editors endeavored to keep each district's rationale intact, trying hard not to change the words which capture the culture, traditions, and values that undergird the educational program of each district. These are, indeed, case studies in the practitioner's voice. These case studies carry good news about the difficult but rewarding work that is associated with school improvement.

For over a decade the people involved in school improvement programs in these districts have been experimenting with "what works." In some school systems, long before the more popular buzz words of "renewal," "empowerment," "restructuring," and "shared decision-making" were known, these educators were setting up **systems** that could **renew** schools, designing new organizational arrangements and reporting **structures** which would **empower** teachers by supporting them in their work with students, and participating in decision-making procedures which were collaborative and **shared.**

The language of the Effective Schools process for school improvement is now commonly used wherever school reform or renewal is attempted: stated and clear mission, instructional leadership, a school climate conducive for learning, high expectations for students and staff, student performance outcome measures, data-driven improvement planning. These phrases began with Effective Schools Research and are now the common language of school improvement today. Even **disaggregation of data** is now being legislated by some states in an effort to help districts to determine the distribution of subgroups of students' achievement scores, by socioeconomic status, race, ethnicity, and gender. The word **disaggregation** was used by early Effective Schools researchers to describe the process by which student outcomes, usually normed scores on standardized achievement tests, were broken into student subgroups and compared.

Of course, many school improvement components were developed outside of Effective Schools Research: time-on-task considerations, active-learning time, and academic press were all names of concepts formed to identify pedagogical concerns in the classroom having to do with student achievement. The synthesis of research on teaching and learning behaviors proposed in the principles of Madeline Hunter, Cooperative Learning, Teacher Expectations and Student Achievement processes, and Mastery Learning are all examples of programs which promote teacher effectiveness. These concepts continue to be developed simultaneously as Effective Schools Research evolves.

Effective schools and effective teaching are complementary literatures in the field, and they intersect at classroom management concepts. Although the instructional program is the primary *target* of Effective Schools Research (ESR) efforts, interesting questions *focus* on school and district policies, programs, procedures, and practices and their relationship to student performance. Effective Schools Research attempts to create a framework for addressing organizational, instructional, and institutional issues which are encountered as practitioners address and implement school improvement based *both* on quality in educational program and equity for all students in program and process.

Based upon the belief that "all children can learn," the Effective Schools model develops from a simple logic: If all students can learn, then we must structure school and district policies and procedures so that faculty are supported in their daily work of teaching all children. Specifying the locus of responsibility for student learning with the faculty, the Effective Schools model centers around organizational feedback systems such as the student academic monitoring system and school accountability systems, which inform the classroom teacher and the school principal about how well each of them is doing with regard to specific criteria.

In this process, the unit of change is the school building organization. The faculty and principal in each building form a decision-making team that frequently includes parent and support staff representatives. Each team is designed in accord with the culture of the school and the characteristics of the neighborhood or community the school serves.

Over time, school-based management (also called site-based management), a governing and planning structure for school improvement, has developed alongside the Effective Schools model. In the late seventies and early eighties school-based management and the Effective Schools model were combined in the minds of some practitioners in their efforts to place responsibility for decision-making for day-to-day activities in the hands of the principal and staff at the school site. But without a comprehensive model like the Effective Schools model, school-based management is only a governance structure, not a program for comprehensive school improvement. Educators who were advocating each of these models held the other implicitly in their minds: School-based management people were reorganizing decision-making so that more responsive program decisions could be made on behalf of students and their parents. Effective Schools model researchers advocated a framework which embraced a set of correlates, or characteristics of Effective Schools, which, once in place, would interact to begin the renewal process, as long as the organizational resources were redirected, the monitoring systems were in place, and the school staff was committed to the new belief system that "all kids can learn." Those focusing on school-based management had the "shared decision-making at the school site" part of the model. Those looking at Effective Schools had the "why" of school improvement: to reach and teach all children.

Design of the Present Group of Case Studies

In the spring of 1988, the National Center for Effective Schools Research & Development sent a survey form to personnel in sixteen districts and one educational resource center with whom the center personnel were working. This form was submitted to those districts which had worked faithfully and consistently over time to implement an evolving Effective Schools model. Some districts had been at work for over seven years (Jackson, Mississippi) while others had just begun. San Pasqual, a smaller district, was in the second year of implementation. Eleven of the districts and an educational resource center (the Middle Cities Association in Michigan) responded to the invitation to write their case studies, using a common form (see Appendix A & B). Over the summer the districts wrote reports of what had transpired based on their own observations.

Common Elements of the Comprehensive Model

The editors held two priorities: (1) to keep the case studies in the langauge of the authors and (2) to report the studies in a comprehensive yet comparable way (hence the need for a form for each district's reporting). The paramount attribute to be emphasized was the *comprehensiveness* of the Effective Schools model.

The model's capability for adaptation within the culture and norms of each school and district will become evident to the critical reader. However the reader should pay particular attention to a **number of elements** which comprise the model. These elements or components of the model are embedded in several common themes which run through the case studies:

- **Schools and districts which early on attempted to apply Effective Schools Research realized that they could do better, especially in reaching and teaching high-risk students in their instructional procedures and educational programs.** This primary motive for school improvement was instigated by the educational "accountability" movement of the seventies.

- **"Accountability" is encouraged on different levels and is a highly valued motive for change.** Pride and professionalism seem to promote the belief that school people can perform their roles to certain agreed-upon standards, and can be held accountable for that performance:
    - the schools are accountable to the community and parents;
    - the board of education to the citizens of the community;
    - the superintendent to the board and the community;
    - the principals to the superintendent and the community the school serves;
    - the teachers in a school to the principal;
    - the students to the teacher;
    - the support staff to the principal, teachers, and central office administrators.

  Accountability demands that goals be defined, that a district mission be stated as well as school missions, and that the work and policies in the district be consistent with the district mission. Evaluation processes proceed from these agreed-upon goals and evaluation measures decided upon by district consensus, as well as by federal, state, or local law.

  By agreeing upon a mission, the people in a district pull together. The mission then acts like a rudder on a ship: it gives direction and stability to what otherwise would be a jagged course, depending upon prevailing winds and ocean currents. Accountability in this way promotes cohesion, a sense of "what we are about," and cuts down on counterproductive or diverse efforts. Accountability for an agreed-upon goal lessens political infighting among various outside and internal special interest groups.

  Finally, by stating district and school missions and operationalizing them with realistic goals and objectives, the organizations involved plan for "organized abandonment" of counterproductive policies and procedures. There will be more realistic annual plans written once they are operationalized, and each year prudence will dictate only two or three major goals be attempted. The stated mission should assure that these goals are consistent with one another as well as with the mission.

- **School improvement leaders recognized that small incremental changes or adjustments in teaching techniques are not the answer, in and of themselves.** Changes in the classroom procedures and activities are necessary but not sufficient for beneficial and lasting change. Practitioners who started with pedagogical adjustments in classroom techniques soon learned that school and district policy and procedures often prevented implementation of new teaching innovations. Certainly those teachers "going it alone," unless they were experienced and exceptionally talented, were not able to sustain their efforts over time. This is especially the case with regard to the coordination and coverage of subject matter and teaching objectives from one level to the next.

- **Education leaders who saw a need for change were hesitant about how to start the Effective Schools Research improvement process.** Team building, training in group dynamics, communication skills, and skills of planning are necessary training areas for teachers and principals so they can conduct day-to-day decision-making at the school site. Most school teams and school faculties decided to develop these skills by working on a specific school project such as implementing a schoolwide discipline code. Projects such as these provide a beginning and a foundation for school improvement.

- **Those who plan improvements need appropriate, ongoing dialogue about staff development which links each school with central office staff or the superintendent's office.** The importance of up-to-date training for principals, teachers, support staff, superintendents, and the board of education cannot be overemphasized. New ways of carrying out ESR are constantly being discovered. Barriers to school improvement, which usually center around the belief system and the reallocation of resources in target areas, are being addressed successfully across the country.

- **Finding time to meet, to plan, and to oversee the implementation of the Effective Schools process is one of the most difficult tasks practitioners undertake.** Most of the added resources needed (and most districts feel that little new money is required once the staff development program is adequately funded) are needed in this area, in terms of released time. Also, certain official "waiving" of parts of the teacher contract for a specified period of time, and according to the rules of the teacher's association, needs to be negotiated.

- **Effective planned change requires a central system that monitors student progress and reports to teachers and principals in an accurate and timely fashion.** Deciding what student outcomes to measure, and how to measure them for decision-making and planning purposes at the school site level, is not an easy task. The process of disaggregating data demands sophisticated interpretation, and the reporting of these data to internal and external constituencies is a sensitive issue. Such a system needs to document student scores and give fast and accurate feed-back to teachers for re-teaching. Because these structures have been difficult to design, and because the amount and kind of testing best suited for teaching for learning for all varies across districts, regions, and even countries, student monitoring is often put on the back burner until other assessment questions (like teacher evaluation) are settled. The student monitoring system should be held separate from the teacher evaluation system, as far as employment questions are concerned. The student monitoring system is part of the teacher conferencing system, and for the use of the principal and teacher to improve instruction in the classroom.

- **As early in the process as possible, teachers and other personnel need to align curriculum and develop criterion-referenced tests which measure mastery.** For most teachers, knowing that their students will be tested on the topics and objectives that are being taught takes much of the uncertainty out of relying on standardized achievement test scores. Curricular alignment is also the first step in preparing criterion-referenced tests for the district, so that teachers using these tests can cover subjects adequately and know that all children are keeping up to date.

- **"Quality" and "equity" must be defined and their measures specified.** Definitions clear up misunderstandings about goals and objectives. Effective Schools advocates are aware of the role public perception plays in assuring success, both within the school system and in the community it serves. Good public relations gives pride in accomplishment, to the people achieving, and to the community reaping the rewards of their endeavors. Early in the process, indicators of school improvement (see Appendix C, page 215) should be decided upon by the school board and the district planning team. These indicators should be used to make decisions internally. Certain indicators should be reported regularly to the community.

- **The "correlates" of Effective Schools Research are a means to an end, and not an end in themselves.** One of the best indicators of a good understanding of Effective Schools Research is when a practitioner or researcher realizes that the correlates are characteristics of effective schools, not the goals of the Effective Schools process. The goal is to design district and school policies and procedures so that they support the classroom teacher in his or her effort to teach for the learning of all students.

- **Leadership on the part of the superintendent, principals, teachers, and outside consultants is an essential part of the process of school reform and renewal.** Because the process of change does not take place overnight, or even in a year or two, practitioners must have the determination to see things through when they get bogged down. The model is specific enough to point to the areas of concern; the people responsible for implementation must make their own decisions and be innovative in finding solutions to the problems they encounter. Commitment, enterprise, and persistence are especially crucial in large school districts, where organizational momentum can be slowed easily, in some cases without warning, when internal or external political questions remain unresolved. Internally there is always the possibility that the school improvement process will become the target of unrest within the ranks of teachers, principals, or support staff associations. Usually, the key question to be resolved centers on the traditional bargaining arenas of working conditions, salary, and fringe benefits and not the school improvement program. It is important to separate the issues early on in negotiations and keep the improvement process moving.

The case studies should be read, then, with a focus on pragmatism. The threads running through these reports are dynamic, often a product of mutual causations in the district.[1] (A good example of mutual causations is the development of "high expectations." This belief on the part of teachers in part proceeds from *experiencing* higher student achievement and in part *fosters* higher student achievement.) Phenomena which result from mutual causation are hard to research. So is a non-linear process of development, which the Effective Schools Research process of school improvement most certainly is: iterative at every step. Involving many complex, interlocking decisions, and many actions on the part of various persons, the model makes sequential analysis difficult, and predictive and explanatory analysis almost impossible.

To understand better what seems to be confusion, a new philosophical underpinning is needed. In his book, *After Virtue*, Alisdair McIntyre describes the essence of a good leader in reorganizing for a specific goal:

> Clearly his first step would have to be the creation of an organization to provide an instrument for his project and equally clearly his first task would have to be to render the activity of his own organization wholly or largely unpredictable. For if he were unable to achieve this, he could scarcely achieve his larger goal. But he would also have to render his organization efficient and effective, capable of dealing with its highly original task and of surviving in the very environment which it is committed to changing. *Unfortunately these two characteristics, total or near total predictability on the one hand and organizational effectiveness on the other, turn out on the basis of the best empirical studies we have to be incompatible* (italics added). Defining the conditions of effectiveness in an environment that requires innovative adaptation Tom Burns has listed such characteristics as 'continual redefinition of individual task,' 'communication which consists of information and advice rather than instructions and decisions,' 'knowledge may be located anywhere in the network' and so on (Burns 1963, and Burns and Stalker 1968). *One can safely generalize what Burns and Stalker say about the need to allow for individual initiative, a flexible response to changes in knowledge, the multiplication of centers of problem-solving and decision-making as adding up to the thesis that an effective organization has to be able to tolerate a high degree of unpredictability within itself* (italics added). Other studies confirm this. Attempts to monitor what every subordinate is doing all the time tend to be counterproductive; attempts to make the activity of others predictable necessarily routinize, suppress intelligence and flexibility and turn the energies of subordinates to frustrating the projects of at least some of their superiors (Kaufman 1973, and see also Burns and Stalker on the effects of attempts to subvert and circumvent managerial hierarchies).
>
> Since organizational success and organizational predictability exclude one another, the project of creating a wholly or largely predictable organization committed to creating a wholly or largely predictable society is doomed and doomed by the facts about social life (pp. 105–106).

The Effective Schools Research model is a process, a framework for decision-making by educators who would make their schools places of learning for all students. These case studies illustrate common practices, describe the more pervasive program barriers and opportunities encountered, and show that increased staff and student morale can come from shared decision-making in a collaborative enterprise that owns regular success.

This model is descriptive, not predictive, except for a list of the general types of work to be done by the people involved. The outcomes of that work are politically and socially different for each district and each school. The outcomes are related to an increase in higher academic achievement for all students. Further systematic research is needed to substantiate these findings.

However, the lessons we have learned from this pragmatic knowledge-base are important and useful. Dr. Lezotte's summary chapter weaves the threads together in a descriptive and explanatory text

---

[1] See Lincoln and Guba (1985), *Naturalistic Inquiry* (Beverly Hills: Sage Publications), pp. 150–157. The authors' discussion of "mutual simultaneous shaping" is worthy of study by practitioners and researchers alike.

which adds to our understanding of the Effective Schools model and its application in a variety of districts.

The National Center for Effective Schools Research and Development thanks all the authors of the case studies, their boards of education and superintendents for allowing the case studies to be written and published. The degree of forthrightness demonstrated by their candid contributions to the field of education reflects the openness of the districts involved and their commitment to the Effective Schools process for school improvement.

Barbara O. Taylor, Ph.D.

The Language of Practice

Barbara O. Taylor, Ph.D.

The Language of Practice

The language of educational practitioners is distinctly different from the language of educational researchers. The language of researchers is typically third person, present or past tense with passive verbs, and in its attempt to be accurate often seems quite stilted to the untutored mind. The language of practitioners is typically first or third person, with active verbs in the present, past, or past progressive tense—or all three within the same paragraph—and changes easily to tell a moving story.

In their effort to represent interesting day-to-day experiences practitioners design sentences which pull together many threads or elements of which they are aware, knowing that this whole cloth is the way things happen in school. The researcher's job is to take these tapestries and sort out the patterns, the paths, the relationships, and the symmetry of development. Indeed, most practitioners would argue that it is impossible to separate content and process elements in daily deliberations at the school house; only the researcher can do that on paper and at a distance, looking back on what happened and trying to see what is process, what is content.

The language of practice in this way often appears too personal, too anecdotal, even disorganized in its presentation. And yet practitioners' reflection upon their actions, decisions, and roles played is an authentic genre of applied research. What practitioners link together and the emphasis they give each action mentioned tells the researcher a great deal. Indeed research on language should be developed and its protocols made more systematic. Building on the strengths of direct experience and the immediacies of special situations, of constant synthesis in interpreting organizational dynamics, which include a bias for what really matters, the spoken word of practitioners is invaluable data (Mintzberg et al., 1976). The practitioner's written work is just as helpful, and is easier to analyze because it is permanent and decidedly thoughtful.

Each language is instructive to the other. While the language of practice generally describes, and that of research analyzes, each language does both; it is a question of emphasis. The practitioner is a constant interpreter of what is going on, and "makes sense" of the actions and discussion and behaviors of the school as they take place. Analysis for the practitioner is almost coexistent with description. The "why" of practice is generally up front: Give reason to the student, give reason to the teacher, give reason to the administration, as the conversation happens.

The researcher, on the other hand, is told to keep distance from whatever is being studied in order to analyze after the fact what indeed did occur. And *then* the researcher must interpret and answer why it occurred. The "why" of research comes after lengthy methodologies, as mature evidence manifests itself within an accepted paradigm.

Both languages are important sources of social data, but the data of practitioners are more difficult to recognize. In these case studies the hard data are only suggested by the narratives, and are interpreted within the rich context of daily work and professional judgment. Disaggregated test scores and other indicators are compared over time, and then each school's educational program and procedures are called into question where student outcomes are not improving. Precise delineation (the researcher's hallmark) gives way to breath of description in the practitioner's language, and the phenomena being discussed are rendered extremely complex.

Mintzberg, H.; Raisinghani, D.; Theoret, Andre. "The Structure of 'Unstructured' Decision Processes." *Administrative Science Quarterly* 21 (June 1976):246–75.

The language of practitioners is not easy for the novice to understand, and the analytic process needed to understand it is only now being developed. The first requirement for doing naturalistic research is to understand the context of the situation. The researcher then has two fundamental jobs to perform: to delineate the contextual milieu, and then to report clearly the specific elements or components of interest. This makes an investigation very risky and time-consuming.

The National Center for Effective Schools hopes that these case studies will intrigue educational researchers and compel them to test a few of the hypotheses they find within them. We hope the educators in the field will read these case studies, find enough evidence of what works to build confidence, and then get about the business of improving schools for all children, using action research and trial and error strategies.

There are many conversations to be held between researchers and practitioners, and they proceed from both parties. The language of both actors has instruction for each, if only each will listen carefully and reflect on what is being said. There are many roles to be played in school improvement, and all of them are important.

Barbara O. Taylor, Ph.D.
Madison, Wisconsin
October 1989

Reaching for Excellence and Equity in Prince George's County Public Schools

John A. Murphy
Superintendent of Schools

Louise F. Waynant
Associate Superintendent for Instruction

Prince George's County, Maryland
Became involved in Effective Schools process in 1985

Community

Population
710,014 (Prince George's County)

Type
Located in the Washington, D.C.–Baltimore corridor. Economic base—Workforce comprised of federal employees, military personnel, and employees of high-tech businesses. Per capita income is $18,477. County has a 50 percent minority population and therefore reflects a high degree of diversity.

Socioeconomic Description
Predominantly middle class, urban/suburban geographic mix, 50 percent minority population. 16,230 students qualify for free lunch; 7,083 students qualify for reduced lunch.

School District

Enrollment
104,140

Ethnic Composition, (percent)
African-American	63.2
American Indian	.3
Asian-American	3.9
Caucasian	29.7
Hispanic	2.5

Per Pupil Expenditure
Year 1988–1989	$4,353
Year 1989–1990	4,710

Percent bussed
72.6

Area (in square miles)
489

Schools
Elementary schools	114 (K-6)
Middle schools	26 (7-8)
High schools	20
Other	10
(special education)	

Number of Staff
Administrators	150.5
Certified Teachers	6,728.8
Support staff	4,714.8

(including 102.5 administrative support)

Student-Teacher Ratio
Average class size:
Kindergarten	21.3
Grades 1–6	26.3
Middle	24.3
High school	25.1

Percent college-bound (approx.)
61

Abstract

Prince George's County Public Schools played an important role in the development of the Effective Schools Research model: This was the first time a diverse district decided at the beginning of the process that every school in the district, a large, county-wide system, would embark on a school improvement program based on Effective Schools Research (ESR). In previous years (1978–84) ESR consultants had often helped districts design student academic monitoring and personnel assessment systems when they found they needed them. However, in Prince George's County, these systems were **designed and installed** (using disaggregated analysis procedures) early in the improvement program, along with the training components for the school improvement teams. In addition, training in team building for school personnel was carried out in the first two years of planning and implementing and is an ongoing part of staff development.

The results of Prince George's County efforts have been reported coast-to-coast. Especially interesting for the reader are detailed descriptions of the impact of the Effective Schools process upon the student monitoring system, including how student achievement is measured and analyzed, the impact of ESR implementation on curricular and staff development systems, and the impact of the process on personnel evaluation.

The communities served by this county system also profited from the ESR comprehensive plan for school improvement. Most importantly the model had positive effects on desegregation efforts and on achievement for "at-risk" students.

Overview

In January 1988, the eyes of the nation were on the Prince George's County Public Schools as the President of the United States visited the school system to recognize progress the system had made in improving student achievement and establishing magnet schools to address desegregation issues. Following his visit, President Reagan wrote to Superintendent John A. Murphy, "Great things are happening indeed in the Prince George's County Public Schools. Please tell the students, the teachers, and the administrators to keep up the outstanding work."

During the months following the President's visit, educators throughout the country called or visited to learn more about the exciting and innovative programs underway in the school system. The question visitors asked most frequently was this: What has made such a dramatic difference in the school system? A significant part of the response to this question is the impact made by implementation of the Effective Schools process.

Prince George's County Public Schools, located between Washington, D.C., and Baltimore, Maryland, is the 16th largest school system in the nation: a heterogeneous, urban-suburban school district in which over 104,100 students are enrolled. The 172 schools in the district include 114 elementary schools, 26 middle schools, 20 high schools, 2 vocational schools, and 10 special education centers. Often called a "school system of choices," the Prince George's County Public School system offers magnet programs in 44 schools. The racial composition of the school system is approximately 64 percent black, 30 percent white, 4 percent Asian, 2.5 percent Hispanic, and .3 percent American Indian. The school system employs over 6,700 teaches, 29 percent of whom are black, and 71 percent other.

The early years of the 1980s marked a very difficult time for Prince George's County Public Schools. A devastating tax referendum led to budget reductions that cost the school system 500 teaching positions. As a result of lost revenues, Prince George's class sizes were among the highest in the state and teachers' salaries had dipped to the bottom of systems in the Washington, D.C. metropolitan area. Exacerbating the plight of the school system were unresolved desegregation issues which created tensions throughout the community. Although student achievement had been increasing gradually, the average achievement scores for the school system still were below state and national averages. Of even greater concern to school system educators and the community was an unacceptably large gap between the performance of black and white students on state-mandated standardized and functional achievement tests.

The story of Prince George's journey from the troubled days of the early 1980s to its current position as a pacesetter for minority student achievement and innovations in the instructional program began with a simple, but dramatically important, step: identifying the major problem of student achievement and taking ownership of that problem. At the heart of the problem was low expectations for students' achievement and, in particular, for the achievement of minority students. In the difficult fiscal and political climate that pervaded the school system, its educators had begun to question their power to make a difference and had limited their expectations for students' achievement.

John A. Murphy, newly hired superintendent of schools for Prince George's County Public Schools, provided the vision that led to dramatic improvements in the school system, and, most significantly, dramatic improvements in minority student achievement. Among the actions the superintendent initiated to address student achievement was implementation of the Effective Schools process. With its dual focus on quality **and** equity, the Effective Schools process was a means to improve achievement for **all** students, while closing the gap between performance of black and white students.

Implementing the Effective Schools Process

Year I: Preparing for Effective Schools Process Implementation

In preparation for initiating the Effective Schools process, the superintendent sent a team of school system educators to an Effective Schools Leadership Training Institute in Phoenix, Arizona, in January 1985. Later in the year, he met personally with Lawrence Lezotte, then chairman, Department of Educational Administration, Michigan State University, to outline a broad strategy for school system implementation of the process. Board of education members met with Dr. Lezotte during a breakfast meeting at the National Federation of Urban-Suburban School Districts Conference in Jackson, Mississippi, in May 1985, to discuss implications of implementing the process in Prince George's County Public Schools. Additionally, the six area assistant superintendents and the directors in the division of instruction participated in the Summer 1985 Effective Schools Institute held in Williamsburg, Virginia.

Principals' Leadership Training

The Effective Schools process was "officially" launched in July 1985 when Dr. Lezotte met with all school system principals during their three-day Summer Leadership Training Institute to describe the research on which the Effective Schools correlates were based and to outline the steps schools need to follow in implementing a school improvement effort. Dr. Lezotte served as consultant to the school system throughout the planning and implementation process and led a series of leadership seminars for principals which explored in depth the topics introduced during the Summer Leadership Training Institute.

The leadership seminars emphasized the steps to follow in conducting a needs analysis which would guide development of local school improvement plans. The needs analysis to be conducted in each school would consist of three parts: analysis of disaggregated student achievement data, assessment of the strength and presence of Effective Schools correlates, and use of archival information such as suspension and attendance data. At several seminar sessions the principals developed or adapted a survey instrument for their school staffs to use in assessing the degree to which effective schools correlates were in evidence in the schools. Instruments were developed for elementary, middle, and high school as well as for special education centers.

A first-year seminar of particular interest to principals described how to select and work with school improvement teams. Guidance was provided concerning ways to create a representative team and to initiate the process of shared decision making at the local school level. The seminar provided a forum to discuss how teachers could become involved in the process of needs analysis, goal setting, and evaluation.

Preparing for Local School Implementation

The opening of the 1986-87 school year was designated as the time to "launch" local school improvement activities. In preparation for implementing the Effective Schools process in their schools, each principal developed a plan which described how the Effective Schools process would be introduced to his or her staff, and how the School Improvement Team would be formed. To assist principals with implementation of school-based staff orientation activities, an Effective Schools reference notebook was provided for each school, along with a videotaped interview with the superintendent, the associate superintendent for instruction, and Dr. Lezotte.

Year II: Implementing the Effective Schools Process at the School Building Level

Effective Schools implementation activities during the 1986-87 school year were focused at the local school level. Each school completed four implementation activities by

- providing an orientation to the Effective Schools process for the total school staff
- selecting a school improvement team
- conducting a needs analysis which featured (1) use of the Effective Schools surveys, (2) analysis of disaggregated student achievement data, and (3) review of all other data which could inform the needs analysis process
- developing a school improvement plan based on the needs analysis.

Schools organized their first school improvement plans around the Effective Schools correlates which seemed most relevant to their needs. Implementation strategies and activities were selected, and resources and technical assistance needed to implement the plans were identified. Completed plans were sent to the superintendent of schools and area assistant superintendents for review.

Providing coordination for implementation of the Effective Schools process during this second year of implementation was a newly appointed Director of Effective Schools and Principals' Leadership Training. The director selected a principals' advisory committee to provide dialogue for leadership training activities which would continue to support Effective Schools process implementation. A major focus of the leadership seminars during the second year was how to use disaggregated data to analyze and monitor student achievement at the local school level.

Year III: Refining the Implementation Process at the School Building Level

When school improvement plans for the 1987-88 school year were reviewed, it became apparent that additional guidance from central office in three areas would help schools refine their plans by

- aligning strategies with objectives to assure that strategies selected were likely to lead to the outcomes identified by the school
- identifying formative and summative evaluation strategies to help schools assess whether goals and objectives had been reached
- selecting objectives which were significant, nontrivial, in nature and addressed the correlates, or goals, selected for implementation.

The Washington Post

AN INDEPENDENT NEWSPAPER

Promises Kept in Prince George's

THREE YEARS ago, Prince George's County School Superintendent John A. Murphy promised that his students would reach the 75th percentile on standardized tests by 1990. When pupils reach that level, they have scored higher than 75 percent of the students tested nationally. That's an important threshold, within reach of highly regarded schools such as those in Montgomery County, where students have hit the 80th percentile. Black students in Prince George's, as a group, had test scores far below those of whites. The superintendent promised to close that gap. Few believed that both things could be done at the same time. They were wrong.

The California Achievement Test (CAT) measures the reading, math, spelling and language skills of third-, fifth- and eighth-grade students. Recently released scores show that Prince George's third-grade students hit the 73rd percentile on the total battery of tests, the highest score ever for Prince George's and an increase of nine points since 1986. Both fifth- and eighth-grade students improved by nine points, up to the 69th and 67th percentiles respectively.

Some black students in Prince George's had already recorded high scores, but more and more have excelled on the CAT. In 1987 black students ranked above the 50th percentile for the first time. This year, third- and fifth-grade black students surpassed the 60th percentile, and the gap in test scores is also shrinking. Black third-grade students, for example, trailed whites by 25 points in 1984, but by only 17 points this past year.

Higher budgets, more teachers and a back-to-basics curriculum have helped produce the overall improvement. Schools such as Dodge Park Elementary have shown that black students (96.4 percent of enrollment) can score as high as any others.

At Dodge Park, teachers expect more from their students. More homework is assigned, and regular exams test skills needed for the CAT. A computer lab has helped math students, and parents are given booklets to test their children over the summer. In 1986 Dodge Park's third graders scored at the 77th percentile. They reached the 94th percentile on the last CAT. That type of performance has helped lift the Prince George's schools to the threshold of excellence.

© The Washington Post

This revision process caused some concerns. Although initially an issue of much concern to teachers and principals, the revision process initiated by the central office ultimately improved the likelihood that schools would reach the goals they had established.

The Department of Staff Development analyzed school improvement plans and computerized a "mini-profile" of each school's plan to assist with providing requested resources and support. The mini-profiles included the correlates each school had selected for implementation and summarized requests schools had made for resources and staff development assistance. The three correlates most frequently included in the school improvement plans were (1) positive home-school relationships, (2) high expectations for success for all students, and (3) safe and orderly school environment. Staff development topics most requested were establishing high expectations for student achievement, approaches to classroom management, and communicating with parents.

Throughout the third year of Effective Schools process implementation, principals continued their participation in monthly leadership seminars. The central theme of this group of seminars was establishing excellence **and** equity.

At the end of the school year, each school improvement team gathered and analyzed results from the current year's school improvement activities to determine which objectives were reached and what next steps were needed. If objectives were not reached, reasons were discussed and a decision was made whether the objective should be refined or even included in the plan for the following year.

Year IV: Extending the Implementation Process at the Local School Level

As a result of experiences gained during the initial years of Effective Schools process implementation, several changes were made in the guidance provided for the development of school improvement plans.

- Rather than developing a one-year plan, schools were asked to develop long-range plans.
- Rather than selecting Effective Schools correlates as the basis for developing school improvement plans, schools were asked to identify two to four long-range goals which reflected the results of their needs analysis, and then to select specific objectives which addressed the long-range goals.
- Rather than have the plan signed only by the principal, all members of the school improvement team were asked to sign the plan before sending it to their area assistant superintendent for review.
- Rather than limiting schools to "traditional" solutions to identified problems, schools were encouraged to try innovative strategies to address their objectives.

Taken together, these revised guidelines invite schools to try strategic, long-range planning to promote and assure a higher degree of teacher involvement. They encourage school staffs to think beyond traditional solutions to shape school improvement.

Placing the Effective Schools Process in the Context of an Effective School System

When Prince George's County Public Schools initiated the Effective Schools process in 1985, emphasis was placed almost exclusively on the process as it related to each local school and the roles and responsibilities local school personnel should assume in implementing the process. As individual schools "launched" their Effective Schools activities, numerous requests for resources and technical assistance were made to central and area offices. The requests for support of local building school improvement activities, the need for coordination of response to these requests, and the compelling message of the Effective Schools Research for broader school system decision making clearly identified the need to involve every component of the school system in the Effective Schools process. Simply stated, effective schools needed to exist within the supportive context of an effective school system.

Although much research was available to inform local building implementation of the Effective Schools process, little was known about organizing an entire system to support this effort. Nor was it clear from existing research and experience what the characteristics of an effective school system should be.

Defining the School System Mission and Goals in "Effective Schools" Terminology

The first step toward becoming an effective school system was defining a new mission statement and new school system improvement goals as a springboard from which local schools could develop their statements of mission and goals. The new **mission statement** clearly reflected the dual focus of quality and equity: the belief that **all** children can learn, and that teachers are able to reach and teach all children.

> **Mission Statement of Prince George's County Public Schools**
>
> The mission of the Prince George's County Public Schools is to assure that all students acquire knowledge and develop the skills and work habits to enable them to become productive members of society. This mission is best accomplished in an environment characterized by strong instructional leadership, high expectations for success for all students, sufficient time for teaching and learning, a safe and orderly school environment, frequent monitoring of students' progress, and effective home-school communication.

Next, school system improvement goals were developed and announced to the community and the press, putting system educators "on the line" for improved student achievement. These goals state clearly what expectations for student achievement will be:

- Standardized test scores for Prince George's County Public Schools will show annual increases in the percentages of students within the upper quartile, and annual decreases in the percentage of students in the lower quartiles.
- Functional test scores for Prince George's County Public Schools will show annual increases in the percentage of students at grades nine and ten who reach or exceed the criterion for mastery.

- The gap between achievement scores for black and non-black students will diminish annually, while achievement scores for all students will increase.
- Criterion-referenced test scores will show annual increases in the percentage of students at each grade level who attain essential objectives.

These school system improvement goals became the foundation for the school system's **strategic action plan** which details both short term and long term action needed to reach the goals, indicates the individuals responsible for this action, and describes the specific evaluation strategies to be followed to determine if the action has been successful.

Defining an Effective School System

After considerable discussion and examination of the literature, Prince George's County Public Schools' personnel created their own definition of an effective school system. Characteristics of an effective school system were identified and implications for planning and action suggested by these characteristics were developed. (See Appendix A in this case study) Additionally, each central office division and area office within the system defined its roles and responsibilities in supporting implementation of the Effective Schools process.

Prince George's County Public Schools defined an effective school system as ". . . one in which all resources are organized and delivered in such a way as to assure that **all** students within that system . . . regardless of race, gender, or socio-economic status . . . learn the essential curriculum as defined by that system. An effective school system, through its statement of mission and goals, its instructional program and support services, and its allocation of resources, assures that its priorities are teaching and learning, and that its focus is on both quality and equity."

Ten characteristics of an effective school system were identified as:

1. strong, instructionally focused leadership
2. clear and focused mission
3. frequent monitoring of student progress
4. climate of high expectations for success for all students and staff
5. purposeful and supportive involvement of parents, other citizens, and business and community groups
6. curriculum and instructional programs that assure opportunities for every student to learn
7. support for schools to assure a safe and orderly learning environment for students
8. high rate of attendance for students and all school and non-school based staff
9. strong staff development program which reflects and supports the implementation of the Effective Schools process
10. clear understanding on the part of all staff as to their specific roles and responsibilities in contributing to the Effective Schools process, and an evaluation process which supports this understanding.

This school system commitment to and involvement with the Effective Schools process have significantly influenced "mandating and prescribing" to "helping and supporting." A second difference has been the increased emphasis on school-based decision making and innovation.

As a symbolic way to illustrate this change in focus, the 1986–87 school year was launched with a summer leadership training workshop during which principals were given red buttons which stated "Priority" and central and area office personnel wore green buttons which asked, "How Can I Help?" Additional examples of the impact the message of the Effective Schools Research has had on the **school system** are described in other sections.

Creating an Effective Schools Steering Committee

Just as each school needs a school improvement team to guide its implementation process, so a school system needs a system-wide steering committee to provide input to the superintendent to help "monitor and adjust" the system-wide implementation process. The Prince George's County Public Schools Effective Schools Steering Committee, formed at the end of the third year of implementation, had three primary responsibilities:

- overseeing the implementation process, and making recommendations for change, as needed
- designing and updating a comprehensive, long-range plan for staff development, and communication about Effective Schools process implementation
- advising on the collection, analysis, and use of data in instructional decision making.

Members of the steering committee include principals, teachers, parents, and representatives from each central office division and each area office.

Impact of the Effective Schools Process on How Student Achievement Data Are Gathered, Interpreted, and Used

The Effective Schools process has had a major impact on how student achievement is measured in Prince George's County Public Schools, and how achievement data are interpreted and used. The most significant change in how student achievement is measured has been the development and use of criterion-referenced tests which are based upon the objectives which form the curriculum for Prince George's County Public Schools. These tests are developed by teacher teams who work with curriculum supervisors. Currently, the tests at the elementary level are administered in September, January, and June. At the secondary level, tests are administered at the beginning and end of courses. Eventually, items will be available in computerized banks which will enable teachers to access the items immediately after a unit of work has been completed.

A second change the Effective Schools process has made in how student achievement is measured has been the use of multiple sources of data to create a more comprehensive "picture" of student achievement. Data from grade distributions, criterion-referenced tests, placement in instructional groupings, standardized and functional tests, enrollment in and level of success with higher level courses, and scholarship awards are among the types of data now used to assess student performance.

Analyzing Student Achievement Data: Disaggregation of Data

The primary impact made by the Effective Schools process on how student achievement data are analyzed has been the disaggregation of data by race and sex. Procedures soon will be available to analyze achievement data in terms of socioeconomic factors as well. Disaggregation of data from criterion-referenced tests, standardized and functional tests, grade distributions, course assignments, and attendance enable educators to determine if student progress is shared across all groups of students within the school or school system.

Using Data for Instructional Decision-Making

As a result of implementation of the Effective Schools process, decisions made about the instructional program at the school and school system level are decisions now based upon extensive data analysis. The school system has become a "data-driven" organization at every level. Student achievement data form the heart of the needs analysis process at each local school, in each area office, and at the school system level.

Summary

In summary, the Effective Schools process has significantly influenced procedures used by the school system to assess, interpret, and monitor student achievement. A strong emphasis is placed on **frequent monitoring** of student performance, **adjusting instruction** based upon analysis of achievement data, and **accountability** for student outcomes. Because we know that "what gets measured gets taught," our measures of student achievement reflect the **significant** objectives and skills upon which our curriculum is based. Because we know that "who gets measured gets noticed," our assessment is **inclusive** in nature. Special needs students are included in the assessment and accountability measures used by the school system.

In the superintendent's conference room—called by many the "applied anxiety room"—are graphs charting the trends in student achievement for every school. Effective Schools Research illustrates that the achievement gains made by many schools can be made by all schools. The graphs are an ever-present reminder of this goal.

Impact of the Effective Schools Process on Curriculum and Instruction

The body of research which informs Effective Schools process implementation has strong implications for curriculum and instruction. The message of Effective Schools states clearly that **all** students can learn; therefore, all students must have access to quality instruction in both essential basis skills and higher level thinking skills. All students must "see themselves" in the curriculum—thus, their education must be multi-cultural in nature. Teaching for learning implies use of a broad range of instructional strategies, attention to students' learning styles, and incorporation of instructional technology in the learning process.

Higher Level Thinking Skills for All Students

For too long instruction in higher level thinking skills has been limited to highly able or talented and gifted students. Yet we know from Effective Schools Research that high expectations for achievement must be maintained for **all** students. Higher level thinking skills must be taught to all students if we truly believe in quality **and** equity. Curriculum revision, staff development, enrollment in higher level courses, and use of more challenging texts are among the actions currently underway in Prince George's County Public Schools to upgrade the teaching of higher level thinking skills.

A specific example of the school system's commitment to higher expectations for all students is the system-wide goal that by 1990, pre-Algebra and Algebra I will become courses in which at least 80 percent of the students in Prince George's County Public Schools will enroll. Approximately half of Prince George's students currently enroll in these courses.

Multicultural Education: A Feature of Effective Schools

The Prince George's County Public School System has a remarkably heterogenous student population and is often called a "patchwork quilt" with respect to its diversity. Effective Schools Research clearly illustrates that all students can learn, yet unless students can identify with the curriculum and participate in classrooms where teachers are sensitive to their needs, they may not perceive themselves as individuals with the potential to succeed in school and society. Many "at-risk" students have little sense of belonging and identification. Additionally, future graduates will live in an international society and must know the skills of collaboration and communication with individuals different from themselves.

In May, 1987, the board of education passed a resolution in support of multicultural education. In addition, a school system-community task force has worked for a full year to identify curricular changes, staff training needs, and instructional materials which will support an emphasis on multicultural education.

Instructional Use of Computers

The Prince George's County Public Schools' focus on success for **all** students has significantly influenced the system's approach to the instructional use of computers. Use of computers is not seen as a "reward" for interested and/or able students, but as an important learning tool or resource for **all** students.

In 1984 fewer than 950 microcomputers were available in the 171 schools within the system. Currently, that figure has expanded to more than 6,500. Used with high quality software, computers can bring about measurable gains in student achievement. Prince George's County Public Schools is on the "cutting edge" of using computers for instructional purposes. IBM (International Business Machines) and ESC (Education Systems Corporation) have joined forces and resources to offer a highly innovative computer installation. Students will have computers in their classrooms with "state of the art" software and an easy-to-use management system.

Teaching for Learning

Teaching for learning calls for a focus on both the process of teaching and the outcomes to be reached. Because effective teaching is teaching that leads to desired student outcomes, it is important to assure that the outcomes selected are significant, and the teaching strategies and materials used are ones which will help reach the identified outcomes. To support teachers in their teaching effectiveness, several initiatives have been taken.

- Standards for Excellence for Teaching have been defined, and all new and tenured teachers are given staff development options to grow in these standards' areas.
- Research-based teaching strategies such as Cooperative Learning have been emphasized and school system educators work with personnel from colleges and universities in the area to identify and apply these strategies.
- Elements of effective lessons have been defined and are featured in staff development activities.
- To create more **time for learning,** new ways to organize classroom time and provide more direct teacher-student contact have been initiated. Use of parallel block scheduling, re-grouping students for specific instructional tasks, and using a two-group instructional model are examples of ways to increase instructional time.

Impact of the Effective Schools Process on Staff Development

Creating Strong Instructional Leadership

Instructional leadership is a correlate of the Effective Schools process which has been strongly emphasized in Prince George's County Public Schools. Evidence from past and recent research continues to confirm that the school reflects its leader. If the leader focuses on academic achievement and high expectations in a business-like atmosphere where time and resources are efficiently used, learning occurs. **Every** principal must be an outstanding instructional leader. The principal must have the vision to chart the course for the school, and the skills to guide staff, students, and the community toward that vision.

In Prince George's County Public Schools, strong instructional leadership is fostered through providing regularly scheduled, high level training and constant feedback. Every principal goes "back to school" once a month for intensive leadership training. Principals come together to work with nationally respected consultants and their own peers to enhance their skills in all dimensions of leadership. The Principals' Leadership Training Committee has been formed to analyze leadership needs and plan a variety of professional development programs to meet these needs. Many of the topics included in the Advanced Leadership Training Program have been directly related to Effective Schools Research and implementation.

Providing School-Based Staff Development

One of the least popular—and least effective—staff training procedures formerly used in Prince George's County Public Schools was the "one shot mass meeting" where all teachers were given the same in-service at the same time. These sometimes frustrating and non-productive experiences did little to stimulate professional growth. The Effective Schools focus provided the impetus to change our staff development activities to combine school based planning with a wide selection of offerings from which teachers can select. Many staff development activities now occur at the school building level. Plans currently underway for creative use of cable TV and videotapes will enhance our efforts to bring quality inservice programs to the building level.

A directory of "In-House Consultants" has been compiled for reference and use by every school. This helpful directory, organized by Effective Schools correlates, features and nurtures in-house talent for professional growth.

Impact of the Effective Schools Process on Personnel Evaluation

During the 1987–88 school year the personnel evaluation process for principals and central and area office staff who work with the instructional program was expanded to include the extent to which targeted outcomes related to student achievement and attendance were reached. Additionally, a teacher evaluation process which includes a section on student outcomes was developed and has been piloted in eight schools. The process involves collaboration on the part of teachers and principals in establishing student outcome goals at the beginning of the school year, and identifying the evaluation procedures to be used to determine if goals had been met at the end of the school year. These new approaches to evaluation will be carefully monitored to determine what adjustments are needed prior to extending their use.

Impact of the Effective Schools Process on Home and Community Involvement

Guided by the Effective Schools Research which emphasizes home, school, and community collaboration, deliberate efforts have been made to involve parents and the broader community in the school and the school system improvement activities. Examples of parent and community involvement which have been influenced by the Effective Schools Research are summarized below.

Parent Involvement

- Parents participate on school planning and management teams and school improvement teams.
- Weekend conferences and workshops for parents have been designed to help parents help their children.
- Parent representatives are invited to join school system committees and task forces.
- A parent involvement specialist position has been created to help school personnel link home and school to support students in their instructional program.
- Schools sponsor special programs and activities designed to involve parents in their children's learning.

Community Involvement

- The Community Advisory Council advises the board of education on desegregation issues.
- The Community Advisory Board for Suspension Reduction examines suspension rates, school by school, and offers recommendations.
- The Business and Industry Advisory Council supports the school system with community relations, fund raising, teacher recruitment activities, and specific instructional improvement activities such as identification of key employability skills.
- The Interfaith Advisory Council made up of clergy from various denominations within the county helps school personnel address issues such as dropout prevention, drug abuse, teen pregnancy, and values and ethics in the curriculum.

Summary

As the need for well informed citizens and a well educated workforce increases, one thing is clear: Schools cannot do the job alone. Only when schools enter collaborative relationships with parents and the community can they fully respond to the challenge of educating students for the twenty-first century.

Impact of the Effective Schools Process on Programs for "At-Risk" Students

At the top of the education agenda today is the pressing issue of dealing with the "at-risk" student. Defined as those students most in danger of failing or dropping out of school, "at-risk" students pose the greatest single challenge for every school system, including Prince George's. Schools cannot afford to lose any students to failure and must reverse the alarming increase in the number of students considered "at risk."

The Effective Schools process affirms that **all** students can learn, and illustrates that high expectations result in improved achievement. Effective Schools Research has influenced how the Prince George's County Public Schools work with "at-risk" students in two major ways: establishing high expectations for all students, including "at-risk" populations and strengthening the emphasis on **preventing** learning problems through greater emphasis on meeting students' unique instructional needs in the early grades.

In Prince George's County Public Schools, a three-fold approach to working with "at-risk" students has been taken: prevention, intervention, and remediation. Our greatest emphasis is on prevention.

Prevention strategies have included:

- A strong instructional program with frequent monitoring of student achievement as the single best prevention program.
- A program for four-year-olds in nine elementary schools with large numbers of students from low socio-economic backgrounds and low achievement scores. This has given young children opportunities to develop oral language skills, "social skills," and familiarity with the school setting.
- Full-day kindergartens in our predominately black schools (using the Milliken II plan). These have given five-year-olds the extra time needed to develop "school skills," along with building a solid foundation for reading and mathematics.
- Transition programs in grades K-2 featuring small class sizes and intense multisensory instruction for students with greatest potential to become "at-risk."

Intervention strategies have included:

- The SUCCESS Program, in intensive academic program for grade nine students with highest rates of suspension and absence and lowest academic achievement. The program has been a promising intervention strategy for secondary "at-risk" students. In addition to a strong emphasis on academic content, students learn study skills, "coping skills," and have the opportunity to participate in summer work-study programs.
- Programs for pregnant and parenting teens to encourage pregnant teens and teen parents to stay in school.
- Special reading programs and Chapter 1 programs which give additional assistance to students in need of instructional support.

Remediation strategies have included:

- Summer programs in math and reading for elementary students who have failed or are in danger of failing. These have enabled hundreds of students to move successfully to the next grade level.
- After-school workshops for students who have failed high school competency tests. These build skills in small class settings with active learning.
- Saturday School offering remedial programs for students with academic problems and students whose excessive absences demand "make up" time.
- Two vocational high schools with a job-oriented, hands-on approach to learning with caring, specially trained teachers providing educational options for "at-risk" youth.

In each instance, consistent with the premises of Effective Schools Research, programs for "at-risk" students are designed to keep students in the mainstream or return them to the mainstream classroom as soon as possible.

The Impact of the Effective Schools Process on Desegregation

Blending Effective Schools Concepts with Magnet School Choices

During the 1984–85 school year Prince George's County Public Schools was confronted with new, court-ordered desegregation guidelines; no school within the system was to have a black student population exceeding 80 percent or below 10 percent. The board of education as well as black and non-black citizens within the community rejected mandated busing as the school system's response to the new guidelines. Instead, an instructional alternative—implementation of a variety of magnet school programs—was proposed by the superintendent. Now in their third year of implementation, the popular magnet programs have been featured in newspapers throughout the nation, and have been enthusiastically received by parents.

Magnet schools are just as intensely involved in Effective Schools implementation as are non-magnet schools. Magnet programs offer choice, but must be characterized by quality and equity as well. Like non-magnet schools, all magnet schools have the responsibility for addressing correlates of Effective Schools. Magnet schools have school improvement teams, develop school improvement plans, establish goals for student achievement, and disaggregate data to adjust and improve instruction.

Milliken II Schools Feature a Unique Approach to Effective Schools Implementation

Sixteen Prince George's elementary schools with populations that fall outside court-ordered desegregation guidelines and cannot, at this time, be further desegregated due to demographic factors, have been given compensatory resources to enhance instruction for students. Among these resources are computer labs, new texts, and a 20 to 1 pupil-teacher ratio. Termed Milliken schools after the Governor of Michigan who worked with a similar desegregation action in Detroit in 1976, the Milliken II elementary schools implement the Effective Schools process in a special way known as the Comer School Development Program. Dr. James Comer, director of the Yale University Child Study Center Schools Program and a recognized authority on implementing successful programs for minority students, has consulted with Prince George's County Public Schools to help develop a highly successful program which emphasizes principles of child development, high expectations, and extensive parent involvement.

Each Milliken II elementary school has a school planning and management team which includes parent representatives. A calendar of events which involves parents in school activities is developed each year to foster home-school relationships. To prevent problems related to achievement and discipline, as well as to provide support for students with special needs, each Milliken II school has formed a student staff services team (SSST). The SSST promotes a positive school climate and works closely with the school planning and management team. The school improvement plan developed by Milliken II schools focuses on three areas: student achievement, school climate, and home/school relationships.

Evidence of School Improvement

Gains in Student Achievement

Average student achievement in Prince George's County Public Schools has continued to improve, nearing the fourth, or highest quartile on standardized achievement measures and reaching or exceeding state averages on high school competency exams. Criterion-referenced test results show steady gains in the number of students who demonstrate mastery of essential objectives.

Standardized Test Results

During the 1987–88 school year, third grade students in Prince George's County Public Schools moved into the top 30 percent nationally on the California Achievement Test by scoring at the 73rd percentile—the first time any grade in the school system has surpassed the 70th percentile on the total exam. Students in grade five reached the 69th percentile and those in grade 8 reached the 67th percentile. (See Figures 1 and 1a.)

Black students in grades three and five entered the top 40 percent nationally by exceeding the 60th percentile on the test for the first time. Black third graders scored at the 66th percentile while black fifth graders reached the 61st percentile. Black eighth graders system-wide scored at the 58th percentile.

The gains by black students, system-wide, continued to narrow the gap between white and black student achievement. The gap was reduced to 17 percentile points in grade three alone—the first time the gap has been less than 20 percentile points. Gains made by black students in Milliken II schools were particularly impressive, exceeding the county-wide average as well as the gains made system-wide by black students. Average achievement for white students moved into the top 20 percent nationally at all three grade levels for the first time. White third graders reached the 83rd percentile, while white fifth graders scored at the 81st percentile. White eight graders reached the 80th percentile.

Results from High School Competency Tests

Students must pass four high school competency tests as part of the graduation requirements for the

CALIFORNIA ACHIEVEMENT TEST
Percentile Scores for Grade Eight
Black and White Students

Year of Testing	Black	White
Fall 1984	46	70
Fall 1985	49	72
Fall 1986	56	77
Fall 1987	58	80

CALIFORNIA ACHIEVEMENT TEST
Percentile Scores for Grade Five
Black and White Students

Year of Testing	Black	White
Fall 1984	47	72
Fall 1985	51	74
Fall 1986	54	75
Fall 1987	61	81

CALIFORNIA ACHIEVEMENT TEST
Percentile Scores for Grade Three
Black and White Students

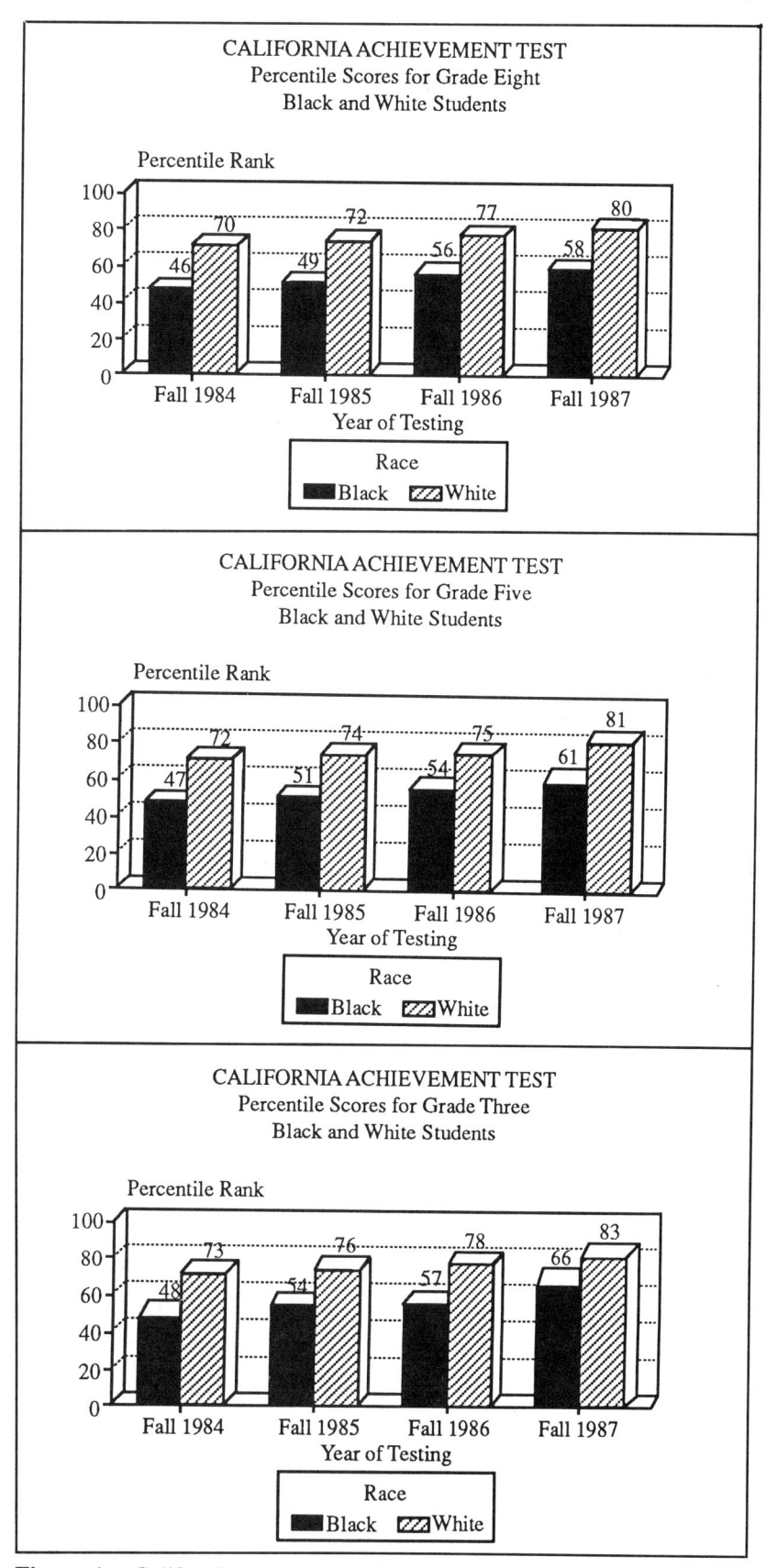

Year of Testing	Black	White
Fall 1984	48	73
Fall 1985	54	76
Fall 1986	57	78
Fall 1987	66	83

Figure 1. California Achievement Test Percentile Scores, Grade 8
California Achievement Test Percentile Scores, Grade 5
California Achievement Test Percentile Scores, Grade 3

California Achievement Test Percentile Rank Summary, Total Battery

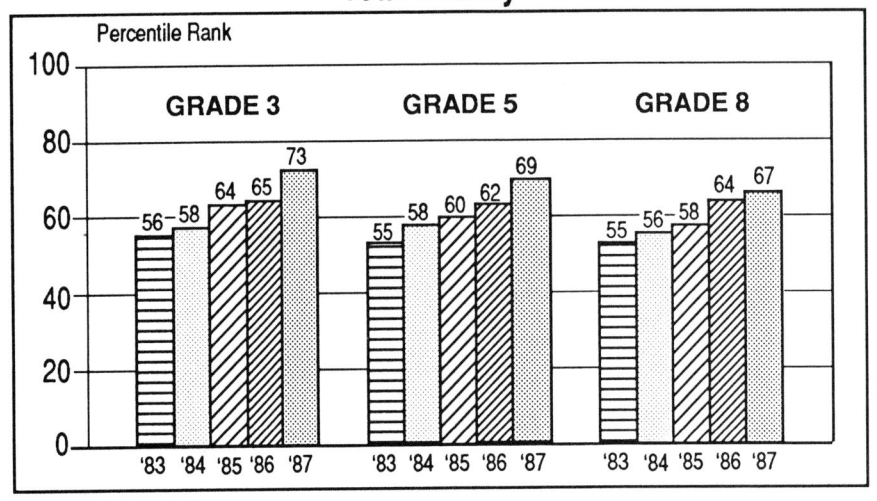

Grade 3: '83: 56, '84: 58, '85: 64, '86: 65, '87: 73
Grade 5: '83: 55, '84: 58, '85: 60, '86: 62, '87: 69
Grade 8: '83: 55, '84: 56, '85: 58, '86: 64, '87: 67

Figure 1a. California Achievement Test Summary

State of Maryland. These state-developed tests measure student competency levels in reading, writing, mathematics, and citizenship. Three of the tests have been developed in a multiple choice format, but the writing test requires students to write narrative and expository passages on prescribed topics. Students have their first opportunity to pass the tests in grade nine and may take the tests each subsequent year until mastery is achieved. The results have been positive.

- On the Maryland Test of Citizenship Skills, achievement for grade nine black students improved from 55 percent passing in 1985–86 to 67 percent passing in 1987–88, and achievement for grade nine white students improved from 75 percent passing in 1985–86 to 80 percent passing in 1987–88. See Figure 2.
- On the Maryland Functional Mathematics Test, achievement for grade nine black students im-

Black and White Ninth-grade Students who Passed the Maryland Test of Citizenship Skills, 1986-1988

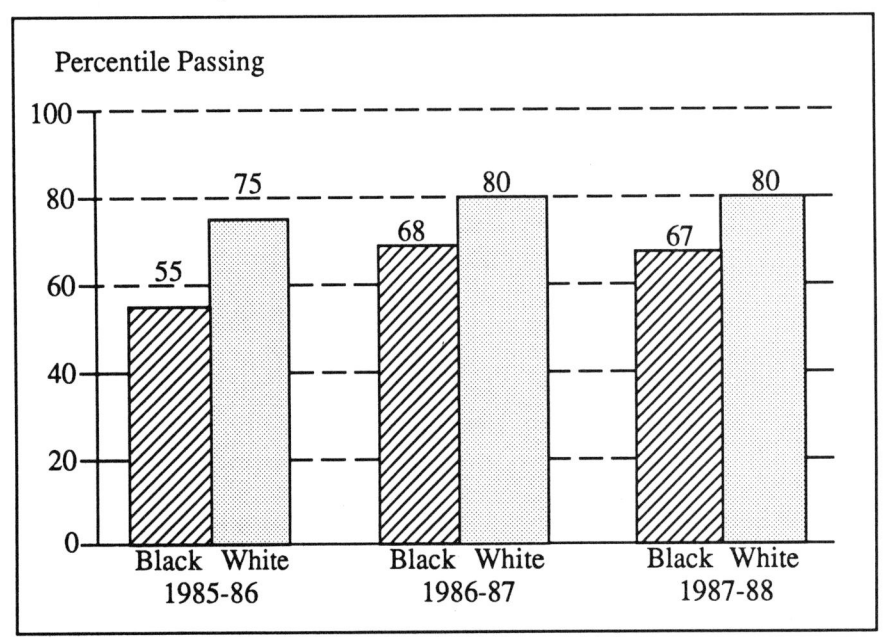

1985-86: Black 55, White 75
1986-87: Black 68, White 80
1987-88: Black 67, White 80

Figure 2. Black and White 9th Grade Students' Results: Maryland Test of Citizenship Skills

The Maryland Functional Mathematics Test Black and White Ninth-grade Students Who Passed, 1985-1988

Percentile Passing

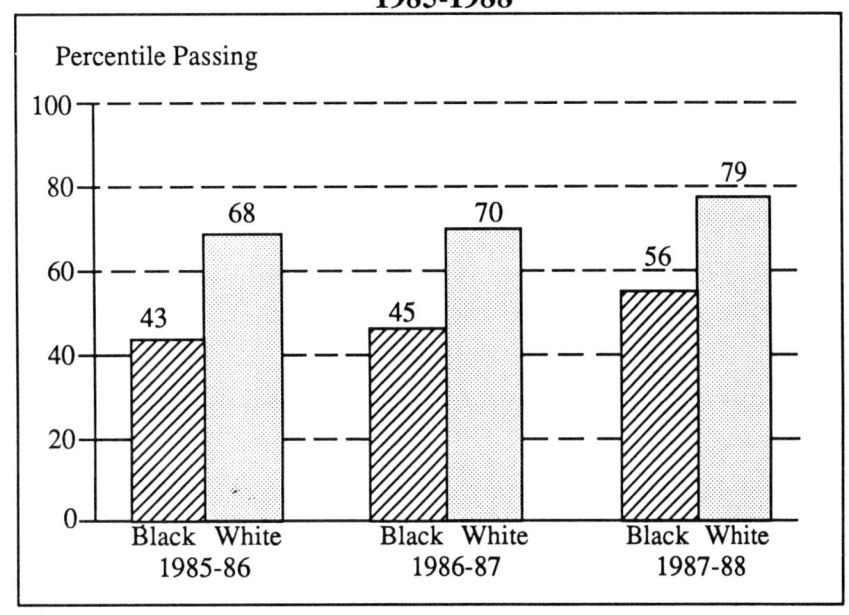

	Black	White
1985-86	43	68
1986-87	45	70
1987-88	56	79

Figure 3. Maryland Functional Math Chart

The Maryland Functional Reading Test Black and White Ninth-grade Students Who Passed, 1985-1988

Percentile Passing

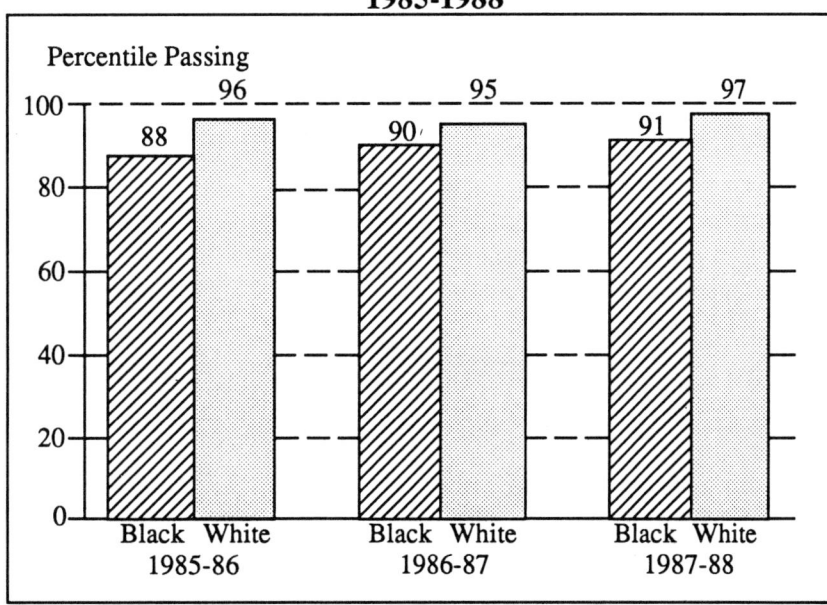

	Black	White
1985-86	88	96
1986-87	90	95
1987-88	91	97

Figure 4. Maryland Functional Reading Test Chart

proved from 43 percent passing in 1985–86 to 56 percent passing in 1987–88, and achievement for grade nine white students improved from 68 percent passing in 1985–86 to 79 percent passing in 1987–88, as shown in Figure 3.

- Grade nine black students who passed the Maryland Functional Reading Test increased from 88 percent in 1985–86 to 91 percent in 1987–88. See Figure 4.

A Comparison of Black and White Ninth-grade Student Performance on the Maryland Writing Test

Percentile Passing - Grade Nine

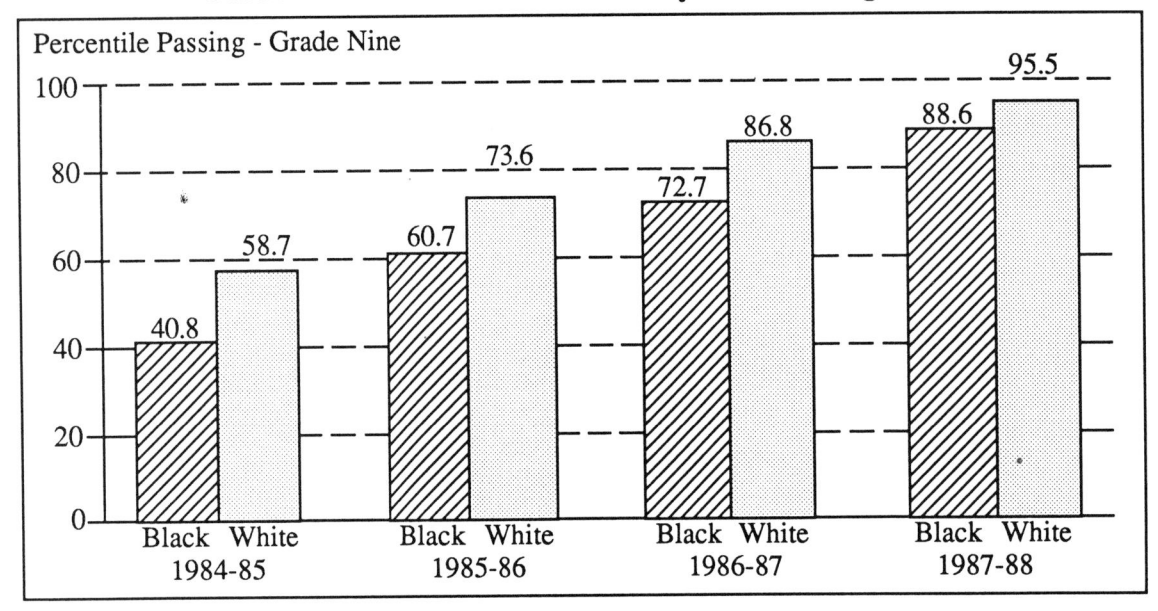

	Black	White
1984-85	40.8	58.7
1985-86	60.7	73.6
1986-87	72.7	86.8
1987-88	88.6	95.5

Figure 5. Comparison of Black & White Students' Results

- Grade nine black students who passed the Maryland Writing Test increased from 41 percent in 1984–85 to 89 percent in 1987–88, while the number of white students who passed the test increased from 59 percent to 95 percent during the same period. See Figure 5.

Strength and Presence of Correlates of Effective Schools

An Effective Schools Audit Advisory Team process was developed as a monitoring strategy to give feedback to schools concerning the extent to which their school improvement activities are being implemented as described in their school improvement plans. The audit advisory process also provides a measure of the strength and presence of the correlates of Effective Schools within the schools and the school system.

Each audit advisory team is chaired by a principal and includes classroom teachers and a central or area office representative. The team spends one day in a school, interviewing the principal and staff, visiting classrooms, and reviewing data. The team prepares an audit report which gives feedback to the principal and staff. Problem areas are identified and a plan to address these areas is developed by the principal and school improvement team.

During the 1987–88 school year, 37 schools were visited by an audit advisory team. Reports from the visits indicated the level of staff **awareness** of the Effective Schools Research and process; the degree of **involvement** staff members felt they had in developing their school's improvement plans; and the extent to which staff members felt they were actively participating in the **implementation** of the process.

Data from the audit reports indicated that in over 95 percent of the audited schools, staff awareness of the Effective Schools Research and process was evident. Similarly, staff involvement in development of school improvement plans was evident. The widest range of responses occurred with questions that focused on the staffs' active participation in the implementation process, particularly in the classroom setting. Later, audit report data are used by individual schools to assist school personnel in refining the implementation process within their school.

Resolving Concerns Related to Effective Schools Process Implementation

As The Effective Schools process was implemented in Prince George's County Public Schools, several issues and concerns emerged. A summary of these issues and a description of how the issues were resolved is presented below:

Gradual vs Total System Implementation

Issue: Should the Effective Schools process be implemented gradually, school by school, over an extended period of time, or should a system-wide commitment to implementation be made from the outset?

Resolution: Early in the implementation process a commitment to system-wide, rather than school by school implementation, was made due to the significant impact the process could make for all students.

The Mission vs the Means

Issue: How can the school system keep a strong focus on the message and mission of Effective Schools—quality and equity, and not confuse the means to reach the ends, the Effective Schools correlates, with the ends themselves?

Resolution: During the first two years of Effective Schools process implementation, school improvement plans were built around implementation of the correlates of Effective Schools. With such an intense focus on the correlates, the means to achieve the goals of quality and equity became confused with the goal itself. This issue was resolved in part by changing the focus of school improvement plans from implementation of correlates to development of long range goals related to **student outcomes**, and by renewed emphasis on quality **and** equity.

Dynamic vs Static Process

Issue: Must all parts of the implementation plan be "in place" before a system-wide commitment is made to implement the Effective Schools process?

Resolution: As stated above, at the time Prince George's County Public Schools implemented the Effective Schools process, there was little research to guide school systems in ways to establish a total commitment to accomplish implementation. The resulting implementation process has been a dynamic—but sometimes fragmented—one. Because some features of accomplishing implementation were incorporated after the initial introduction to the process (e.g., audit advisory teams, outcomes-based planning, steering committee guidance), it was sometimes confusing to school-based educators exactly what was meant by the Effective Schools process. In spite of the issues raised by this "dynamic" implementation process, the process has been successfully implemented and has had a profound impact on the total instructional program.

Local School Decision-Making vs School System Priorities

Issue: How can a balance between local school decision-making and school system priorities best be reached?

Resolution: School system priorities and local school priorities have become much more closely matched as a result of Effective Schools process implementation. Effective Schools Research provides a mission, a common language, and a collaborative implementation process for the entire school system.

Time for Planning vs Time for Teaching

Issue: How can sufficient time for school improvement teams to meet be provided?

Resolution: Finding time for school improvement teams and total school staffs to meet for planning and staff development has been an ongoing challenge. The issue of time was partially resolved through creating four "early closing" staff development days in the school calendar when school-based development activities related to Effective Schools were scheduled.

Process vs Outcomes

Issue: To what extent should the success of school improvement efforts be determined by the **process** followed and to what extent by **outcomes** reached?

Resolution: During the four years Prince George's County Public Schools has been involved with the Effective Schools process implementation, the process vs. outcomes discussion has surfaced in many forms and in a variety of settings. Educators traditionally have been process oriented. Although process is important, the Effective Schools Research clearly points to **student outcomes** as the final indicator of success. Prince George's County Schools has addressed the process vs. outcomes issue by demonstrating how the process becomes the **means** to the desired ends of positive student outcomes.

Effective Schools as Schools of the Future

Effective Schools Research points educators in the direction of school-based decision making and school-based management. Prince George's County Public Schools is looking toward the year 2000 with a new initiative called Project 2000—an invitation to ten schools to create a vision of education for the future. Principals and teachers participating in Project 2000 are exploring questions such as these: Given what we know about the projected student population for the twenty-first century, how should we organize for instruction? How should we staff our schools? How do we create teacher leadership? How do we meet the increasingly diverse needs of students? How can home and school be linked so closely that one is an extension of the other? How can schools capitalize on the advancements in technology to improve instruction for all students? How might the traditional school year and patterns for school organization change? However these questions are answered, one thing is certain—schools of the future must be Effective Schools.

Summary

A clearly defined mission and school system improvement goals, higher levels of student achievement, positive results from audit advisory team visits, increased accountability, greater levels of teacher involvement in decision-making, and implementation of an instructional management system with criterion-referenced tests are some of the many indicators that the Effective Schools process is well on its way toward full, successful implementation in Prince George's County Public Schools, and most significantly, to improve the achievement of minority students.

Appendix A

Characteristics of an Effective School System

As noted earlier, until recently research has focused on what makes a school building effective without regard to the contributions that the rest of the system makes toward achieving that effectiveness. The following are characteristics that the system must have in order to support, reinforce, and help guide the process at the local building level.

- Strong, instructionally focused leadership
- Clear and focused mission
- Frequent monitoring of student progress
- Climate of high expectations for success for all students and staff
- Purposeful and supportive involvement of parents, other citizens, and business and community groups
- Curriculum and instructional programs that assure opportunities for every student to learn
- Support for schools to assure a safe and orderly learning environment for students
- High rate of attendance for students and all school and non-school based staff
- Strong staff development program which reflects and supports the implementation of the Effective Schools process
- Clear understanding on the part of all staff as to their specific roles and responsibilities in contributing to the Effective Schools process, and an evaluation process which supports this understanding.

On the following pages are specific implications for planning and action which must be considered by any school system engaged in the school improvement process.

Characteristic	Implications for Planning and Action
Strong, Instructionally focused leadership	1. The superintendent of schools assures that a school system plan for implementing the Effective School Process is developed and assigns responsibilities for implementing the plan. 2. Associate superintendents assure that resources within their divisions support school by school implementation of Effective Schools School Improvement Plans. 3. Assistant superintendents assure that each school in their administrative area develops and implements a school improvement plans. 4. Subject area supervisors and program coordinators provide assistance to schools in implementing school improvement plans as the schools define a need for such assistance. 5. Subject area supervisors and program coordinators provide assistance to schools in implementing school improvement plans as the schools define a need for such assistance. 6. Principals provide leadership for and assure staff participation in developing, implementing, monitoring, and evaluating their local school improvement plan. 7. An Advance Leadership Training Program provides principals with information required to develop and maintain an Effective Schools Program within their buildings. 8. A Pre-Leadership Training Program provides professional employees who aspire to positions of leadership with information related to implementation of the Effective Schools process at the local school level. 9. A variety of staff development programs is available for teachers to strengthen their instructional expertise in assuring that **all** students learn the essential curriculum.
Clear and focuses mission	1. A school system mission statement is developed which includes the expectation that all students will learn the essential curriculum, and highlights characteristics of Effective Schools as a means to reach that end. 2. The school system Strategic Management Plan includes school system improvement goals that define high expectations for all students and reflect focus on quality **and** equity. 3. School system policies and administrative procedures are reviewed on a regular basis, and strengthened or adjusted, as needed, to increase support for the school system's mission and improvement goals. 4. Goals and objectives for each division within the school system clearly reflect and support the school system mission and improvement goals and priorities identified from local school improvement plans. 5. Each school develops its statement of mission and goals which reflect the school system mission and improvement goals.

Characteristic	Implications for Planning and Action
	6. Each school has a school improvement team representing the entire staff of the school which guides the school improvement process within the school. 7. Each school improvement team, with staff input and involvement, develops a school improvement plan that provides direction in accomplishing its mission and reaching its goals.
Frequent monitoring of student progress	1. Criterion-referenced tests based upon essential curricular objectives are developed for all grade levels, and used in a manner designed to enhance the learning process. 2. Data from system-wide achievement measures are prepared in disaggregated form to facilitate planning for program development or adjustment, and are provided for schools in a timely manner. 3. Data are provided to assist local school personnel in analyzing relationships between student achievement and the instructional delivery system within the school. 4. Student grade distributions, analyzed by sex, race, and attendance, are provided to secondary schools to assist in assessing the day-to-day impact of the instructional program as evidenced by student achievement. 5. Assistance with interpreting and using disaggregated student achievement data to improve instruction are provided for principals and staff. 6. Classroom observations and follow-up conferences provide teachers with opportunities to analyze the impact on student achievement of selected instructional strategies used for classroom instruction. 7. School instructional teams and/or supplemental services teams (SIT/SST) assist in identifying student needs and planning appropriate instructional adjustments. 8. Case review teams provide monitoring and assistance with program planning for students with identified needs beyond their present placements. 9. Psychological services personnel provide classroom observations and consultations with teachers.
Climate of high expectations for success for all students and staff	1. The school system mission statement states that **all** students **will** learn the essential curriculum. 2. The school system develops improvement goals which clearly reflect quality **and** equity. 3. Staff development programs are established to help principals and teachers identify the relationship of high expectations to success, ways to communicate high expectations to all students and staff, and strategies to help different types of learners succeed.

Characteristic	Implications for Planning and Action
	4. The school system's curriculum presents clearly stated objectives which challenge students to achieve at optimum levels. 5. Programs are in place which meet the special needs of students so all may learn the essential curriculum. 6. Teachers and guidance personnel encourage students to enroll in more challenging courses to promote optimum achievement and opportunities for **all** students. 7. Teacher recruitment efforts focus on identifying prospective teachers who have or wish to develop proficiency in assuring that **all** students learn the essential curriculum.
Purposeful and supportive involvement of parents, other citizens, and business and community groups	1. Parents (citizens) are included on major school system committees, task forces, and advisory councils. 2. Parents (citizens) assist with selection of instructional materials. 3. Members of the business and industry community are invited to provide input for school system instructional and management planning. 4. Parents are given assistance in supporting their children's learning through specially designed programs and materials. 5. Parents are represented on school improvement teams and school planning and management teams. 6. Support is provided for schools to develop "social calendars" of events which encourage parent participation/involvement. 7. The school system offers parents/guardians a "system of choices" so they have an opportunity to select from a variety of educational alternatives those most appropriate for their children. 8. Parents (citizens) are encouraged to complete system-wide surveys to evaluate programs of the school system. 9. Parent/teacher organizations are made aware of and encouraged to participate in the Effective Schools process. 10. Parents are made aware of and encouraged to participate in educational and career planning activities. 11. Members of the business and industry community are invited to provide information for students about careers and job-seeking skills.
Curriculum and instructional programs that assure opportunities for every student to participate and to learn	1. The school system's mission and instructional goals are clearly reflected through well designed curriculum documents which are provided for every teacher in the system. 2. Programs are in place to support the special needs of students.

Characteristic	Implications for Planning and Action
	• Special Education • ESOL • TAG • Chapter I • Head Start • State Compensatory Education • Project SUCCESS • Vocational High Schools 3. Magnet programs are offered in response to students' special interests and needs and reflect quality and equity by design. 4. Course offerings are provided which meet students' current skill levels and challenge them to reach and aspire to high levels of achievement. 5. The school system curriculum assures systematic instruction in basic skills for all students. 6. The school system curriculum promotes development of higher order thinking skills for **all** students. 7. High quality, current instructional materials are provided for schools. 8. All curriculum and instructional materials support instruction that is multicultural. 9. Resource assistance is provided for new and experienced staff to assure that appropriate instruction in the essential curriculum is provided for all students. 10. Workshops which include correlates and processes of Effective Schools implementation are provided to assist and support those teachers who are new to the profession or to the schools system. 11. Disaggregated data on student achievement are provided for schools to use in adjusting and enhancing curriculum and instructional programs for students.
Support for schools to assure a safe and orderly learning environment for students	1. A code of student conduct is established and communicated to students, parents, and the community to help schools promote a safe and orderly learning environment. 2. Pupil Services' support is readily available to schools to assist with implement of school improvement plans. 3. Alternative programs are provided for students with special needs. 4. The Supporting Services Division collaborates with schools to help them develop and maintain preventive maintenance programs which are part of a safe and orderly environment. 5. The Supporting Services Division collaborates with area assistant superintendents and local school principals in enhancing the physical teaching-learning environment. 6. Pupil Services personnel support school staffs in efforts to eliminate distractions that interfere with learning.

Characteristic	Implications for Planning and Action
High rate of attendance for students and all school and non-school based staff	1. The relationship between student and staff attendance and student achievement is clearly recognized and documented. 2. Programs are in place which appropriately address students' learning strengths and needs. 3. System-wide and school-by-school attendance data for students and staff are provided on a regular basis. 4. Working conditions promote a high level of staff interaction and involvement. 5. Procedures are in place to communicate with families of students with frequent absences. 6. Pupil Services staff are available to assist schools with identified school attendance problems. 7. Pupil Services staff are available to assist in developing and implementing preventive strategies that result in improved student and staff attendance.
Strong staff development program which reflects and supports implementation of the Effective Schools process	1. An orientation program which features elements of the Effective Schools process is provided for staff new to the school system. 2. Pre-Leadership Training Programs, and Advanced Leadership Training Programs which feature elements of the Effective Schools process are provided. 3. Each department and division within the school system arranges appropriate staff development programs that feature elements of the Effective Schools process. 4. School-based staff development programs which feature elements of the Effective Schools process are provided during the school day. 5. Staff development councils that include representatives from every school provide input for system-wide staff development activities which support elements of the Effective Schools process. 6. School-based staff development coordinators are members of their respective school improvement teams and provide linkage for staff development initiatives and school improvement efforts. 7. A directory of staff development resources is developed by the Department of Staff Development and made available to all schools. 8. School system support for inservice needs identified in school improvement plans is provided.
Clear understanding on the part of all staff as to their specific roles and responsibilities in contributing to the Effective Schools process	1. The superintendent of schools arranges for system-wide implementation of the Effective Schools process and identifies resources needed in support of the process.

Characteristic	Implications for Planning and Action
	2. Each non-school based division, department, and office defines its roles and responsibilities in contributing to the Effective Schools process in the form of a written document widely circulated throughout the school system.
3. Each local school, through its school improvement team, identifies roles and responsibilities of local school personnel in implementing the Effective Schools process.
4. A system-wide Effective Schools Implementation Plan is developed which summarizes the specific roles and responsibilities of all staff in contributing to the Effective Schools process.
5. A system-wide Effective Schools Audit/Advisory Team Process is established which assists schools to monitor and adjust implementation of school improvement plan.
6. Standards for Excellence which reflect the Effective Schools process and outcomes are developed for all staff and form the basis for all staff evaluations.
7. A continuing staff development program is in place which introduces new employees to the Effective Schools process.
8. All components of the school system collaboratively work to fulfil the school system's mission and reach its improvement goals.

A Case for Equity and Quality: How One Team Is Making it Happen In Norfolk, Virginia

Dr. Gene R. Carter, Superintendent of Schools,
Norfolk Public Schools

Mrs. Ann B. Madison, Director,
Human Relations/Staff Development

Mr. Eddie D. Hall, Principal,
Larchmont Elementary School

Dr. Thomas B. Lockamy, Director
Instructional Support Services

Norfolk Public Schools
Became involved in Effective Schools process in 1982

Community

Population
276,000
Urban. Economic base—military, coastal and harbor occupations, light industry. World's largest naval base, inner city under reconstruction with middle/upper income homes, landmark case in bussing for desegregation. 20 percent military—highly transient.

Predominantly middle class 58 percent white, 38 percent black, 54 percent qualify for free-and-reduced lunch. The black/white ethnic composition of the school division is just the opposite of that of the city.

School District

Enrollment
36,000

Ethnic Composition, (percent)
African-American	58.0
American Indian	.1
Asian-American	3.0
Caucasian	38.0
Hispanic	.9

Per Pupil Expenditure
1986–87	$3,854
1987–88	4,139
1988–89	4,303

Percent bussed
47

Area (in square miles):
64

Schools
Elementary schools	37
Middle schools	8
High schools	1
Other—Vocational	1
—Pregnant teens	1
—Sev. handicap	3
—Skills center	1
—Gifted alter.	1

Number of Staff
Administrators 206
(100 principals, 106 central)
Certified Teachers 2,600
Support staff 1,794

Student-Teacher Ratio
Elementary	23.5:1
Middle	24.0:1
High	22.2:1

Percent college-bound (approx.)
62

Abstract

Although many components for school district improvement were in place when Norfolk Public Schools embarked on the Effective Schools process in 1981–82, without SPIRAL (Systematic Process for Instruction, Remediation, and Acceleration of Learning), based on the ESR framework, increased achievement for all students may not have become a reality.

A comparison of the district and schools' involvement in "effectiveness activities," and the systematic management of the school improvement process components implemented in 1982, are described in this case study.

Innovative staff development programs are at the heart of the Norfolk Effective Schools process, with a wide variety of training programs utilized to address the needs established by school faculties and the district's staff development department.

Norfolk, like Prince George's County, established a comprehensive system that tended to keep the school improvement effort mobilized no matter how the political, economic, or community environment changed around it. Prince George's was able to go forward in spite of negative connotations of a desegregation compliance order. Norfolk continued its school improvement efforts in spite of the fact that poor neighborhoods were demolished and replaced by neighborhoods of middle- and upper-income families. This led to the reestablishment of "neighborhood elementary schools," which meant over one-third of the schools were comprised of poor and predominantly black students. Norfolk treated this development as a challenge, and continued to move forward toward "teaching for learning for all children."

The importance of a new set of beliefs which staff, administrators, students, and parents must share that "all children can learn" is well articulated in Norfolk Public School's report. This belief set flows from decisive, positive actions on the part of all constituencies, documented results, and collaborative planning, teaching, and learning in the district and the schools. From the new belief system and incisive actions commitment to the Effective Schools process is realized.

Success for All Children

Imagine a school where **each** child experiences success daily. Visualize the teachers of these students happily discussing creative ways to make learning relevant and ardently seeking avenues for students to apply what they learn. Also listen with your mind's ear to the principal, members of the faculty and staff, several central office support staff members, and two parents gathered around a conference table in the bright, sunlit media center. They are generating ideas for a master plan that will move the school closer to the descriptors used to define an effective school. Two key words heard throughout their discussion are "equity" and "quality." Their conversations focus on where the school stands in relation to providing educational opportunities for *all* students that reflect both terms. This is the goal for each of the 53 schools that comprise the Norfolk Public Schools System.

The Norfolk (Virginia) Public Schools (NPS) System serves 36,000 students in an elementary (pre–K–5), middle (6–8), senior high (9–12) organizational setting. Additionally, a technical vocational center, an outdoor education camp, and several supplementary facilities offer alternative programs for students with special needs.

Norfolk is a highly transient, urban city which houses the world's largest naval base. The district has diverse socioeconomic strata. The city is 58 percent white; the school system is 58 percent black and 42 percent white or other. Approximately 44 percent of its students are from middle to upper income families; 56 percent are from the lower socioeconomic stratum. Of the families in the district, 20 percent are from a highly transitory military population.

The school system welcomes the challenge inherent in its mission to provide a quality educational program that is equitable for each of its students. In fact, its mission is that "All students will master the established educational objectives required for graduation with **no differentiation** in the **proportion** of students demonstrating mastery of the essential educational objectives among the various socioeconomic levels." SPIRAL (Systematic Process for Instruction, Remediation and Acceleration of Learning) is the school improvement process to be described. It provides the means for answering the question, Can a large, complex, inner-city school system which serves a highly transient and relatively low socioeconomic population make equity **and** quality a reality?

What follows is an overview of the progress the school system has made since its implementation of the system-wide school improvement process in 1981–82. Next, the process will be explained; finally, recommendations for initiating, refining, or extending a school improvement process are offered.

It must be mentioned first and foremost that "equity" does not mean equal, and "quality" does not mean the 50th percentile on standardized tests. Equity, by NPS definition, means that resources and opportunities are based on need; quality is a direction partially measured by test scores reflecting a steady increase over time. Both provide each student the greatest number of options when exiting school. With this clearly in mind, it is evident that never before has there been such a deliberate and unified effort to ensure that *all* students succeed, regardless of previous academic performance or socioeconomic status.

What has this done for the mission of teaching and learning? The results speak for themselves. The bottom line is increased student achievement, higher employee personal efficacy, and a more satisfied parent and community population. In fact, in a 1988 national poll conducted by the University of Kentucky, Norfolk, Virginia, was cited as being the second most desirable place to live in the United States. It goes without saying that the public schools play a big part in public opinion about a particular demographic area.

Highlights of the progress made toward equity and quality since 1982 are reflected in the representative graphs included in this chapter. These constitute evidence that schools are improving. For the first time in over a decade, composite scores on standardized tests system-wide are at or above the national norm at every grade level tested, and are maintaining an upward trend. Criterion-referenced test results show similar gains. The retention and dropout rates have been reduced significantly, and the percent of high school graduates continues to rise in spite of increased requirements for graduation. Attendance and discipline at all grade levels have improved. The number of schools meeting the criteria for effectiveness is also increasing.

A number of distinguished awards and commendations have been bestowed upon the school system for its systematic efforts to implement Effective Schools Research. The school improvement process has been featured nationally in publications and at conferences (American Association of School Administrators (AASA), Virginia Association of School Administrators (VASA), Virginia Association of Supervision and Curriculum Development (VASCD), and NASCD, National Staff Development Conference, *The Effective School Report, HRD=P*). It is recognized as an exemplary model for school improvement by the National Center for Effective Schools Research and Development. The process is a major component in the staff development model which received one of AASA's nineteen National Exemplary Staff Development

Awards in 1987. SPIRAL has received Excellence in Education Awards from Virginia Polytechnical Institute in the areas of staff development, dropout reduction, new teacher orientation, and community involvement. (NORSTAR, a collaborative program between the schools and governmental community, is also recognized in the *American School Board Journal Executive Educator.*) AASA selected Dr. Gene R. Carter, superintendent, as its first National Superintendent of the Year in 1987–88. Moreover, both the elementary and secondary State Principals of the Year are members of the NPS team.

How Have These Results Been Attained?

Prior to the implementation of the systematic process for system-wide school improvement, many Effective Schools activities took place. Locally generated performance-based curriculum guides and criterion-referenced tests were available. Continuous coaching of teachers and administrators in the application of the effective teaching research received top priority. A promotion/retention criterion had been established and a task force formed to study the dropout problem. The school division participated in both the state and the Southern Association of Colleges and Schools (SACS) Accreditation programs. A system-wide Six-Year Improvement Plan was in place and reviewed annually. However, without SPIRAL, many efforts became fragmented and the focus (mission) became diffused.

In 1981–82 the school board, in conjunction with the superintendent, established several priority goals for the system. The development of a comprehensive system-wide school improvement plan, to be funded by the regular operating budget, was one of these goals. Under the direction of the superintendent, with the support of the school board, and guided by the research of the late Professor Ronald Edmonds and Dr. Lawrence W. Lezotte, the members of the NPS School Improvement Planning Committee (i.e., teachers, principals, administrators, classified staff, parents, and members of the community) structured the SPIRAL plan. It was designed to provide an educational program of the highest quality for each student. Implementation would be system-wide, beginning first in each of the 40 elementary schools in 1983. Because it produced highly favorable results in 1985, it was extended to include the system's five senior high schools and vocational education center. In 1987 the eight middle schools became involved. The middle schools were last in the evolution cycle because the district was in the process of transition from a junior high school organization to a middle school configuration.

Norfolk's school improvement plan was structured to be consistent with the "correlates" identified in Effective Schools Research as being characteristic of typical Effective Schools.

1. A system-wide mission is clear and focuses on teaching and learning. It incorporates the belief that **all** students can learn.
2. The principal is a strong instructional leader and an effective and competent manager.
3. Staff members hold high expectations for the educational accomplishments of their students and for themselves.
4. A safe, orderly, caring, goal-oriented environment is essential to teaching and learning.
5. Acquisition of essential skills takes precedence over all other school activities.
6. Frequent and thorough monitoring of student performance is required and results are used to make educational decisions.
7. Parent and community involvement is actively sought.
8. Human, fiscal, and physical resources are equitably distributed among the schools and tailored to students' needs.

The system-wide implementation plan follows this process: Need—School Board/Superintendent Goals—System-wide Planning Team—Cadre Training in awareness of the Model—Needs assessment—Inbuilding and System-wide Staff Development Committees—Staff Development (Awareness, Training)—School-based Implementation—Evaluation—Curriculum/Testing/Staff Development Alignment-on-Maintenance—Extension—Celebration—Continuous Assessment of Need, Planning, Implementation—Need, Planning, Implementation.

The thrust has been on improving schools from *within,* one at a time. The district-level coordination team consists of the superintendent, a principal, and the directors of human relations/staff development, instruction, and research/testing/statistics. Coordination responsibilities fall within the parameters of their regular duties.

Each principal establishes a school improvement planning committee to coordinate the school improvement process, and to write the annual school improvement plan. Although a smaller steering committee leads the process, larger correlate committees are also established to make shared leadership effective. Teachers, classified and support staff, parents, members of the community, students (at secondary levels), and central office support staff are members of these committees. Every employee has a part in the joint effort to create equity and quality in an optimal teaching, learning, and caring environment. The Annual

School Improvement Plan is developed by the staff, guided by the school board's goals, the superintendent's objectives (upgraded annually), state standards of quality and accreditation, results of the needs assessment (conducted every three years), and analysis of the disaggregated student achievement, attendance, and computerized data (provided annually). The plan and its results form the basis for discussion in the semiannual interviews conducted by the superintendent with each principal. In this sense, the Effective Schools process can be described as a "top down-bottom up" process.

The Effective Schools thrust has had a tremendous impact on curriculum, staff development, program implementation and evaluation, personnel evaluation, and the general practice of running schools. The student, and what is best for him or her, is the pivotal point of reference for all decisions regarding the aforementioned areas. Some of the primary changes will be described now in the sections that follow.

Measurement of Student Achievement

Test results are now disaggregated by SES (socioeconomic status). Standardized and criterion-referenced test scores are administered at every grade level, not just those designated by the Virginia State Department of Education. In the area of communication skills, criterion-referenced tests are now administered quarterly, rather than twice a year. Analyses of test results provide the basis for determining instructional priorities.

How well is Norfolk doing? Some representative results show steady gains. Figure 1 shows increases in composite SRA scores for grades 2, 4, 6, 8, and 11; increases from 1982 to 1987 range from 5 percent to 17 percent. Figure 2 illustrates the increases achieved by grades 1, 3, 5, and 7 from 1983 through 1988. Increases ranged from 1 percent to 15 percent. Not only has student achievement improved notably, but the dropout rate (see Figure 3) has decreased markedly, from 15.8 percent in 1980–81 to 8.1 percent in 1987–88. In addition, need for formal disciplinary procedures (including suspensions and expulsions) has decreased. Figure 4 reports heartening progress in preventing disciplinary problems and in more effectively handling problems that arise.

Curriculum and Instructional Management

Norfolk Public Schools incorporates the belief that schools can and will make a difference in the learning process and that all students can and will learn. There must be congruence among written, taught, and tested curriculum. A standardized method for curriculum development, based on the Quality Control Triangle created by Dr. Fenwick English of the University of Cincinnati, is being implemented to produce an effective instructional management system.

Norfolk has implemented SPIRAL (Systematic Process of Remediation and Acceleration of Learning), a strong alternative program for remediation of essential skills of students at all levels. Unique promotion options exist for elementary and middle school students previously retained. These students may join their former peers at midyear or at the end of the year if they have demonstrated the competencies needed to be optimally successful at that grade level. Teachers of these classes are carefully selected because of their previous success rates with lower achievers. These teachers also receive intensive and specifically tailored inservice training to increase their probability of success. SPIRAL was designed in Norfolk to help teachers be more effective with at-risk students. SPIRAL teachers learn to use five to six major approaches to teaching the existing curriculum. SPIRAL training includes mastery of the TESA (Teacher Expectation and Student Achievement), modality-based instruction, experience in how to plan and deliver interdisciplinary studies (including coordination of objectives across the disciplines), training in reinforcement theories, cooperative learning (with special attention given trust-building skills), study ways to raise student expectations, and organizational skills (because some at-risk students are very disorganized), creative discipline (using ideas from Lee Canter and Associates and other consultants, such as posted rules, positive and negative consequences, school-wide support for consistency, parent involvement), intensive instruction using the Effective Teaching Model (Madeline Hunter), training in how to teach students to keep records of their own progress, and how to use test data in making instructional decisions. Many regular teachers apply to take the training out of a desire to improve their effectiveness.

The need for SPIRAL-trained teachers is declining, a sign of success. More teachers than are needed apply to take SPIRAL training. When the SPIRAL effort began, the school district identified eleven schools, largely in poorer neighborhoods, and systematically trained teachers to teach in those schools. Every year staff members conduct a needs assessment and talk over how problems were solved and how to solve remaining problems.

A longitudinal study of the results of student performance over time, 1983–87, clearly provides evidence that continued student success is maintained. Not only has the total number of SPIRAL-taught stu-

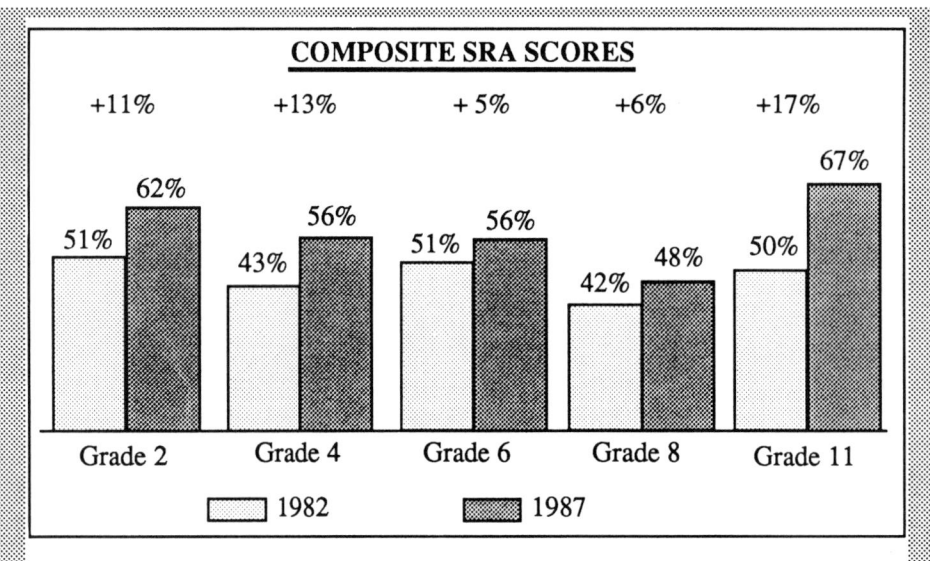

Figure 1. Inceases in Composite SRA Scores, Grades 2, 4, 6, 8, 11

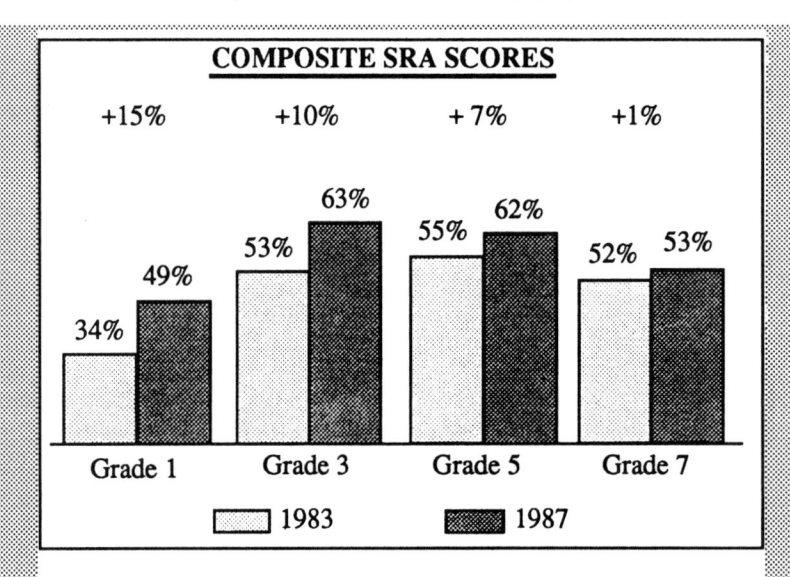

Figure 2. Increases in Composite SRA scores, Grades 1, 3, 5, 7

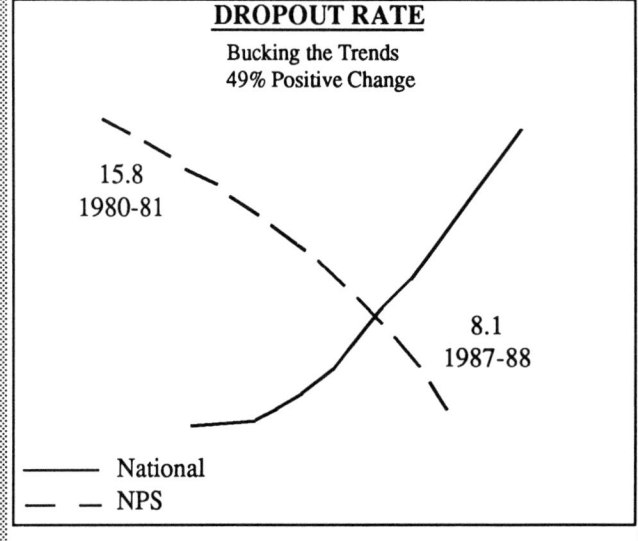

Figure 3. Dropout Rate, 1980–81 through 1987–88

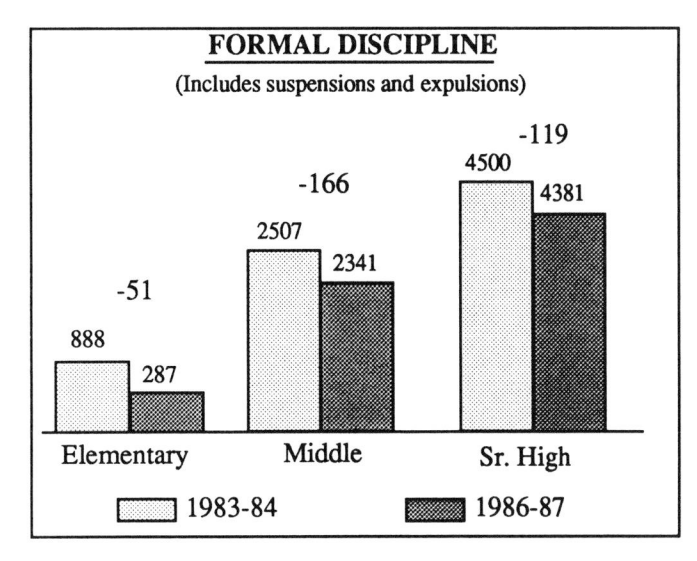

FORMAL DISCIPLINE
(Includes suspensions and expulsions)

	Elementary	Middle	Sr. High
1983-84	888	2507	4500
1986-87	287	2341	4381
Change	-51	-166	-119

Figure 4. Need for Formal Discipline

Mid-Year Spiral Class Promotions
1983-84 through 1986-87

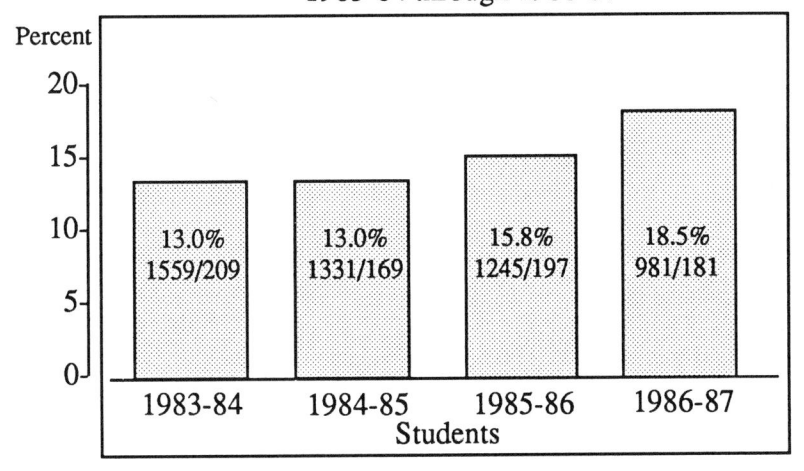

Year	Percent	Ratio
1983-84	13.0%	1559/209
1984-85	13.0%	1331/169
1985-86	15.8%	1245/197
1986-87	18.5%	981/181

Figure 5. Mid-Year SPIRAL Class Promotions, 1983–84 through 1986–87

Spiral Class Students Who Rejoined Peers Total 1,297 over 4 years

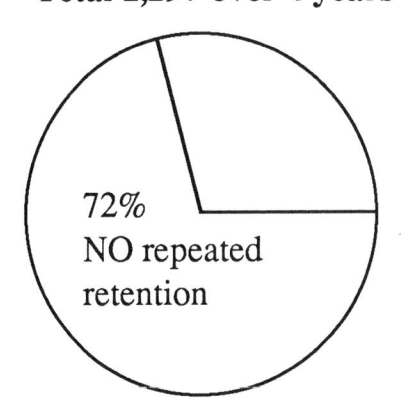

72% NO repeated retention

Figure 6. SPIRAL Class Students Who Rejoined Peers, Total 1,297 over 4 years

dents dropped, but the percentage of students who join their peers is increasing. Figure 5 shows the consistent trend. Additional students rejoin their peers after a full year in the SPIRAL program rather than at mid-year. In the long run the SPIRAL program saves money and enables more students to be successful. This program also keeps some students from dropping out. (Figure 5)

Norfolk teachers and administrators are pleased that 72 percent of the SPIRAL students have successfully rejoined their peers and have not repeated being retained. (See Figure 6.)

Schools where the student population consists of predominantly low-income families have been identified as target schools. Additional resources, a parent activity leader (PAL), and a lower student-teacher ratio have been established to intensify efforts to maximize student achievement. A monitoring mechanism operates under the name "Oversight Committee." After ten years of court-ordered desegregation, Norfolk, in a landmark decision, won the right to return to neighborhood schools because of its efforts to bring about equity in all of its schools. In the city of Norfolk, massive renovations have renewed the downtown. Now all but 12 of the city's schools are racially mixed. Schools that aren't racially mixed are in unmixed neighborhoods. Ron Edmonds, who was consulted by the district toward the end of the study that led to the landmark decision to return to neighborhood schools, said that the district could return to neighborhood schools and still have equity, especially if they continued the school improvement based on Effective Schools Research. He also said that Norfolk should have an oversight committee to monitor the use of resources. The Oversight Committee consists of business people, clergy, city council members, principals, teachers, and parents, for the purpose of monitoring equity and quality.

Another approach to achieving quality and equity in a new way came through a state grant. NPS was awarded the three-year grant to create a model elementary school to develop innovative approaches for accomplishing the system's mission. The plan includes specially trained teachers, a writing-to-read laboratory (using computers), new approaches to scheduling, and more. At the outset the teachers attended an intensive one-week training session just before classes began.

A number of other special programs to accommodate the unique needs of the urban learner in the acquisition of essential skills include the Holding Power Plan, Project Rescue (funded by U.S. Government Vocational Education Entitlement), and Dropout Hotline (dropout reduction and retrieval for at-risk students), Homework Hotline, and Writing to Read (IBM Grades K–1). Additional enrichment programs for acceleration of academic performance include CHROME (Cooperating Hampton Roads Organizations for Minorities in Engineering, grades 7–12), NORSTAR (Norfolk Public Schools Science and Technology Advanced Research, grades 9–12, in conjunction with NASA, National Aeronautics Space Academy), Work-Study Plan in conjunction with Norfolk Sentra Hospital, and a Magnet School for Health Professions (grades 10–12) in conjunction with the Medical Center of Hampton Roads.

Professional and General Staff Development

Commitment to becoming better is contingent upon relevant professional growth activities. All employees are involved in needs assessment, planning, implementation, and evaluation for staff development purposes. Whether at the district, school, or individual employee level, professional growth activities are related to the correlates that characterize an Effective School. Focus is on support for student outcomes for long-term benefits. Activities are meant to raise the levels of proficiency and increase self-confidence in job skills. They are intended to raise expectations of self and others; the needs of both the organization and the individual are important.

The umbrella of the school improvement process gives professional development continuity and direction. Programs focus beyond a single topic or isolated skill; "Dog and Pony Shows" are a thing of the past. Furthermore, the school improvement plan emphasizes the importance of addressing the needs of **all** employees. School improvement and staff development have become synonymous.

Topics that have been covered include empowerment, curriculum alignment, critical thinking across the curriculum, whole-language approach to communication skills, leadership training for the school improvement process, training/coaching (of central office personnel and principals) related observing teacher instruction and holding feedback conferences on professional development, training for teachers coaching teachers on new concepts, skills, and strategies, middle-school teachers and teacher advisor programs, meeting the needs of the gifted, multi-cultural education and international studies, literature-based reading instruction, and effective questioning strategies to promote higher-level thinking skills (including how to individualize instruction in whole-group instruction by the manner in which you ask questions). New teachers and other new employees learn about improving schools based on Effective Schools Research. Ongoing training is available to virtually all employees. For example, by training maintenance personnel in boiler repair, money has been saved. Workshops on bathroom and floor care have been beneficial. Classified personnel have become more versatile.

Overall, Norfolk has sent cadres to receive training so that they can return and train others. That way the district saves on the expense of sending many people outside the district for training, yet further reaps the benefits of their new knowledge by having them become district trainers. The beauty of this approach is the large extent to which the system maintains itself. The Training the Trainers Model has brought awards: the American Association of School Administrators in 1986, and the Virginia Governors Award for Excellence in 1986.

Because schools improve one at a time (Goodlad, 1984), it is logical to conclude that staff members also improve one at a time. Consequently, the System-wide Staff Development Advisory Council has been formed with representation from every employee classification, at both building and central office levels. The council's major responsibility is to ensure that each member of the teaching and learning team, from the superintendent's level to the support staff levels, engages in practical, relevant, and visionary opportunities to grow professionally, systematically, and continuously. Priority is given to developing the leadership skills of building-level administrators, both

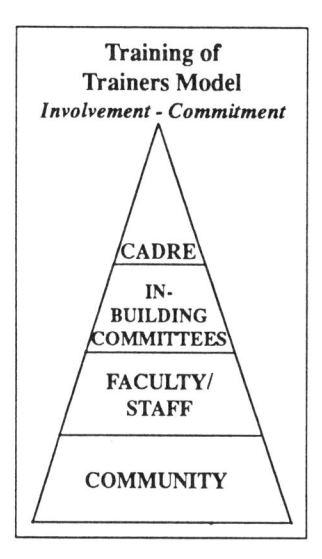

Figure 7. Training of Trainers Model

professional and classified. The council provides input to the director of human relations and staff development, who develops the comprehensive biennial system-wide plan. This plan is based on State of Virginia Standards of Quality, school board goals, superintendent's objectives, and results of the system-wide needs assessment. Major thrust is on developing skills and extending building-level expertise.

The primary basis for professional development plans is the identification of the schools' needs by the Inbuilding School Improvement Team. The team interprets student performance on standardized and criterion-referenced tests. It examines attendance, discipline reports, parent and community involvement, accidents, perceptions of the physical environment, and the extent to which the eight correlates have been implemented. Professional development activities address these needs. An award-winning, cost-effective Training of Trainers model is the primary vehicle used to maintain and enhance employee skills that support the mission. (See Figure 7.)

Personal Evaluation

"Knowing that we can make a difference, and knowing how, we must then decide that we will" (Edmonds, 1982). What gets monitored gets done! "The best way to show a stick is crooked is not to argue about it, or spend time denouncing it, but to lay a straight stick alongside of it" (Dwight Moody). It is upon these postulates that the personnel evaluation process rests as an integral component in the overall school improvement process.

Staff development is evaluated in terms of the positive changes in behavior that directly or indirectly impact on the overall mission. Several examples of positive change are:

- Participation in continuing education coursework has increased 135 percent.
- Reduced tuition rates at nearby universities resulted in personal savings of over half a million dollars.
- 12,768 **partnership** classroom observations and instructional conferences between school and central office administrators were conducted.
- School-based, on-site, professional development activities average 24 hours per year; some involve professional and classified staff members together.
- 96 percent of the teachers new to the system, or returning from a leave of absence, voluntarily participated in review and extension sessions on Effective Schools Research.
- 1,000 teachers and 88 substitute teachers voluntarily participated in a series of workshops to address low achieving students. These were planned and conducted by a total of 377 teaches, central office and building-level administrators.
- 44 percent of the approximately 5,000 NPS employees are involved in providing leadership for employee growth activities.
- One-third of the elementary schools (a total of 304 staff members, professional and classified) are voluntarily participating in shared leadership training with members of the business community.
- 132 **prospective** administrators are participating in a series of effective leadership orientation and skill-building sessions.
- A National School Improvement Institute for Practitioners has been hosted by NPS for two consecutive years, and attracted educators from 22 states and several provinces in Canada.
- An advisory council for classified support staff (i.e., office personnel, custodial workers) provides input and direction for continuous staff development based on Effective Schools Research and related job skills.

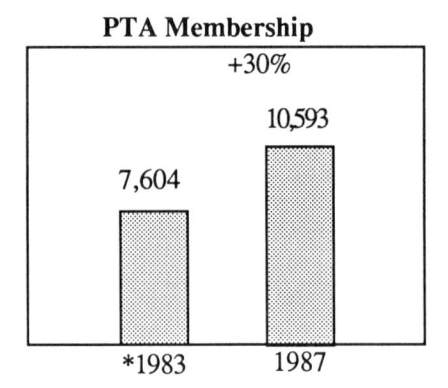

PTA Membership

```
                +30%
              10,593
     7,604
    *1983      1987
```
*Records of PTA Membership not kept prior to 1983

Figure 8. PTA Membership

Evaluation has always existed for improving job skills; however, major changes in the frame of reference, the focus on an individual employee's skills, and the process and procedures for evaluating staff was a result of the school and teacher effectiveness movement. The major changes are listed below:

- Emphasis on reinforcing employee strengths to correct weaknesses.
- Direct observation, anecdotal notes, post-observational conferences, and inservice replaced checklists of specific characteristics and rating scales. Focus is on measuring outcomes and performance behaviors against their impact on the overall mission. The evaluation instrument indicators of proficient performance are based on Effective Schools Research.
- In evaluating administrators, particularly principals, **instructional** leadership is weighted heaviest among the performance behaviors. Student and staff outcomes are an integral part of the overall evaluation.
- Peer observation, coaching, and self-evaluation are encouraged.

Parent and Community Involvement

Local universities are joining forces with NPS in pursuit of more Effective Schools. Partnerships have been established for coursework to address present and future needs. Tuition rates for school system employees have been reduced.

"Directions Toward Excellence," a school system publication, is mailed to all residents of Norfolk four times a year. It communicates the system's goals and objectives and highlights student and staff accomplishments. This effective public relations tool is augmented by the NPS Channel 28 Update News broadcast.

The public image of the school system is changing as is evidenced by positive media coverage, increased student enrollment, numbers of volunteers, and school "adopters." An increase in PTA membership over the past five years is another indication of the community's confidence in the school system (Figure 8).

Further evidence of positive school-community relations can be found in the support and commitment of community services and funding agencies. Each school has been adopted by one or more business or community agencies. The Academy for Educational Development, supported by the Ford Foundation and Carnegie Institute, sponsors the Urban Middle School Adolescent Pregnancy Prevention Project; The Tidewater Scholarship Foundation assists average college-bound students in completing the application process and securing financial resources; the Danforth Foundation provides funds for several professional development activities for school board members, principals, and teachers.

With any change, and especially one that is as far-reaching as the SPIRAL process, a certain number of problems, issues, or concerns are expected. Problems that have been encountered evolve around external mandates, changes in the community, and confusion over roles and responsibilities. Although these were few in number, they were important. Because of the system-wide *team* effort to ensure equity and quality, problems have been minimized.

The first of the concerns was the short time (six months) that the school division had to develop and implement a comprehensive, **system-wide** school improvement plan as the result of a school board mandate. At that time (1982) no one had knowledge of any school divisions in the United States where plans, broad in scope, were in place. A planning committee with a strong belief in students was appointed. Members of this committee were committed to the mission, and believed that the NPS team could accomplish it. At the recommendation of the late Ron Edmonds, a cadre was trained at the Michigan State University Summer Institute on Effective Schools. Also, members of the staff visited several school districts that were in the initial stages of implementing a school improvement program. These resources provided the foundation for the development of the model (SPIRAL) Norfolk Public Schools was to implement.

The second major issue dealt with the changes in the community. Many of the formerly urban poor neighborhoods were demolished and replaced by neighborhoods of middle- and upper-income families. Massive crosstown bussing was eliminated and neighborhood elementary schools were reestablished. As a

> **MY MISSION**
>
> Teaching and Learning
> Equity/Quality
> For All
>
> _____
> Signature

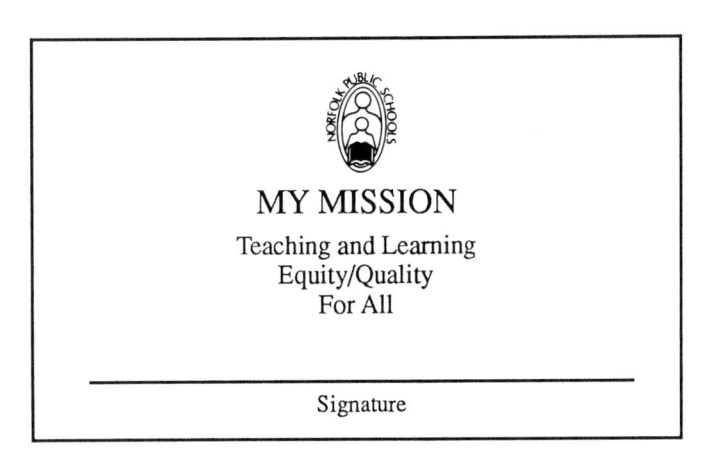

Figure 9. Norfolk Commitment Card

result, one-third of the schools were comprised of poor and predominantly black students. The burden of equity and quality for all presented challenges. The Target Schools Program, previously mentioned, is providing the means by which the needs of these students are being met. In addition, the Multicultural Education and Enhancement Program was established to afford students of all races, cultures, and socioeconomic classes an opportunity to interact and develop an appreciation of one another.

Another concern was the closing of the secondary alternative school due to limited space. It had been established to prevent extremely high-risk students from dropping out of school due to very low achievement and severe behavior problems. The teachers and counselors assigned to the school were involved in designing the new program, which was relocated in the regular high schools. Inservice sessions were conducted to prepare them for the change and support groups were formed among the three centers.

The Definition of "Effective Schools"

The major problem in applying the research of the Effective Schools movement has been the acceptance of the belief that "All students can learn." Great strides are being made to strengthen the belief system of both staff and students through professional growth activities. Instead of giving "lip service" to the notion, staff members are **demonstrating** behaviors that prove that belief, commitment, acquisition of skills and knowledge, determination to "follow through," and willingness to pull together as a team, make the mission of teaching and learning attainable. Taking time to celebrate student and staff success is a top priority! In fact, staff cannot help but be reminded that the mission is possible, when they are adorned with a wallet-sized commitment card pictured above, a logo pin, mission statement briefcase tote, pencil, T-short, sun visor, coffee cup, paperweight, bookmark. . . .

The interpretation of the definition of an Effective School has caused some to dispute the logic of the statement. Many interpreted it to mean that NPS expects all students to learn the **same things** at the **same rate.** At every opportunity, visual examples are shared to help all understand that the key point of comparison in disaggregated data is **proportionate rate** of improvement.

The initial perception that the Effective Schools movement was solely for remediation of low-achieving students was another obstacle to overcome. SPIRAL, along with the system-wide goals and objectives, as well as the goals and objectives of the individual schools, has virtually eliminated the problem. All students, staff, and programs are monitored, supported, and reinforced.

The Issue of Finding Time

Last, but not least, time for building school improvement teams, to evaluate progress, and to make future plans is limited. Therefore, this year, early dismissal of students during the last week of school has allowed more needed time for building teams to become operational.

No matter how many roadblocks appear, or how much effort and *time* it takes, the school improvement process is worth implementing because of what it does for the students and staff. Nothing can do more for making schools places for optimal teaching and learning, where caring and celebration are prominent, than a systematic plan which involves all who are to be affected by its implementation—students, staff, and the community (Gross and Gross, 1985).

The following advice is offered to those who are interested in initiating or refining a school improvement plan:

1. **Obtain commitment** and support for school improvement from the **school board** and **superintendent.**
2. Address the plan as a **continuous process** and not a program; programs are often short-lived, and narrow in scope.
3. Label budget requests according to Effective Schools criteria and correlates so that commitment to the Effective Schools process is evident and so that the most crucial needs relative to improvement are addressed.
4. Require that central office school improvement plans **support** the process of **school-based** improvement.
5. Provide **time** allotted during the workday for school staffs to develop, assess, and acquire skills needed to implement school improvement plans.
6. Implement a remediation component for students who have not previously been successful in the regular educational setting (**alternative instructional approaches**).
7. **Sustain** the **momentum** of the process and **keep** the **mission focused** through **visual** reminders such as buttons, pins, T-shirts, and cards.
8. **Align** curriculum, testing, and staff development with needs assessments and data that reflect student achievement.
9. **Monitor** program implementation and outcomes **continuously.**
10. Disaggregate student data on the basis of SES (socioeconomic status) and gender.
11. Schedule **superintendent interviews** with principals and their school improvement teams, as well as with central office departmental heads and key members of their staffs, to discuss school improvement.
12. Develop **biennial** school improvement **plans;** assess and modify them annually. Goals, objectives, and strategies should be limited in number but high in quality, eliminating those which have **not** brought about positive results in the past. **Correlate** the plan with the system-wide Six-Year Improvement Plan and the regional **accreditation processes** (SACS—Southern Association of Colleges and Schools) to unify efforts and to avoid creating a feeling of being overwhelmed when involved in the self-study/accreditation process.
13. Practice impatient patience; recognize that **school improvement takes time.**
14. **CELEBRATE** successes!
15. Concentrate on **team-building!**
16. Make all decisions based on "what is **best for the student!**"

Commitment to school improvement is a heavy responsibility, but a **shared** responsibility. It requires a plan, strong support, leadership, staff development, and accountability. Norfolk Public Schools' process (SPIRAL) represents research into practice. The present picture is one of systematic planned progress for improved performance for students, teachers, administrators, and support staff members.

Periodic progress reports are presented to the school board and to the local citizenry. Reports focus on student achievement, attendance, dropout rates, promotion/retention statistics (disaggregated data). Parents and community members are heavily involved in planning, implementing and evaluating school improvement. Through the Adopt-A-School program, business and agencies support the goals and objectives which reinforce the belief that **all** students can learn and are entitled to equitable opportunities for a quality education. The school board and administrative staff demonstrate continuous support by providing the means by which the school improvement process can operate.

High instructional expectations and commitment of all personnel to the mission will produce desired pupil achievement. The school district's belief system—symbolized by the theme "Believe—Achieve—Succeed!"—undergirds everything that the school system is about. The results speak for themselves!

References

Edmonds, Ronald. (1982). School Improvement Summer Training Institute presentation.

Goodlad, John. (1984). *A Place Called School.* New York: McGraw Hill.

Gross, Beatrice and Ronald. (1985). *The Great School Debate.* New York: Simon and Schuster.

Alma Public Schools

William R. McKinstry
Superintendent

George R. Gibbs
Assistant Superintendent

Alma Public Schools
Became involved in Effective Schools process in 1983

Community

Population
10,000

Alma, predominantly middle class, is located in an agricultural area in the center of lower Michigan. The seven townships that make up the Alma school district are primarily agricultural. In Alma the four major industries important to the economy are the Total Refinery (petroleum), Lobbell Emory (auto-related), Alma Products (auto-related), and Alma Plastics. Alma College, a small liberal arts college with an enrollment of 1,200 brings a number of professional educators to the community.

Thirty-three percent of the public school students are from low-income families as measured by applications for free-and-reduced price meals.

School District

Enrollment
2,710, about half live outside the city in an area covering 100 square miles.

Ethnic Composition (percent)
Caucasian 92
Hispanic 7
Other 1

Per Pupil Expenditure
1988–1989 $3,448

Percent bussed
51

Schools
Elementary (K–4) 3
Middle schools (5–8) 1
High schools (9–12) 1
Alternative high school 1
Adult ed. high school 1

Number of Staff
Administrators 19
Certified teachers 150
Support staff 7

Student-Teacher Ratio
Elementary 25.:1
Middle 25::1
High school 24.:1

Percent college-bound (approx.)
NA

Abstract

Alma has identified its present state and its goals for the future (mission, vision, beliefs, exit outcomes). The challenge is to get there. An individual school improvement planning process is essential for accomplishing these goals. Mistakes will be made along the way, but the school district believes it is moving in the right direction ensuring that **all** children be adequately prepared for the future.

A small district, Alma has proceeded to build upon its strengths. The board of education, superintendent, and building staffs and principals are all committed to the Effective Schools Research model for school improvement. From the start organizational mechanisms such as a teacher evaluation system and a new school monitoring system have been integrated with established procedures. The role of the District Coordinating Committee (DCC) is to carry on the discourse on school improvement and to initiate a district focus on school improvement.

In spite of a good staff development program, Alma has not seen "remarkable instructional improvement" or improved student achievement test scores overall, but is moving in that direction. In addition, data were not disaggregated until the second year. Perhaps too much emphasis was placed on staff development for teacher effectiveness **before** these information feed-back mechanisms were in place. Nevertheless, these components to the process are now in place, and increased achievement for **all** children should occur. Because the district has very good achievement levels for grades 2–8 (in the sixtieth to sixty-fifth percentile on average) their effort is commendable. Many districts with this level of average student achievement might not expect to improve significantly and would not entertain "school improvement." Alma, however, knows that many of its students are not performing to their potential and are fully implementing the Effective Schools process for purposes of equity in their program.

Alma Public Schools

Alma, a small, rural community in the center of lower Michigan, with a population of 10,000, is the home of Alma College, a private 4-year liberal arts college of 1,200 students. About one-half of the 2,710 K–12 students live outside the city in an area covering 100 square miles. The ethnic composition of the students in the school district is 92 percent white, 7 percent Hispanic, and the remainder American Indian, Asian, and black. Thirty-three percent come from low-income families as measured by the number of student applications for free-and-reduced price meals. The total general fund expenditures per pupil are $3,448, about the same as the state average of approximately $3,560 per pupil.

In the Alma school district there are three small private schools: St. Mary's (80 students), Grace Lutheran (19 students), and Seventh Day Adventist (7 students). Alma has one high school (757 students), one middle school (772 students), three elementaries (1,181 students), an alternative high school (80 FTE students), an adult high school (61 FTE students), and an adult basic education program (40 FTE students).

Why Did Alma Launch the Program?

The superintendent and the assistant superintendent were aware of Effective Schools Research, and in particular, some of the early published reports by Ronald Edmonds and others. In the summer of 1983, the Institute on Effective Schools Research was offered at Michigan State University, and the superintendent and assistant superintendent attended. Effective Schools Research appeals to Alma because it attempts to identify the positive characteristics of exemplary schools, especially those associated with optional student performance. The research provides the value system and tools to establish schools where all children can learn.

Following the summer institute, the district investigated further the research on Effective Schools by visiting Dr. Lawrence W. Lezotte at Michigan State University to get guidance as well as to help in locating research abstracts. In the fall of 1983, at the urging of central office administrators, the Alma Board of Education created a 25-person "Effective Schools Task Force" to review the literature and research on Effective Schools and to make judgments about the applicability of that research to school improvement planning. That task force, made up of principals, teachers, parents, and non-parent representatives, reviewed the literature and research on "teacher" and "school" effects that correlated with student achievement. They proposed the following definition of an Effective School and selected the following seven characteristics as being the ones they would most like to see in the Alma school district:

1. *A clear and focused school mission.* There is a clearly articulated mission of the school through which the staff shares an understanding of and commitment to instructional goals and objectives, priorities, assessment procedures, and accountability.
2. *Instructional leadership.* The principle acts as the instructional leader, supported by the building staff, and together they effectively communicate the mission of the school to the community, parents, and students. The principal understands and applies the characteristics of instructional effectiveness in the management of the instructional program, including well-planned and systematic staff development programs.
3. *Teacher effectiveness.* Classroom instructional leadership reflects enthusiasm, resourcefulness, knowledge of the subject matter, and the ability to relate to students. An effective teacher stimulates interest by utilizing a variety of techniques which provide for individual differences and learning capabilities.
4. *High expectations.* There is a climate of expectation in which the staff believes and demonstrates that all students can attain mastery of basic skills and where students are encouraged to attain their highest potential.
5. *Frequent monitoring and evaluation of student progress.* Student academic progress is measured frequently. Multiple assessment methods are used. The results of assessment testing are used to improve individual student performance and the instructional program.
6. *A safe and orderly environment.* There is an orderly, purposeful, and cooperative atmosphere. The climate is conducive to teaching and learning. Discipline policies are clear, firm, and consistently enforced.
7. *Good home/school relations.* Parents are given the opportunity to understand and support the basic mission of the school. Schools actively encourage positive and constructive relationships between the school and the community.

Instructional leadership inservice was provided for all building administrators on a regular basis. The district testing policies and practices were revised. All performance objectives (K–12) were reviewed and updated. All district newsletters began to contain information on the Effective Schools process, and Effec-

Priorities

The board of education goals for 1983–84 included:

- the development of individual school improvement plans
- consideration of board policies specifically dealing with school improvement
- formation of a district coordinating committee (DCC) to carry on the discourse on school improvement
- a monitoring process for the school improvement plans
- board direction to focus on the needs of at-risk and disadvantaged students

The board adopted a mission statement and endorsed a rationale and assumptions:

Mission Statement

The Alma School District believes that all students, regardless of family background, socioeconomic level, or sex, will achieve mastery of the essential objectives in each subject area or course. Each student is encouraged to achieve to his/her highest potential.

Rationale and Assumptions

1. It is essential that a public institution clearly define itself; i.e., what it believes in and stands for.
2. All schools should be held responsible for effectively teaching basic skills to all students.
3. The school building is the key unit for change.
4. Focus must be on the organization of the individual school to bring about desired change and improvements.
5. Local school organizations with adequate assistance can create conditions required for change and improvements.
6. School improvement can be planned and managed. Meaningful change occurs through a systematic process, not as an event.
7. Large amounts of money to initiate and sustain educational innovations are not essential.
8. Local improvement efforts produce desired changes in pupil performance.
9. Continuous personal participation by the implementing staff is needed to firmly root and sustain the change.
10. Administrators play a crucial role in supporting the utilization process of a new method or idea.
11. The main focus of school improvement is instructional effectiveness and school effectiveness.
12. The improvement of schools is a task requiring community commitment. It cannot be left solely to the schools.
13. Constructive change is encouraged through a process calling for an objective assessment of school programs followed by articulated building improvement plans.
14. All staff members must believe that all students can learn.

tive Schools Research abstracts were purchased and placed in every building. The administration encouraged principals to make instructional effectiveness a topic in faculty meetings. Finally, the school system hired school improvement and testing consultants to help with the initial efforts.

Finances

Because the Alma school district already had a commitment to professional development for all staff members, school improvement efforts in these early years did not require large amounts of money. In 1985–86 the individual school improvement plans cost $25,000 and this year, 1988–89, the cost is $33,100 or 0.3 percent (.003) of the budget.

Individual school improvement plans and their cost have become part of the budget-planning process in the spring of each year. All funding has come from the general fund. Each building has a line item for school improvement to cover the cost of implementation, as well as a separate line item for professional development, created for each principal's use in the building. In addition, significant district-wide commitments were made for professional development activities related to school improvement. For example, the board adopted a three-year budget for voluntary teacher effectiveness training. At the end of two years, 90 percent of teachers and 100 percent of district administrators had completed the 30 hours of "ITIP" (Instructional Theory into Practice) training and many of them were taking advanced training. The number of days per year devoted to professional development has risen from 1.6 days per year in 1983–84 to 5.6 days per year in 1987–88. The district has allocated for 1988–89 a budget of $168,105 or 1.7 percent of the budget for staff development.

Program Implementation and Evaluation: Monitoring

The district found out that programs *can* be reorganized to meet the needs of a diverse body of students. Large amounts of additional money were not required, instead the district placed much stronger reliance on research and data. Individual school improvement plans, based on assessment data and student achievement data, brought requests for program improvements such as: Math Their Way, DIP (Discovery in Phonics), QUEST, and Writing Across the Curriculum Program, to mention a few.

Greater emphasis was recently placed on closer monitoring of instructional programs and school improvement plans to make sure they actually benefit all students and bring about positive change. The district began to monitor and adjust programs rather than implement programs and then forget about them. By paying more attention to the test data from the Michigan Education Assessment Program (MEAP) and the California Achievement Test, Alma public schools personnel are better able to improve individual student performance as well as the delivery of instructional programs.

Even though the district had written performance objectives in 1975 for each subject and each grade level, and these are updated regularly, one need that surfaced was realigning the written, taught, and tested curriculum. Teachers and administrators needed to clarify what to teach and what students needed to learn, and then how to test for achievement. The district is presently working to realign the math, reading, and science curriculum with student performance objectives of the State of Michigan and with textbook objectives. Alma has also developed competency exams in the areas of writing, language arts, and mathematics at the secondary level. A science competency exam will be ready in 1989. In developing criterion-referenced tests, Alma is using technology and software available (TestMate, item banks, etc.) to make the process efficient.

Disaggregated Data

Since Alma is now disaggregating data on a district-wide and building-level basis, the staff can look at achievement scores (state, local, and CAT) to determine whether all students are mastering the basic/essential skills and knowledge and whether there are differences in learning among the subgroups of the student population (boy/girl, black/white/Hispanic, middle income/low income). The individual school improvement planning process will help in developing plans and programs to address deficiencies shown in the data.

Norm-referenced Assessments

California Achievement Tests (total battery group scores—national percentile) in elementary grades 2, 3, and 4, indicate a significant and consistent improvement, as shown in Table 1. Group aptitude scores are consistently at the 55 percentile with a variance of plus or minus 3 percent. California Achievement Tests (total battery) in grades 5–8 have not indicated significant gains and maintain achievement levels in the 60–65 percentile. Table 2 shows the MEAP Math test results, 1984–1988, at grades 4, 7, and 10. All have improved, with significant numbers moving into the fourth quartile.

Local Writing Scores

All students in grades 3, 6, and 9 also complete a holistically scored writing assessment. Competency has been increasing slowly but steadily since its introduction in 1984. In 1986–87, twenty (10 percent of the grade 9 students) failed the writing test. Through use of a peer tutoring program all but two students have reached competency prior to grade 11.

More Documented Changes

The Connecticut School Effectiveness Questionnaire was administered in 1985 and 1987 by all six schools. Each of the three elementary schools has demonstrated significant increases in their scores. The combined scores for the schools indicate an approximate 10 percent increase for each correlate, averaging the following for 1987:

School and community relations	67
High expectations	69
Opportunity for learning/time on task	82
Safe and orderly environment	85
Instructional leadership	85
Frequent monitoring	87
Clear mission	92

The middle school and high school showed relatively little change.

Specific Areas of Improvement

Each school has identified specific areas of need from the correlate results which have been addressed in school improvement plans producing excellent results. These specific improvements may not always improve the overall assessment.

Program Implementation and Evaluation: Evaluation of Staff

The board-approved teacher performance criteria and evaluation instruments were not changed. Also, correlate assessment data and teacher effectiveness training were not used as a tool in formal evaluations. Administrators did not want the teachers' union or individual teachers to see teacher effectiveness (ITIP) training or the use of data as threatening. Because of this approach, over 90 percent of the teachers completed the 30-hour ITIP training in the first two years of the three-year program. Advanced training workshops have been instituted, as have peer coaching, scripting, and the development of a common language for improving teaching. All are now well accepted by teachers.

Furthermore, the building principal's job description now ties in closely to the characteristics of Effective Schools. For example, the principal is responsible for assuming a major role in the development of a safe and orderly environment. Principals are to develop and clearly articulate the mission of the school. They are to provide instructional leadership and a climate of high expectations. They chair building school improvement teams, assume major responsibility for planning and operationalizing the student testing procedures, and involve staff members in decision-making. The board also adopted several school improvement policies concerning staff involvement in decision-making, professional staff development opportunities, professional travel, and conference attendance.

Alma's policies now clearly spell out the board's commitment to an individual school improvement planning process. The superintendent is responsible for implementing an annual school improvement planning process, making reports to the board of education on the progress of each school's improvement plans, and making recommendations for future plans. Evaluation of staff on a formative basis is an ongoing **systematic** process which generally results in improved teaching and classroom management techniques on the part of most teachers.

Staff Development Programs Have Been Modified

In the past, Alma has participated in many excellent staff development programs through the Intermediate School District (county level), Professional Development Consortium, the Michigan Institute for Educational Management Network, and district-initiated efforts. However, these programs are generally designed to appeal to a varied audience and were not particularly focused on a goal or a theme for any one year. Alma is now focusing efforts on a five-year professional development plan for the district.

The Effective Schools thrust caused Alma to look strongly at instructional effectiveness because that was one of the characteristics they wanted to see in the district. Besides the three-year ITIP training program (12 district-run workshops to date) Alma sponsored clinical supervision programs for administrators and interested teachers. In addition, the central administration secured strong board support for professional development activities in the face of severe financial problems (school closings, wage freeze, layoffs, and budget cuts). The board's commitment to school improvement and professional development is a critical component of school improvement that has remained strong.

Program Implementation and Evaluation: Recognition of the School Instructional Process

When the district made the commitment to be goal-directed, research-based, and data-driven, it was necessary to take a closer look at the instructional process. One of the characteristics the Alma Effective Schools Task Force sought was "teacher effectiveness." The Alma District Coordinating Committee instituted a three-year ITIP training program on a voluntary basis. In addition to the ITIP training, the district began to disaggregate the student achievement data by building and started addressing the equity issues in our district.

Alma Public Schools has no data that show remarkable instructional improvement, but the system has identified the discrepancies and plans are being implemented to correct the problems. Staff has developed a district mission statement, a district slogan (Believing in Achieving), revised the testing program for students, initiated cooperative learning inservice activities, updated student performance objectives for all grade levels, and revised courses across the district. This year, administrators and teachers developed desired student exit behaviors and a common belief system as part of their involvement in an Outcomes-Driven Developmental Model for school improvement. The Effective Schools process focuses more attention on the instructional processes within the school district and classroom.

The district also recently received a grant from the Michigan Department of Education to work on "alternatives within special education." The grant will allow the development of new teaching/learning units in grades 2–6 in math. All special education students will receive math instruction in regular classes, not through pull-out programs. This is in keeping with our belief that all students will obtain mastery of essential skills.

Because of Alma's long-term involvement in the Effective Schools process, administrators and staff are developing a common belief system to encourage common understanding and philosophy about teaching and learning. This solidifies staff commitment to the mission.

In addition, Alma is establishing a common vision for students about what they should accomplish by the end of the 12th grade (after thirteen plus years in the Alma system). A common set of student exit behaviors (outcomes) might include (see pgs. 60 and 61):

- mastery of basic skills
- concern for others
- self-esteem as a person
- self-directed learner
- process skills: problem solving, accountability, communication, decision-making.

Table 1
California Achievement Tests, Grades 2, 3, 4.

	1984	1985	1986	1987*	1988*
Grade 2	60	58	59	62 (76)	66 (80)
Grade 3	61	64	66	68 (80)	73 (85)
Grade 4	64	64	64	65 (76)	74 (85)

*New edition (1985) of test, which was much more difficult—scores in parentheses are comparisons to the 1980 edition.

Table 2
Criterion-referenced Assessments

The Michigan Educational Assessment Program (MEAP) results show notable improvement for students in the fourth quartile form 1984 to 1988.

MEAP Math Tests, Fourth Quartile.

	1984	1985	1986	1987	1988
Grade 4	80.3	85.2	88.0	95.3*	94.1
Grade 7	79.1	77.5	74.3	75.0	85.5
Grade 10	64.4	69.9	75.7	76.3	75.9

*Two of three elementary schools scored 100%.

Program Implementation and Evaluation: The District-Level Coordinating Team

The district established the District Coordinating Committee (DCC) made up of at least two teachers and the principal from each building (three elementaries, one middle school, one high school, one alternative high school, and one adult high school completion program). The DCC's main function is to carry on the school improvement efforts on a district-wide basis, and to communicate with the school improvement teams to advance coordination of the improvement program. The superintendent, central office administrators, building administrators, teachers, and board of education have been deeply involved in the school improvement process. However, Alma has had only limited involvement of parents and student groups in the process.

Each building has a school improvement team and that team is chaired by the building principal. In some of the elementary schools, the entire staff sits on the building school improvement team. In the larger buildings, ten to twelve staff members represent the others on the school improvement team. Parent and student representation is allowed, but is virtually nonexistent.

Since board policy and practice call for a systematic school improvement planning process, each building staff develops school improvement plans. Clear targets and deadlines are set following the assessment of needs, strengths, and resources available. To be funded, school improvement activities have to focus on the enhancement of instructional effectiveness, Effective Schools correlate data, and improved student achievement. Desired student outcomes must be identified and prioritized, and staff members must play a key role in determining the direction of their school's improvement efforts. Before plans can be submitted for funding, the whole team must reach consensus and sign the plan. The plan is then reviewed by central office.

In the first three years, 1984–1987, schools developed annual school improvement plans. In 1987 Alma adopted a more practical approach by adopting three-year, long-range plans that are revised annually.

Procedures for Success

It would be a problem if the school improvement plans had a thrust in one direction while the board of education wanted the administration and staff to follow through on activities in another direction. Beginning with the 1983–84 school year the board's goals have coordinated well with the overall school improvement efforts on a district basis. Planning is now even more coherent overall.

It was important that the general fund budget incorporate monies to support school improvement planning efforts. Alma's school improvement plans are due in the superintendent's office in early spring for coordinating budget planning and central district needs with the financial needs for school improvement.

The Effective Schools process has affected community attitudes in a positive way. Home-school relationships are improving. In the community Alma publicizes the district goals and mission statement, student achievement gains, school improvement plans, and progress reports. District goals are published and progress is reported back to the board on a routine basis.

In March of 1988, Alma schools sought 2.5 additional operating mills. The campaign theme dealt with school improvement and the need to maintain good quality schools for Alma's young people. Many community groups gave positive feedback. The millage passed by a rate proportion of almost 3–1. The community seems to know that the Alma schools are good and are willing to support them.

The Alma district has received no additional funds from any service or funding agency because of its involvement in the Effective Schools process. However, the 1987 North Central Accreditation report praised Alma for its work because of its positive impact on school climate and student achievement. In addition, Alma High School was recognized as one of the top ten high schools in the State of Michigan by the United States Department of Education Secondary School Recognition Program in 1987. A great deal of credit for this award goes to the school improvement efforts implemented by the Alma High School staff and administration.

When the board of education approves the school improvement plans in late spring, the board is aware of the financial constraints and the effect on the budget of items that they might consider. Because Alma is in a tight financial situation, parts of school improvement plans have at times been denied. On the whole, large amounts of money to initiate and sustain school improvement innovations have not been essential in Alma.

During this entire process, Alma has attempted to deal with the administrators up-front and prior to dealing with other employee groups. The building administrator, who is expected to be the team leader on the front line, has been kept well informed of what is going on and what is coming along. For example, in looking at test data and correlate assessment data, a testing consultant spends time with the administrators before the school improvement teams and other staff members see the data. This has been helpful and has kept administrators supportive of the process.

Individual school improvement plans have helped the administration to focus on school problems at the level closest to the students being most affected. However, Alma has experienced some problems because the six buildings sometimes go in different directions. At times they compete rather than collaborate. For example, when one building began a breakfast program for those students who came to school without breakfast, the other schools immediately wanted a similar program even though their plans had not called for such a program. The administration is encouraging cooperation. The uniqueness of individual school improvement planning needs to be balanced with district coordination of school improvement activities. This is the job of the district coordinating committee. The mission, vision, common beliefs, district goals, and desired student outcomes should provide that *common sense of direction*, expectations, and outcomes. *How these things are to be accomplished* should be decided at the building level by teachers and their principal working together.

What Problems, Issues, or Concerns Did Your Program Encounter and How Were They Overcome?

External Mandates

External mandates have not caused any serious problems, but they can be a nuisance. For example, the Michigan State Board of Education's incentive monies are tied to increased graduation requirements. Although Alma students are exceeding the requirements set by the State of Michigan, the board formally increased graduation requirements so the district could qualify for the student incentive grant.

Community Changes

The 3 to 1 vote that passed a recent millage increase was heartening. The increased achievement by students as a result of the school system's school improvement efforts have been effectively communicated. The diverse programs Alma offers—special education, vocational education, adult education, gifted and talented programs, advanced placement classes, college classes, and programs for at-risk youngsters—meet community needs.

Despite Alma school system successes, further improvements are needed. Some students are below their grade level, too many high school students exit with low grades, and poorer students generally achieve at lower levels than their wealthier classmates. The "reading" and "science" curriculum (K–12) are also being realigned because of recent research findings. Alma must find ways for all students to be successful learners.

Budget Cuts

Alma has maintained school improvement efforts despite serious financial problems. From 1972 to 1985 enrollment dropped by 1,200 students. Four schools have been closed. In 1983 Alma had a wage freeze. In 1988 the public voted for 2.5 additional operating mills to keep the system from developing a deficit. Alma is working to establish a sound financial base for long-term school improvement and staff development.

Format for School Improvement Plans

School improvement teams now write plans using a specific format and criteria. Not only are plans easier to read, but they are also more apt to better meet actual needs. For example, the plans must describe the focus of change, expected change in student behavior, implementation procedures, how success will be assessed, and what resources will be needed. Plans will also be needed for implementation, then the building team will have to explain the results of their efforts.

Parental Involvement

The early Effective Schools task force involved parents, but getting parents to stay on the committees has been difficult. Parents appeared to be interested, but were not willing to commit so much time to the process. Alma will continue its efforts to involve parents in the process.

Technical Assistance

Alma hired several part-time consultants for assistance. Consultants have played a vital role in the following areas: school improvement planning, testing and the evaluation of data, group processes, writing, computer technology, outcome based education, ITIP training, cooperative learning, assertive discipline training, fitness, and health.

Unions

The Alma district has a good working relationship with its two major unions, the Alma Education Association (Michigan Education Association) and the OCAWIU that represents support staff (cooks, bus drivers, custodians, and maintenance personnel). Grievances and concerns are minimal, but when they do occur, both parties meet and discuss the situation with a spirit of cooperation. Contract problems are corrected during the school year and not put off until bargaining. Staff input in planning and decision-making keeps these relationships healthy.

Strategic Plan

Alma will develop a strategic plan for looking at the entire school organization and its efforts to bring about improved student achievement and desirable student exit behaviors. By matching knowledge (research, experience, data) with goals (desired student exit behaviors and teacher behaviors, philosophy, belief system, commitment, and mission), Alma can assess what it actually does (classroom practices, curriculum planning, leadership behaviors, research and data driven). As Alma achieves a better match, student achievement should be enhanced.

ALMA PUBLIC SCHOOLS
DESIRED STUDENT EXIT BEHAVIORS[1]

Behavior	General Attributes	Sample Measures
I. Self-esteem as a learner and a person	A positive vision of the future Works well with people Personal integrity Views self as successful learner Good self concept Search for the truth Feels lovable and capable	Exemplifies knowledge of self Displays adequate self concept Willing to take risks Good time manager Displays an attitude supportive of inquiry Knows what he/she wants in life and learning Builds overall wellness into life Has a clear value system—acts on values Excels at something
II. Cognitive Learning	Able to function at all cognitive levels—knowledge, comprehension, implementation, analysis, synthesis and evaluation Mastery of basic skills—math, reading, science, social studies, health, vocational skills, language arts, writing, computer literacy Communicates thoughts clearly Parenting skills Extended learning—full intellectual development Career education Fine Arts appreciated Knows a foreign language	Good grades in school Competency exams Academic excellence attained—GPA Kinds and number of courses taken Works up to full potential Demonstrates cognitive learning—low and high Bilingual Presidential Academic Fitness Norm-referenced achievement stats—60% or better Employability skills test Employed
III. Process Skills	Problem solving skills Critical thinking skills Decision-making skills Voting forecasting Goal planning Accountable Communication skills Group process skills Team work How to adapt to change	Demonstrates: Good interpersonal relationships Attendance records Takes leadership roles Completes tasks started in a timely manner Speaks and writes clearly and concisely Takes an active part in political process Gets people to work together Sports: Participation as a team member Extra curricular activities

[1] This is an instrument for discussion to help clarify exit outcomes. The attributes and measures are samples and are not meant to be all inclusive.

Behavior	General Attributes	Sample Measures
IV. Self-directed Learner	Knows how to learn Study skills and research Has a good self-concept Inquiring mind Intellectually curious Reads for pleasure and information Can elaborate upon original ideas Takes responsibility for preparing Goes the extra mile Seeks help when needed Goes beyond the minimum asked Is creative, flexible, has original ideas	Use of library Makes good use of leisure time Comparison shopper Given an idea, he/she can develop it, research options, decide and implement Completes homework Creative problem-solving activities Example: Odyssey of the Mind Quiz Bowl Debate/Forensics
V. Concern for Others	Tolerant of options and values of others Compromise Tolerance Patience/accepting Caring Develops a global awareness Enculturation Sensitive to those who need help A good citizen Thoughtful Involved with volunteer projects, community service Shows respect for others	Observe behavior Participates in volunteer efforts to help handicapped, elderly and poor Demonstrates social courtesies Respectful of all others
VI. Emotional, social and physical well being	Physical fitness Emotional stability Aware of health issues (drug and alcohol abuse) Manage stress	Health test Successful completion of physical education courses Drug free Builds overall wellness into life Fitness Michigan Model Health Fitness measures Quest Builds healthy relationships Demonstrates interpersonal skills

ALMA PUBLIC SCHOOLS
WE BELIEVE

1. We believe that all students can learn, given sufficient time and appropriate support.
2. We believe that schools control enough of the variables to influence student success. The task of schools is to alter the learning environment to provide conditions for success.
3. We believe that the manner in which a student views himself will have direct and important bearing on success for that individual.
4. We believe that one of the most significant roles is to intentionally enhance the student's view of himself as a learner and as a worthwhile person.
5. We believe that all students can be expected to successfully acquire what we identify as essential learning outcomes. The rate at which students will acquire these skills will vary, but the expectations for their success will not.
6. We believe that all students have unique skills and talents. Our task is to identify these skills and talents and then nurture their development.
7. We believe that learning will be more successful when the experiences have meaning for the student.
8. We believe that all students can acquire skills and understandings at higher cognitive levels. We commit to keep opportunities open on each learning task.
9. We believe that the role of all school personnel is to act in the best interest of the students. We will systematically build and maintain positive relationships.
10. We believe that a student's rate of learning may vary from task to task. We are committed to keep opportunity open and provide support until essential learning is in place.
11. We believe that all of our professional behaviors need to be intentionally aligned with the most applicable knowledge, regarding learning and individual behavior.
12. We believe that how fast a student learns does not determine the success of that learner. We believe that the essential requirement is that a student learn and be successful. The rate at which a student learns does not diminish the power of that learning.
13. We believe that learning is an open experience. There are no mysteries or surprises in the total process. What is to be learned, how it is to be learned, and how it will be assessed will be clear and open at all times.
14. We believe that any grouping which places students in situations where learning expectations and opportunities are automatically limited is not acceptable.
15. Educational achievement and opportunity require the responsible commitment and participation of the Board, community, students, parents, and entire staff.

"Every Anoka-Hennepin Student Will Learn"

Claudia Risnes
Effective Schools Coordinator

Original Leadership:
Anoka-Hennepin District No. 11 School Board

Dr. Lewis Finch
Superintendent
Dr. David Wettergren
Deputy Superintendent
Jerome Lerom
Effective Schools Administrator

Anoka-Hennepin
Became involved in Effective Schools process in 1984

Community

Population
129,000

Northern suburban area of Minneapolis (mostly residential, some agricultural areas); all of three municipalities and portions of ten; predominantly middle class. Most residents work in the Twin Cities area in education, government, industries, and business. Within the school district major industries include Federal Cartrage, Hoffman Engineering, and John Roberts Printing. A number of smaller industries and businesses round out the economy. The percent of children from lower socioeconomic levels in the various schools ranges from 4 to 16.6.

(K–12) 8.76 percent on free-and-reduced lunch.

School District

Enrollment
32,190 (second or third largest in state, alternates with St. Paul),

Ethnic Composition (percent)
African-American	.6
Native American	1.0
Caucasian	95.0
Hispanic	.8

Per Pupil Expenditure
1988–1989 $4,253

Student-Staff Ratio: Does not include special ed., paras & adm.; includes all other certified staff and reg. ed. paras.

Percent bussed
77

Area (in square miles)
172

Schools
Elementary schools	27
Middle schools	1
Junior high schools	5
High school	3
Post high school, voc-tech	1

Number of Staff
Bldg. Administrators	55
District Administrators	55
Certified teachers	1,800
Support staff	1,050

Does not include substitutes, community education, or post-secondary

Student-Teacher Ratio
Elementary	27:1
Middle/Junior high	N/A
High school	N/A
Elementary	22:1
Junior High	18.6:1
High school	21.6:1

Percent college-bound
31

Abstract

"A good school district that wanted to get better," Anoka-Hennepin used the Effective Schools process to promote consistency across schools in its educational program. Many excellent educational programs and practices already existed in the district, but there was a lack of focus and many discrepancies within schools and among schools in the implementation of these programs. The Anoka-Hennepin district leadership was not certain that they were serving all children well. Also district personnel believed they had to be more accountable to their communities and families of students. So they gathered data and used them in a systematic way to inform their constituencies as well as principals and teachers about how well all students were achieving.

An excellent description of the change in beliefs and the mind-set of school personnel over the course of the Effective Schools process is found under "Advice for other schools?" (page 70). The importance of training for team building and participative management skills is also described. A plea is made to include curriculum consultants in the same training programs as teaching staff and principals receive, to make the process of integrating curricular and staff development with the school improvement program more efficient.

Brief Overview of the Effective Schools Program

Anoka-Hennepin Independent School District No. 11 is a suburban school district north of Minneapolis, Minnesota. The district covers 172 square miles and enrolls 32,190 students in its regular K–12 education programs. With the opening of Andover Elementary in the fall of 1988, the district has 27 elementary schools, one middle school, five junior highs, three senior highs, and one Area Technical Institute for post high school students. Other important demographic information includes:

- About 5.9 percent (1,830) of the district's school-age children attend non-public schools in the district.
- Sixty-five percent of the dwellings in the school district have school-age children or younger.
- Student enrollment is increasing slightly.
- Another 589 youngsters attended preschool handicapped programs in the district in 1987–88.
- The Anoka-Hennepin School District is the second largest in student enrollment in Minnesota.
- The district's three (grades 10–12) high schools rank first, second, and fourth largest in Minnesota.

What motivations launched the program? Emerging research and literature suggested that in even the best school districts certain educational practices work better than others, and for a district to be truly effective it must discard practices judged to be ineffective. Initiating a school improvement process was, in part, a response to some of the recent criticism of public schools in this country by major reports, study commissions, and critics. The district recognized the legitimacy of some concerns and wanted to respond in a forthright manner where needed. The district also recognized pressure for more public accountability and saw in this process a vehicle for responding to this concern. Perhaps most important, the district saw the Effective Schools program as a process for coordinating the variety of excellent educational practices currently existing in the district under a common plan, guided by a stated mission: "Every Anoka-Hennepin Student Will Learn."

Emergence of Interest

As practical ideas emerged from Effective Schools Research, the district superintendent, administrators, and curriculum consultants began to show an interest in the process. On Superintendent Finch's initiative, an educational consultant group was brought to the district in 1983 so that district administrators could look at the research and consider whether the educational programs and students could benefit from the process.

In March 1984, four district staff members attended an Effective Schools Institute in Scottsdale, Arizona, hosted by the Glendale Union High School District with Dr. Lawrence Lezotte, Michigan State University, and Dr. Mac Bernd, Glendale, serving as conference leaders. The four who attended included the elementary curriculum coordinator, an elementary principal, and district science and reading consultants. On their return, they expressed enthusiasm and support for the Effective Schools process. During April they reported their reaction to various groups within the district, including the Instructional Management Team, the school board, the Staff Development Committee, and elementary and secondary principals.

On June 15, 1984, Dr. Lezotte was brought to the district to meet with consultants and administrators to identify the basic elements needed in a district school improvement plan. Over the summer of 1984, another larger representative group attended an Effective Schools Institute in Michigan sponsored by Michigan State University and organized by Dr. Lezotte. This group of 13 included consultants, nine principals who had volunteered to be part of Phase I, and the teacher's association president. Upon their return they made a presentation to inform other consultants and principals. As support increased for adopting the Effective Schools process, formal committee work began under the direction of Deputy Superintendent Dr. Wettergren, and a formal implementation plan was written. Due to the large size of the district (34 schools), the decision was made to phase in the process over a 3-year period beginning with nine Phase I schools in 1984–85. Principals in these schools, along with their staffs, had chosen to be in the first group. Phase II schools began in 1985–86, with the last 12 Phase III schools joining the process in 1986–87. This allowed the district to provide appropriate and necessary staff development and support for each group of schools as they began.

Funding

Because the administrators considered Effective Schools a process to bring purpose, coordination, and focus to many existing programs, the district did not consider it to be a large additional expenditure. The curriculum study and review process already included committee and curriculum writing time, and the staff development program included an extensive instructional improvement component. The district was already on its way toward consistent district curriculum and a testing program that included both standardized testing and locally developed criterion-referenced testing. In addition to these efforts, several other budget areas were affected.

In January 1985, a central office position was created to coordinate the development and implementation of the Effective Schools process. This temporary position, titled the Effective Schools Administrator, was an additional salary item. Although the position was to have been terminated June 1987, it became important to supporting and sustaining the program once all schools were phased into the process; therefore it has been continued.

As part of the staff development, instructional improvement focus, the district created positions called resource teachers. These positions were developed as a result of research which emphasized the need for highly trained, in-building staff developers to bring instructional skills from awareness levels to levels of classroom application. The staffing allocation is .5 FTE in each elementary school (one staff member) and 1.2 FTE for each secondary school (two staff members). In order to retain their identity as teachers, and credibility with other teachers, each elementary resource person teaches in the classroom approximately one-half time, while at the secondary level, the two people each teach two classes per day. During their non-classroom time, they are responsible for direct instruction and follow-up of their building staff on matters pertaining to instructional improvement. That part of their salary is considered a staff development cost.

Another staff development cost has been released time for building leadership teams (BLTs). BLTs are school improvement teams of building staff members who assume leadership for development and implementation of school leadership for development and implementation of school plans. As each building entered the process, they were allocated four days per BLT member for training and building planning days. That has continued since 1984, but in 1988–89 the allocation will be reduced to three days per BLT member.

The BLT training and building school improvement plans have brought great focus to staff development efforts. Staff members have always been released for a variety of professional pursuits. Now, however, the fragmentation of these efforts is disappearing, and instruction and student achievement have become the focus of attention.

Program Support

In addition to the budgetary support described above, Effective Schools has been supported in a number of other ways over the past 4 years including:

- Continued public verbal commitment from the superintendent and the school board
- District publications featuring articles on varying aspects of Effective Schools
- Visits by the superintendent to BLT meetings
- Visual displays of the mission statement on district banners and stationery
- BLT presentations of their action plans to the school board
- Strong support of Effective Schools by the two associate superintendents
- Continuation of the Effective Schools coordinator position
- High visibility by the Effective Schools coordinator at all BLT training sessions, on district committees, and at many BLT meetings and building staff meetings
- Inclusion of Effective Schools goals in many individual district personnel job targets

Evidence of Improvement: Measured Student Outcomes

What evidence does the district have that schools are improving? The Anoka-Hennepin School District recognizes that formal assessment and evaluation of student achievement is one method of evaluating the effectiveness of instructional programs and of judging the success of students in acquiring essential knowledge and skills. Measurement of student achievement is of greatest value when the information is used in concert with professional observation and judgment.

The student assessment coordinator works with district curriculum consultants and teacher committees to develop learner outcomes and criterion-referenced tests. She also presents sessions to BLTs on interpreting and using test data within their building. Anoka-Hennepin has developed a long-range testing plan to coordinate and integrate all activities in this area. Test results are displayed to the public by district averages, and test results are shared with each school staff by building average and individual score (Iowa Test for Basic Skills) and by classroom average and individual score (criterion-referenced tests). The district started gathering baseline data in 1985–86.

During the 1987–88 school year, Anoka-Hennepin changed from administering the California Test for Basic Skills (CTBS) to the Iowa Test for Basic Skills (ITBS). The ITBS was selected because it was thought to have a better fit to the Anoka-Hennepin curriculum and programs. Norm-referenced tests are conducted for the following purposes:

- to assist in making decisions regarding individual students
- to provide information to curriculum committees to be used in evaluating programs at school and district levels
- to report to parents the performance of each student in the areas tested in relationship to the performance of a much larger group of students
- to report to the community the level of achievement in basic skills attained by students in the district.

Outcomes. While 56 percent of the students ranked above the national average in reading in 1985–86, the number moved to 63 percent in 1986–87. The number of students taking the PSAT has jumped from 937 in 1983 to 1,265 in 1986, a 35-percent increase, while scores have remained stable.

Anoka-Hennepin curriculum teams began writing criterion-referenced tests in limited content area in 1985–86 and have continued to add to the content areas and refine existing tests. The assessment of performance on criterion-referenced tests related to essential learner outcomes is conducted for the following purposes:

- to assess the impact of curriculum and instructional practices within the content areas
- to determine if there are substantial differences in performance among schools or groups within schools in demonstrating mastery of essential learner outcomes
- to determine which individual students are mastering essential outcomes and which students are not.

Several figures are included as examples of how Anoka-Hennepin reports district criterion-referenced test data to the public. Individual buildings have their own data available to interpret. Individual buildings also disaggregate on the basis of gender and children receiving free-and-reduced lunch. The following district examples show specific grade levels in secondary social studies (Table 1) and elementary mathematics (Figures 1 and 2).

In addition to focusing on student achievement, attendance and dropout problems also became a student outcome focus of the district in 1987–88. A major study showed that during 1986–87, 4.5 percent of the total high school population dropped out before graduation. Although that is a small percentage, it still represented 342 individuals who may have been kept in school. These data and the new 1987–88 data will serve as baseline data for Anoka-Hennepin's work in dropout prevention. Consideration is also being given, at this time, to adoption of a consistent attendance policy district-wide next year or in the near future.

How Does the Effective Schools Process Affect the Way Student Achievement Outcomes Are Measured?

Disaggregated data fosters accountability. Disaggregated analysis of norm-referenced data may be conducted for specific purposes. The nature of the disaggregation must be determined each year prior to the administration of the tests. Once the purpose has been accomplished, the disaggregation will be discontinued.

Individual buildings may disaggregate their test data on the basis of gender or socioeconomic status (SES). Anoka-Hennepin buildings range from 7 percent to 23 percent of the students on free-and-reduced lunch programs, one indicator of SES.

Development of criterion-referenced tests. Anoka-Hennepin has a long-range plan for the development of criterion-referenced testing, with the use of computer-managed instruction (CMI) contributing greatly to the efficiency of the program. Mathematics, science, social studies, health, and art administered

Table 1
Social Studies Scores Improvement

Comparison of Percent of Students Who Achieved Mastery in 1986–1987 over 1985–1986

Social Studies, Grade 7

Units of Instruction	Percent of Change
1. Map Skills	Same
2. Graph Skills	+18%
3. A World of People	+16%
4. Feeding a Hungry World	–7%
5. How Much Do People Have	Same
6. Worldwide Communication	+19%
7. World Cultures	Same
8. People in Government	–10%

Comparison of Percent of Students Who Achieved Mastery in 1986–1987 over 1985–1986

Social Studies, Grade 9

Units of Instruction	Percent of Change
1. Roots of American Government	+14%
2. Political Parties/Elections	+29%
3. Executive Branch	Same
4. Legislative Branch	+22%
5. Judicial Branch	+19%

Percent of Students who Achieved Mastery in 1986 and 1987

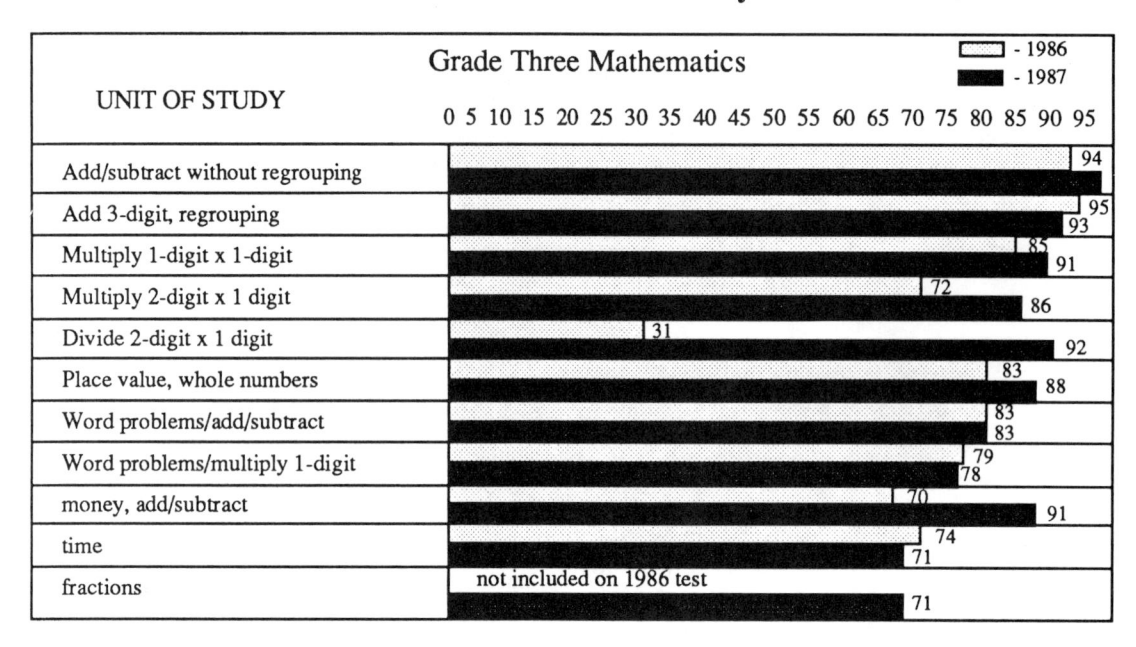

Grade Three Mathematics
□ - 1986
■ - 1987

UNIT OF STUDY	1986	1987
Add/subtract without regrouping	94	94
Add 3-digit, regrouping	95	93
Multiply 1-digit x 1-digit	85	91
Multiply 2-digit x 1 digit	72	86
Divide 2-digit x 1 digit	31	92
Place value, whole numbers	83	88
Word problems/add/subtract	83	83
Word problems/multiply 1-digit	79	78
money, add/subtract	70	91
time	74	71
fractions	not included on 1986 test	71

Figure 1. Percentage of Students Achieving Mastery in 1986 and 1987

Percent of Students who Achieved Mastery in 1986 and 1987

Grade Five Mathematics
□ - 1986
■ - 1987

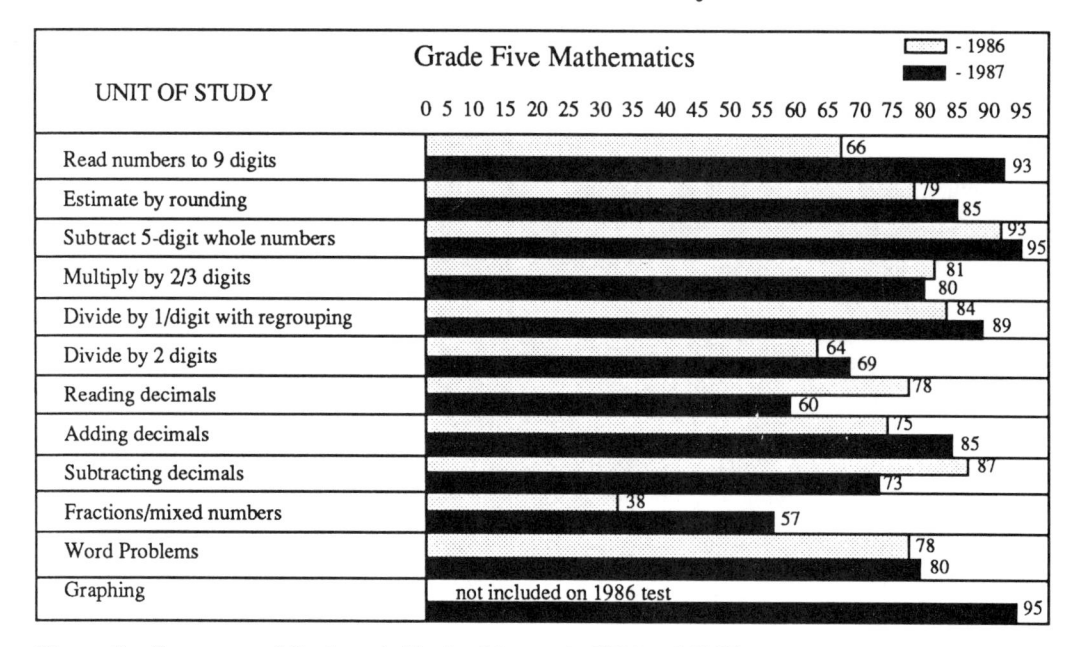

UNIT OF STUDY	1986	1987
Read numbers to 9 digits	66	93
Estimate by rounding	79	85
Subtract 5-digit whole numbers	93	95
Multiply by 2/3 digits	81	80
Divide by 1/digit with regrouping	84	89
Divide by 2 digits	64	69
Reading decimals	78	60
Adding decimals	75	85
Subtracting decimals	87	73
Fractions/mixed numbers	38	57
Word Problems	78	80
Graphing	not included on 1986 test	95

Figure 2. Percentage of Students Achieving Mastery in 1986 and 1987

criterion-referenced tests in 1987–88 to determine whether or not students have learned the skills established as essential learner outcomes in each area. In 1988–89 the elementary schools CMI will function with reading and math. Additions of new content areas to CMI will be based upon readiness of the curriculum, costs of hardware, interest of teaching staff in mastery learning concepts, ability to handle data entry, training, and importance of immediate feedback to achievement of essential outcomes. A plan to guide district assessment has been included in Appendix A because it briefly describes the extent of Anoka-Hennepin's process.

To fulfill the district mission "Every Student Will Learn," a program has been developed titled "Assurance of Basic Learning." Students will be required to demonstrate mastery level in math and reading, and those who do not pass will continue to receive instruction in the basic skill areas they have not yet mastered. Students will be re-assessed yearly until they pass. In preparation for 1988–89 implementation of this program, committees carefully considered questions of mastery level requirements, test selection, counseling services, remediation, and a strong support system for students identified as needing assistance.

How Have Professional and General Staff Development Programs Changed As a Result of the Effective Schools Thrust?

In the past few years, the staff development program has changed extensively. The first change is in the movement toward a building-based approach. This made sense because each resource teacher became a highly trained staff developer conveniently placed in each building. Second, buildings organized their staff development around the goals of their action plans, therefore, district-wide inservice training seemed less appropriate. Also, the goal of staff development became that of application, not just awareness of skills. Last, even though staff development still includes many aspects of education, the major mission is to effect student learning and success. The Effective Schools program has helped to focus on that mission.

During 1987–88, 450 (25 percent) district staff members participated in building-level training on the **Elements of Instruction** by their resource teacher. The training consisted of four days (release time) of direct instruction and opportunities for several classroom follow-ups by the resource teacher and/or other colleagues. The participants were surveyed in late May on the effectiveness of the training "to increase their understanding of 18 teacher behaviors and instructional techniques." With 0 meaning no increase, 1 meaning somewhat of an increase, and 2 meaning a great deal of increase, the average response was a 1.38. Scores ranged from a low of 1.21 to a high of 1.58 on various teacher behaviors of the 18. The strongest results came from the category of teachers with 0–3 years of experience. A very complete statistical analysis of the survey is available, but too lengthy to include in this report.

What Else Has Developed in Relation to the Effective Schools Process?

Policies, procedures, practices. During interviews to hire new employees at both the district and building level, candidates are asked to describe their familiarity with Effective Schools Research and instructional improvement practices. New employees are brought on-line as soon as possible with regard to this knowledge.

Discussion and decision-making about grading and attendance policies, grouping practices, new curriculum adoptions, staff development plans, instructional delivery, and program selections usually consider Effective Schools Research. This focus has not eliminated conflict over these issues, but in general, decisions in these areas focus more specifically on student outcomes and success in Anoka-Hennepin schools. (See Appendix B)

What Other Problems, Issues, or Concerns Were Encountered?

State statute requires each school district to publish annual reports to its citizens on district activities related to planning and evaluating educational programs. These reports are based on the work of the Planning, Evaluation, and Reporting Committee (PRE), composed of Anoka-Hennepin citizens and district staff. As district work on curriculum review, learner outcomes, and criterion-referenced testing has become more sophisticated and complete, the statute requirements of the State of Minnesota have paralleled district direction.

The State of Minnesota recently enacted legislation requiring districts to spend a certain per-pupil allotment of their funding on staff development and to provide proof of that expenditure to the state. Anoka-Hennepin was already in compliance with that spending requirement.

Several issues developed within the district which required consistent communication and perseverance. The message that curriculum, "what we teach," is the heart of the mission needed to be more clearly understood. Staff perceived a definite conflict between the concept of being "building-based" and the concept of "consistent district-wide curriculum." Through continued curriculum committee work and test writing committees, the perceived conflict began to diminish. Also, focusing Effective Schools staff development on curriculum issues, and connecting curriculum development and instruction more tightly, is helping to resolve the issue.

Criterion-referenced testing has also been a district issue. The concept of assessing, at a district level, whether students have mastered what they had been taught was unfamiliar to many teachers. Some teachers had some doubts and misconceptions concerning the use of those test data. The district tried to assuage those doubts by using the test data appropriately to evaluate programs and instructional practices and to assess mastery by individual students. Consistent, appropriate use of those data will develop trust and help overcome that conflict.

Reduced revenue and increased expenses in 1987-88 have required Anoka-Hennepin to enact budget cuts for 1988-89. The district believes that all the programs now offered are important to the success of students. It has been determined that about half the cuts will come through staff reduction and the other half through non-salary items. The Effective Schools staff development budget has been reduced by the same percentage as other budgets.

Advice For Other Schools?

After four years in the Effective Schools process, district programs and priorities seem focused on the tasks of the mission. Staff development is centering on instructional improvement skills and student affective and academic success. Curriculum is being strengthened by development of learner outcomes. The staff in the district is becoming more attuned to student assessment and how to use the data effectively to improve programs and instruction. The question is often asked, why didn't the process start with this focus? The Effective Schools process is a gradual one that involves slow changes in attitudes and practice. To expect an abrupt change in focus and practice would be an unreasonable and impractical expectation. However, several ideas mentioned by different groups and individuals in the district could be added to the steps which were taken.

As a result of staff assessment, the building principal might feel exposed and vulnerable. The process can be harsh and threatening in some situations. For the third phase of school improvement, informal meetings were organized for principals to get together with building staff to share ideas and discuss the process. This might have helped the earlier groups feel more comfortable with the process and feel supported by their colleagues and the central office.

As described earlier, Building Leadership Teams (BLTs) received four days each year in staff development and planning time. The staff development consisted of background on Effective Schools Research, leadership training (trust building, team building, and conflict resolution skills), research on change, training to write action plans, and inservice on specific Effective Schools correlates. Although the principals were part of the team training, they could also have benefited from additional training and support on participative management skills. For some, they were, for the first time, being asked to manage their building in styles quite different from their own leadership. Involving staff in decision-making through the BLT was a new concept to some and additional knowledge and skills might have eased the transition. (See Appendix C)

Although a number of specific curriculum consultants reviewed the Effective Schools Research and were part of the initial training group, they were not involved in the leadership training which BLTs received over the first few years. Therefore, when BLT began to "grab hold" of student achievement data and question curriculum and instructional practices in their buildings, consultants were not in a comfortable position to interact with the groups. The integration of curriculum and instruction might have more naturally occurred if the curriculum consultants had been invited to participate in the same training as the teaching staff and principals had received.

Summary

The original district school improvement plan was to build upon current practice while focusing upon the theme that "things can be better." A significant feature of the plan was to assess existing conditions with specific attention to how the district could improve what it perceives as strengths while also addressing its perceived weaknesses. The Effective Schools process provides a research base to assess the quality of current practices and a building-based process to implement necessary improvements.

The process has not been without conflict. However, many of the disagreements have revolved around issues of significance—funding priorities, curriculum, grouping for instruction, instructional skills, and student assessment and success. The Effective Schools process has provided a vehicle to focus attention on issues of great importance to students in the Anoka-Hennepin School District.

APPENDIX A
Anoka-Hennepin Assessment Plan and Process

A committee of staff and parents examined the district's total testing efforts and developed a plan to guide assessment in the future.

The plan outlines all the district wide tests that will be administered in the foreseeable future. It also explains how the data for each test will be used and who will receive reports of the scores.

The plan, which is required by the 1988 Planning, Evaluating, Reporting (PER) legislation, will be reviewed annually and revised if necessary.

NORM-REFERENCED TESTING PROGRAM
1988–89

TEST	GRADES	RESULTS-PURPOSE	USE OF DATA
Iowa Tests of Basic Skills	2, 4, 6	National percentile score to assess program in basic skills compared to other students in national sample	Parent reports, class placement, remedial decisions,
Tests of Achievement and Proficiency	9	Reading, Math, Language Reference Skills	Assurance of Mastery, school improvement
Cognitive Abilities Test	4, 6, 9	National percentile score to assess strengths and weaknesses in skill areas, and in abstract reasoning. Determine if achievement is at appropriate level.	Parent reports, teacher information, identification for gifted programs.
PSAT, ACT, SAT	11, 12	Special scores for each test to show ability in math and verbal skills.	Required for admission to most colleges
Developing Cognitive Abilities Test	Above 88th percentil on ITBS	National percentile to show differences in ability and achievement among top students.	Identification for gifted program.
Music Aptitude Profile	4	National percentile to show differences in musical talent	Music instruction and guidance of students
Physical Fitness Profile	1-6	District percentile to show level of physical fitness.	Teachers, parent report.

CRITERION REFERENCED TESTING PROGRAM

TEST	GRADES	RESULTS—PURPOSE	USE OF DATA
Reading on CMI	2–6	Mastery of objectives for each unit to guide instruction and evaluate curriculum.	Teachers, parent reports, staff committees.
Math on CMI	1–6		
Degrees of Reading Power	6 & 9 Lower 25% ITBS	Scale score to determine level at which students read. Scale score to determine level at which students read.	Assigning students to reading classes. Assurance of Basic Learning.
ABL Math Test	8	Mastery or non-mastery of 37 basic math skills.	Assurance of Basic Learning.
Language Arts Writing Sample	3 & 9	Score 1–12 to assess writing	Teachers, committees
Spelling test	4 & 6	Assess student learning of words taught in curriculum.	Teachers, committees
End-of-Year Assessments	Math, Science, Social Studies, English, Home Economics	Mastery or non-mastery of essential learner outcomes	Teachers, principals curriculum committees

APPENDIX B
How Has the Effective School Process Influenced and Changed the Various Program Components?

The Anoka-Hennepin Phase I schools have just completed a 3-year cycle which included assessment, planning, and implementation of their school improvement plan. At this time, the only schools which have reassessed the presence of the correlates are schools that changed building principals during the cycle. Throughout Anoka-Hennepin's involvement in Effective Schools, changes have occurred at two levels, district and building. The most crucial changes at the district level were those involving alignment and consistency of the curriculum and development and administration of criterion-referenced tests. These changes are ongoing and are documented through the curriculum review process and the district testing plan.

At the building level, changes focus on the use of test data to improve student learning and the involvement of the staff in making decisions about teaching and learning. This process and an evaluation of its results is documented at each building through its written school improvement plan. These plans are updated yearly.

The curriculum. Effective Schools helped to bring to sharper focus a study and review process that began in Anoka-Hennepin in 1976. The BLT process helped to initiate discussion and research on the issue of curriculum and district mission at the building level. Many elements working together, such as curriculum committees, criterion-referenced test writing, and BLTs, brought curriculum issues to the forefront of district and building effort for students.

Program implementation. At this point, the district is on its second curriculum study and review cycle, and clarification of purpose would naturally be occurring. However, the work of district curriculum committees and BLTs have focused on our basic purposes in education, and have helped determine if implementation of a new program would further that purpose.

Program evaluation. Because BLTs have more access to information about attendance, grades, dropouts, and other data indicating student success or failure, program evaluation has become a more open and informed process. The district also began parent and student surveys during 1987-88. These data will provide baseline information for future comparisons.

Staff evaluation. A Teacher Performance Review System has been functioning in Anoka-Hennepin since 1981-82. The system involves teacher observation, principal feedback and evaluation, and teacher job targets. During 1986-88, a committee reviewed the system and is now formulating recommendations for changes. Possible changes involve timelines and frequency of observation, format for principal feedback, and expansion of the job target idea. Several of these changes may have been partially a result of the Effective Schools process. Through extensive training, principals have become more expert at observing, conferencing, and working with teachers on instructional improvement. Also, resource teachers are available as another source of assistance to teachers for instructional skills. Teachers are also connecting many of their personal job targets to their building school improvement plan goals.

The principals' evaluation now includes observation and feedback on their conferencing skills with the teachers. This is completed by the associate superintendents for elementary and secondary education.

Position descriptions. Several professional positions now include roles and responsibilities related to Effective Schools process. The resource teachers, principals, associate superintendents, and Effective Schools coordinator are such positions.

Community attitudes. Parents appreciate the opportunity to participate in the schools through advisory groups, curriculum committees, volunteer jobs, and parent surveys. Individual buildings are just beginning to focus on establishing parent/school partnerships through their school action plans, so the district is looking forward to continued improvement in the area.

Service and funding agencies. Because of the high visibility of the State of Minnesota Effective Schools program, it is a distinct benefit to be involved in the process throughout the Anoka-Hennepin district. District personnel can gain training through the state Educational Cooperative Service Unit (ECSU) because many of the staff development programs match Anoka-Hennepin's in topic and content. Also, the emphasis on student outcomes and assessment fit the national educational agenda.

Recognition of the instructional process. An awareness and commitment to the importance of the instructional process has greatly increased through Effective Schools. Through study and inservice on the correlates and a commitment to the resource teacher position and role, teachers and principals have focused on the impact of instruction upon student outcomes.

APPENDIX C
What Are the Components of the Effective Schools Planning Process?

District-level coordinating team. A District Effective Schools Steering Committee has been in existence since 1984. The committee's role is to monitor and make recommendations related to the implementation and maintenance of the school improvement process district-wide. In 1988–89, parents will be added to the committee which now consists of teachers, district administrators, and principals.

District-wide involvement. The Effective Schools process has had wide involvement in Anoka-Hennepin since the beginning. Initially, district administrators, the school board, teachers, principals, and consultants all considered research and information about Effective Schools. After district adoption of the process, all central office and building administrators received inservice training from Dr. Lezotte, and the district continues to send new administrators to introductory workshops out of the district. As buildings joined the process through the phases, all BLT members attended workshops to become familiar with the research and the process of Effective Schools.

The school board and superintendent have remained well informed and actively involved in Effective Schools. The school board was involved in a presentation on Effective Schools in 1986–87 at the National School Board Association (NSBA) in San Francisco. Because they initially helped determine the district mission and fully understand the philosophy of Effective Schools, board members show concern that normal operating policies and decisions are in line with the mission of the district. The superintendent attends building meetings when possible and has set a goal to attend at least one meeting at each building during 1988–89.

Beginning last year, 1987–88, parents and students became more involved in the process. Parents, students, custodians, cooks, and paraprofessionals have all served on a number of secondary BLTs, and parent and student surveys have solicited wider input from those two groups. In 1988–89, parents are being added to the district steering committee.

At the building level, BLTs considered their first task to be one of providing meaningful involvement for the entire staff in the process of Effective Schools. Every school has established some form of small, networking groups which serve to enhance clear and two-way communication. With staff turnover and transfers, this issue requires continuing attention by the BLTs to maintain and improve channels of communication.

School-based teams. Building leadership teams, initially consisting of principals and teachers, were established as each school joined the Effective Schools process. Members were selected in a variety of ways, depending upon the process which the building and principal chose. Principals were advised to build a diverse team based on teaching experience, gender, department or grade level, and other factors.

Timelines were suggested for teams, with considerable flexibility available to the buildings. During the first year, teams were identified, orientation and education of the teams took place, teams established communication structures, correlates and indicators were reviewed by the entire staff, and a building assessment of the presence or absence of the correlates was conducted. The second year involved developing school improvement plans, with extensive staff participation in prioritizing, goal setting, and brainstorming ideas. Implementation, monitoring, and review of the plan took place during the third year. From there forward, the process becomes cyclical in nature, with teams and staffs continuing to evaluate their progress and set new goals for the future.

School Effectiveness at the Secondary Level: The Glendale Union Model

Marc S. Becker, Ph.D.
Research Specialist

Janet N. Barry
Associate Superintendent

Glendale Union High School District

Glendale, Arizona

Glendale Union High School District
Became involved in Effective Schools process in 1982

Community

Population
300,000

Metropolitan Phoenix, Arizona

The economic base of Glendale consists of a mix of electronics companies, small businesses, professional offices, construction trades, and tourism (many resorts). Largely residential; some agriculture. Most residents are middle to upper class with a few lower socioeconomic families. About 60 percent of homes have no school-age children. Near Glendale is the Arizona State Extension campus and one of the state's largest community colleges.

School District

Enrollment
14,000

Ethnic Composition (percent)
African-American	2
American Indian	1
Asian-American	3
Caucasian	83
Hispanic	11

Per Pupil Expenditure
1988–1989 $3,264

Percent bussed
12

Area (in square miles)
60

Number of Schools
High schools   9

Number of Staff
Administrators	45
Certified teachers	568
Support staff	608

Student-Teacher Ratio
High school   20:1

Percent college-bound
80 (based on survey of graduates)

Abstract

Although the nation has now developed some knowledge about school improvement in secondary schools, Glendale Union's experience is especially interesting from a research point of view. The district began its school improvement program in 1972 by putting in place an "ambitious accountability program designed to evaluate the instructional program and student achievement in a centralized, systematic fashion." This approach preceded the development of the Effective Schools model by almost a decade.

By 1982, Glendale Union had several additional efforts underway: innovative testing systems, a curriculum planning process, and criterion-referenced tests based on district-wide teaching objectives. The instructional management system (IMS) was probably the first of its kind in the nation. Despite the improvements, there was a feeling that much of the "accountability" had led to more centralized decision-making than many staff members desired. Principals and teachers wished to participate in more decisions, especially those that affected their ability to set the stage for increased achievement for all students. The district sought an organizational structure that would promote the systematic flow of information from campus to district-level personnel with regard to testing, curriculum planning, and school improvement in general.

The evolution of these beliefs led to the creation of a new staff position, Administrator for Effective Schools, and sparked a planned process of change based on the Effective Schools model at all district schools. From the beginning, the superintendent and board supported the process.

Early on, the district had to define terms, including "school effectiveness." From these definitions the interested reader can discover the basic rationale of Glendale Union for introducing and sustaining the process and the philosophical commitment to the measurement of outcomes that undergirds the Effective Schools model. Assessment procedures are also specifically described and their indicators are to this day useful in assessment processes of Effective Schools.

Origins of the Glendale Union School Effectiveness Model[1]

In the fall of 1989 the Glendale Union High School District (GUHSD) began its eighth year of school effectiveness planning, assessment, and improvement. Located in suburban Phoenix, the district contains nine four-year high schools and a student enrollment of approximately 14,000. About 17 percent of the students are from minority backgrounds, with the largest minority group from Hispanic families. The Glendale Union School Effectiveness Model is a product of the district's long commitment to educational accountability. The origins of the model, its unique features, and its influence on students are complex and comprehensive.

All beginnings are difficult. This axiomatic insight became the daily experience of administration and faculty in the district in 1972. During that pivotal year, the district launched an ambitious accountability program designed to evaluate instructional programs and student achievement in a centralized, systematic fashion. At the time, such programs were rare and the term "accountability" was merely the latest addition to the current educational lexicon. Without any models to emulate, GUHSD moved forward by drawing upon the expertise of several measurement researchers. Within five years, the district succeeded in developing an instructional management system, which has become recognized for its leadership role in criterion-referenced testing.

By 1982 teachers were heavily involved in innovative test development and curriculum planning. A variety of staff development efforts were underway and, most importantly, student achievement was moving upward. Yet internal dissatisfactions with the system became evident and had to be understood and resolved. Administrators and teachers within Glendale's nine high schools were concerned that the district's accountability system had become too centralized. Local schools wanted more influence in the decisions that affected student achievement and program planning. Many teachers thought the district-wide testing program was too focused on cognitive achievement and ignored other school-specific variables which contribute to the success of students and programs. Most wanted to know whether increases in student achievement could be sustained among students from lower socioeconomic backgrounds.

The climate of questioning which existed in 1982 gave birth to the Glendale Union School Effectiveness Model. Drawing upon the emerging body of school effectiveness research, the district created a new position, Administrator of Effective Schools, and hired C. M. "Mac" Bernd. Dr. Bernd, who later became superintendent of schools in San Marcos, California, spearheaded a three-year developmental effort which resulted in the model in use. Since its inception, the model was supported by district funds as an integral part of the district's educational program.

School Effectiveness: A Definition

The initial task confronting GUHSD was to establish a model of school effectiveness which would balance the demands of district-wide accountability with school-based decision making. After long debate, a district steering committee arrived at a definition of school effectiveness which would embrace both student achievement and the correlates of Effective Schools, as identified in the research of Curran (1983), Edmonds (1982), as well as Brookover and Lezotte (1979). The correlates, specific to the organizational climate and functioning of schools, laid the foundation for the establishment of a local, decision-making process on each school campus. Before describing this process, it is instructive to examine the Glendale Union definition of school effectiveness and to look at the district's measurement of student achievement.

The GUHSD definition of school effectiveness reads as follows:

> An effective school in the Glendale Union High School District is one which assures (1) measurable academic achievement and (2) observable growth in emotional maturity, physical well-being, and social responsibility by all students.

[Editor's Note: For clarity and consistency we have changed the name "School Effectiveness model" which Glendale Union espouses to the "Effective Schools model" in most references in this case study. When Glendale Union was building its model, effective schools and school effectiveness were interchangeable in most cases (1976–1984). After 1984, the two terms became more specific: "school effectiveness" connoted a school improvement program emphasizing quality considerations, and "effective schools" continued to emphasize quality and equity components.

Today (1989), Effective Schools (capitalized) denotes the comprehensive model espoused by the National Center for Effective Schools (founded in 1987), and Glendale Union has used this model. Glendale Union still uses the term "school effectiveness," however, because it has always characterized the Effective Schools Research this way. The National Center salutes them in their development of the Effective Schools process we espouse today.]

[1] Marc Becker and Janet Barry bring their Effective Schools involvement to the preparation of this chapter. Dr. Becker provides technical support for the district's Effective Schools procedures, including an extensive criterion-referenced testing program. Ms. Barry provides broad leadership in curriculum,

Eight correlates of school effectiveness are known throughout the district as the "eight characteristics." They consist of the following:

1. clear and specific school purpose
2. strong educational leadership by administration
3. high expectations for students and staff
4. school partnership with parents and community
5. positive climate for learning
6. frequent monitoring of student progress
7. emphasis on the attainment of essential skills
8. high level of faculty commitment to the educational program.

Each characteristic is defined by a specific set of indicators developed by faculty representatives from each school. The indicators for each characteristic are listed in Table 1.

School Effectiveness and Student Achievement

The measurement of student achievement occupies a prominent position in Glendale Union's definition of school effectiveness. This is not surprising in view of the district's criterion-referenced testing program and long-term commitment to accountability (see Table 2 for a description of the GUHSD testing program). With the advent of the Effective Schools model, abundant longitudinal data on student performance in the core curriculum was already available. The decision of whether or when to test was not an issue. At stake, however, was the way in which test results were being reported. Administrators and faculty across the district asked that differences in student background be considered in the summary of student achievement (a sample student achievement report appears in Table 3). Some teachers claimed that students from "poor" families could not be expected to learn as much as their more affluent peers, others disagreed. The Effective Schools Research, with its dual emphasis on quality and equity, promised to shed some light on the issue of student background differences and their influence on student achievement.

The concept of quality is certainly not new in education. Few educators would quarrel with the notion that effective schooling can produce high student achievement. In Effective Schools, however, researchers found that achievement was distributed fairly evenly across subgroups in the student body, regardless of differences in family or home background. The term used to describe this distribution is "equity." Equity can be determined by dividing the student population into subgroups, based upon socioeconomic or demographic variables. Student achievement is then reported for each subgroup and is known as the "disaggregation of data."

Like most school districts across the country, Glendale Union had been preoccupied with quality (high scores). The developers of the Glendale Effective Schools model turned the district's attention to equity (well distributed scores) as well as quality. The result of their effort is a school effectiveness profile for each of the district's nine high schools. It is instructive to describe the district's definitions of quality and equity while examining a typical school profile.

Table 4 presents a school effectiveness profile for one school. Part I in the school profile is labeled "Quality Index" and constitutes the district's measure of quality. The Quality Index is the average percent of district objectives that students achieve on the criterion-referenced tests (across subjects). The objectives are weighted on a 1–4 scale according to level of cognition, as determined by Bloom's Taxonomy. (For example, a knowledge level objective receives 1 point. An analysis level objective receives 4 points.) Part I states that, on the average, students in this school achieved between 78 percent and 79 percent of the weighted district objectives over a four-year period. A detailed explanation of how the Quality Index is computed appears in the appendix.

In establishing its definition of equity, the district drew upon a study conducted by Fredericksen and Edmonds (1981). The study identified parental education, specifically mother's education, as the variable most strongly related to student achievement. Part II of the school profile (Table 4) reports the correlation between mother's education and student achievement as measured by the Quality Index. Part II reveals that this correlation, known as the Equity Index, has been relatively small in this particular school over four years (ranging from .14 to .18). In the Glendale Union district, a school is considered effective if the correlation between mother's education and student achievement is small (close to zero on a scale ranging from -1.00 to +1.00).

Part III of the school profile (Table 4) summarizes the Quality Index, disaggregated by five levels of mother's education over a three-year period. An examination of Part III reveals that students from the upper four levels (mothers with some high school through college graduate) are sustaining relatively high levels of achievement at this school. The lower performance of students with mothers who have completed only elementary and middle school is partially a product of the small numbers who fall in this category. Beginning this year, the bottom two categories (elementary and some high school) will be combined, reducing the levels of disaggregation to four at each school.

Table I
Characteristics and Indicators of School Effectiveness in GUHSD

Characteristic	Indicators Within Each School
Clear and specific school purpose	School purpose is —clearly stated. —used in decision making. —understood by students/staff/parents.
Strong educational leadership by administration	Administrators —are visible and accessible. —are responsive to faculty and students. —are responsive to parents/community. —provide instructional leadership. —maintain NCA approved pupil/teacher ratio.
High expectations of students and staff	Teachers and staff —believe that all students can learn. —stress academic achievement. —see teachers as the most important determinants of student achievement.
School partnership with parents and community	The school —communicates positively with parents. —maintains parental support network. Parents —share responsibility for discipline and achievement. —attend school events.
Positive climate for learning	The school —is neat, clean, and physically safe. —is characterized by pervasive caring. —rewards/praises academic achievement. —reinforces positive student behavior. Students —adhere to school and district rules. —display high time on task.
Frequent monitoring of student progress	Teachers give students —appropriate assignments and practice. —prompt feedback for performance. —optimal classroom participation. —multiple assessments.
Emphasis on student attainment of essential skills	Students —are accountable for reading, writing, computing, and spelling in all classes. —receive instruction in essential skills. Administration —shows high commitment to the teaching of essential skills. Teachers —receive adequate materials for teaching essential skills.
High level of faculty commitment to the educational program	Teachers —help students before, during, and after school. —help formulate and implement school improvement goals. Staff —enforce district and school policies. —exhibit professional conduct and attire.

Table 2
District-wide Testing in the Glendale Union High School District

The Glendale Union testing program is the central pillar of the district's Instructional Management System (IMS), a network of personnel and programs concerned with student assessment, staff development, and instructional improvement. The Instructional Management System features:

1. *District-developed criterion-referenced tests.* Teachers representing each of the district's nine high schools are trained in the development of criterion-referenc tests for district-wide use.

2. *Comprehensive pre- and post-testing.* The criterion-referenced tests are field-tested, refined, and administered annually within the district's nine high schools. Testing occurs each fall and spring within 17 courses spanning the district's core curriculum (language arts, math, reading, social studies science). District-wide objectives are the focus of testing.

3. *Dissemination of student achievement data to various publics.* Teachers and principals receive classroom computer printouts showing pre- and post-test performance of individual students. District administrators, school board members, and citizens are provided with aggregate student performance data.

4. *Data-based decision making.* Test results are used by teachers and administrators to make decisions about the planning of instruction, the placement or promotion of students, and the improvement of programs.

5. *Teacher-initiated instructional planning.* Teachers work individually and collectively to diagnose student needs and generate instructional improvement plans in targeted skill areas.

6. *Collaborative development of instructional materials.* Teachers in each of the five subject areas tested attend workshops to develop instructional materials for more effective teaching of major skills. The materials are packaged and disseminated to teachers across the district.

7. *Linkage to staff development programs.* Through its position in the Instructional Management System, the testing program is supported by a variety of staff development programs including Mastery Learning, the Essential Elements of Instruction, and Clinical Supervision.

Table 3
Student Achievement Profile from GUHSD Testing

STUDENT ACHIEVEMENT PROFILE BY TEACHER, SCHOOL, AND DISTRICT

Subject: English -4 Form 510A PROG GEM310
% of Students Proficient

Skills/Concepts	1	2	3	4	5	6	7	8	9	10	11	Mean % Items Corr	Mean % Skls Ach
Teacher 1 Post	55	98	71	70	91	36	54	52	87	84	77	74	64.9
Pre	43	34	4	25	79	18	29	9	36	5	27	54	27.9
Teacher 2 Post	92	100	100	97	100	100	100	100	95	100	97	96	98.3
Pre	73	92	32	62	100	38	81	41	78	35	57	72	62.7
Teacher 3 Post	58	97	67	61	97	47	81	64	89	75	94	80	75.5
Pre	50	47	11	36	89	22	44	6	36	39	28	60	38.9
Teacher 4 Post	81	100	95	76	95	52	100	71	71	95	90	97	84.4
Pre	38	57	5	29	81	10	43	14	48	10	14	54	31.6
Teacher 5 Post	55	98	67	69	86	61	76	47	73	95	88	78	70.5
Pre	35	47	16	14	84	16	27	10	27	30	27	56	32.1
School Post	65	98	77	74	93	56	77	64	75	71	88	82	76.5
Pre	52	53	14	32	86	21	42	15	46	21	34	29	37.8
District Post	74	94	80	69	95	62	81	76	75	74	86	83	78.7
Pre	62	54	23	30	80	23	44	18	52	25	37	60	40.6

Skills/Concepts
1 Literary Analysis: Fiction
2 Literary Terms
3 Figurative Language
4 Spelling
5 Standard Usage
6 Subject/Verb Agreement
7 Punctuation
8 Phrases/Clauses
9 Principles of Multi-Paragraph Writing
10 Pronoun Usage
11 Pronoun Reference

STUDENTS WITH DROP ACTIVITY WILL NOT BE INCLUDED IN SUMMARIES

GUHSD reports district test data to all schools in varying formats. The profile above summarizes pre- and post-test student achievement by teacher, school, and district. The percent of students proficient in each skill is reported along with mean figures. In GUHSD, students demonstrate proficiency in any given skill by answering 75% of the test items correctly.

Table 4
High School Student Effectiveness Profile*

PART I   Quality Index, 1983–87
                     percent

Year	Percent	
1986–87	78	Explanation: The Quality Index is the mean % of weighted skills that students achieve in the priority programs (core curriculum). Each skill was weighted according to cognitive level, using the Bloom Taxonomy. A SCHOOL IS CONSIDERED EFFECTIVE IF THE QUALITY INDEX IS HIGH.
1985–86	79	
1984–85	79	
1983–84	78	

PART II   Equity Index, 1983–87

Year	Value	
1986–87	.14	Explanation: The Equity Index is the correlation between mother's level of education and student achievement (as defined by the Quality Index). A SCHOOL IS CONSIDERED EFFECTIVE IF THE CORRELATIONS (relationship) BETWEEN MOTHER'S EDUCATION AND STUDENT ACHIEVEMENT IS LOW (close to zero).
1985–86	.14	
1984–85	.18	
1983–84	.16	

PART III   Quality Index by Five Levels of Mother's Education, 1984–87

	1984–85 percent	1985–86 percent	1986–87 percent
Elementary	70	69	62
Some High School	73	72	74
High School Graduate	77	76	75
Some College	81	80	78
College Graduate	84	84	82
Across All Levels	79	79	78

PART IV   Coefficient of Determination (Percent of Student Achievement Affected by Mother's Education)

Year	percent
1986–87	2
1985–86	2
1984–85	3
1983–84	3

*All figures rounded

Quality and Equity: Major Findings

Since adopting the Effective Schools model, the district has collected four years of longitudinal data on quality and equity. The following findings have emerged within GUHSD schools between 1983 and 1987:

1. The Quality Index (average percent of weighted skills achieved) ranged from 61 percent to 81 percent.
2. The Equity Index (correlation between mother's education and student achievement) ranged from .07 to .30.
3. The percent of student achievement affected by differences in mother's education ranged from less than 1 percent to 9 percent.

These findings suggest that student achievement in GUHSD schools is more a product of educational programs and bears less relationship to differences in student background. The quality of student achievement is relatively high in most schools, yet there is room for improvement. As the model enters its seventh year, the district has witnessed an upward trend in student achievement, accompanied by growing faculty commitment to the ideals of Effective Schools. According to teachers, this growing commitment is a product of the decentralized decision-making process which supports the assessment of student achievement in the Glendale Union model.

Part IV of the profile (Table 4), labeled "Coefficient of Determination," indicates the percent of student achievement affected by mother's education. The data reveal that only 2–3 percent of student achievement at this school has been influenced by differences in mother's education over a four-year period. This finding reinforces the conclusion that equity combined with high quality (achievement) make this school Effective.

Assessment of School Effectiveness and Faculty Empowerment

A strong commitment to educational accountability necessitated an expanded role for teachers and staff in decision making. In 1982 Glendale Union faculty

COMPUTATION OF QUALITY INDEX

STEP

1. ASSIGN A WEIGHTED NUMERICAL VALUE TO EACH SKILL IN THE GUHSD CORE CURRICULUM ACCORDING TO COGNITIVE LEVEL. The Bloom Taxonomy is employed to determine the cognitive level of each skill.
   The following weights are employed:
   1 = knowledge, 2 = comprehension, 3 = application, 4 = analysis.

2. Compute PERCENTAGE OF WEIGHTED SKILLS ACHIEVED BY EACH STUDENT, where
   - S = Individual skill in the core curriculum
   - Sw = Weighted numerical value assigned to EACH SKILL in the core curriculum
   - $\Sigma(Sw)$ = Weighted numerical value ACROSS ALL SKILLS ACHIEVED BY A GIVEN STUDENT within the core curriculum
   - n(Sw) = Weighted numerical value ACROSS ALL SKILLS POSSIBLE FOR A GIVEN STUDENT TO ACHIEVE IN THE CORE CURRICULUM
   - $\dfrac{\Sigma(Sw)}{N(Sw)}$ = PERCENTAGE (%) OF WEIGHTED SKILLS ACHIEVED BY GIVEN STUDENT

3. Obtain the mean percentage of weighted skills achieved ACROSS STUDENTS WITHIN EACH SCHOOL, where:
   - Ns = Total number of students in a school
   - % = Percent of weighted skills achieved per student
   - $\dfrac{\Sigma\%}{Ns}$ = MEAN PERCENTAGE OF WEIGHTED SKILLS ACHIEVED ACROSS STUDENTS IN A SCHOOL

asked for a greater share in decisions that affect individual programs. They also said that accountability extends beyond cognitive achievement into the daily functioning of the school environment. The Glendale Effective Schools Model, with its dual focus on student achievement and school functioning, established a successful, faculty-based decision-making process. The primary vehicle for local decision making is the School Effectiveness Team (SET) that provides leadership at each school.

Each SET is responsible for the annual assessment of school effectiveness. A local SET, typically numbering about 15 persons, contains a broad representation of teachers and administrators. Counselors, staff developers, clerical support staff, and one or two students may also participate. Teacher representatives are elected for a one- to two-year period. The main function of the SET is to assess systematically the performance of the school on student achievement (as described previously) and the eight school effectiveness characteristics in the GUHSD model (see Table 1). The goal of assessment is to create an annual school improvement plan that addresses the strengths and weaknesses of faculty and staff. The school improvement plan contains specific action plans and goals, some of which call for inservice training or program development. Each SET receives discretionary funds from the district in order to carry out its yearly goals for improvement. Since the operation of each SET is tied to assessment of the district's eight characteristics of effective schooling, the reader will be served by a brief overview of this assessment process.

Assessment of the Eight School Effectiveness Characteristics

Assessment begins with the administration of surveys to faculty, administrators, students, classified staff, and parents. The surveys address issues related to Glendale's eight school effectiveness characteristics. Survey development encompassed a seven-month period, involving extensive field testing and consultation with prominent Effective Schools researchers.

At each school, survey administration takes two forms: (a) paper-and-pencil questionnaires, and (b) telephone interviews. Due to costs, the telephone interviewing of parents is not conducted every year. Virtually the entire population of teachers, administrators, and classified staff complete the questionnaire in an auditorium at one sitting. Approximately 300 students, sampled from heterogeneous intact classrooms, also complete the questionnaire in the auditorium over a two-day period. Telephone interviews are conducted with 100 randomly selected parents.

Shortly after administering the survey, usually at mid-year, the local SET receives a summary of the results. The associate superintendent and administrator of research schedule a data review session with SET members in what is called a "School Effectiveness Institute." They introduce the data to the school team and model a procedure for analysis.

The SET follows the institute with a series of planning sessions which culminate in a school improvement plan. The school improvement plan is a school-based action plan for maintaining strengths or realizing improvements in school effectiveness. The action plan is tied to each of the district's eight characteristics. Table 5 illustrates one page from a typical school improvement plan. The plan, created by the SET at one high school, outlines responsibilities, activities, and timelines for strengthening the teaching of basic skills across subject areas. The column labeled "Evidence of Success" is particularly important. It lists locally determined indicators of effectiveness beyond those contained in the district model. In this example, the action plan for the teaching of basic skills across disciplines is related to the seventh school effectiveness characteristic: emphasis on student attainment of essential skills.

When formulating its school improvement plan, each SET obtains extensively faculty input, usually through a network of subcommittees. The subcommittees span job titles, including clerical support and maintenance staff for some areas of school functioning. In this way, decision making becomes a vehicle for empowerment, enabling each school to complement standard district policies with local autonomy. Figure 1 depicts a model of school decision-making, beginning with the dual assessment of student achievement and the Effective Schools characteristics (correlates).

Table 5
One Page from a School Improvement Plan for a High School

EFFECTIVE SCHOOL CHARACTERISTIC: EMPHASIS ON STUDENT ATTAINMENT OF ESSENTIAL SKILLS

Area for Improvement/Strength: All teachers (do not) consistently identify and demonstrate which basic skills (reading, writing, speaking, listening, or computation) are required in the lessons and subjects they teach.

RESPONSIBILITY	ACTIVITY	DATE BEG. END	EVIDENCE OF SUCCESS	MONITORING ACTIVITY
Language arts department chair, department chairs, teachers, administrator evaluator	Language arts department chair will encourage teachers from other departments to look at how writing can be used to increase learning in all content areas.	1988–89 School Year	Information was disseminated among department members.	Language arts department chair will keep record of writing uses and check with other chairs to ascertain departments' use.
Language arts team, team leaders, department chairs	Language arts teams will approach same class level teams in other content areas to cooperate on a writing assignment.	Fall 1987 Pilot in science	All departments approached.	Keep record of who was approached when and what response was.
Sub-SET team, principal	Grammar tip charts will be provided for each classroom	11/87	Grammar tip charts present in each room and displayed prominently.	Sub-SET team will check for presence of a grammar tip chart in each room.
Sub-SET team, principal, English teachers	Grammar tip sheets will be provided for each staff member and student, and the use of it will be explained by each student's English teacher.	11/87	Each student has a grammar tip sheet.	Sub-SET team will check with their students for chart.

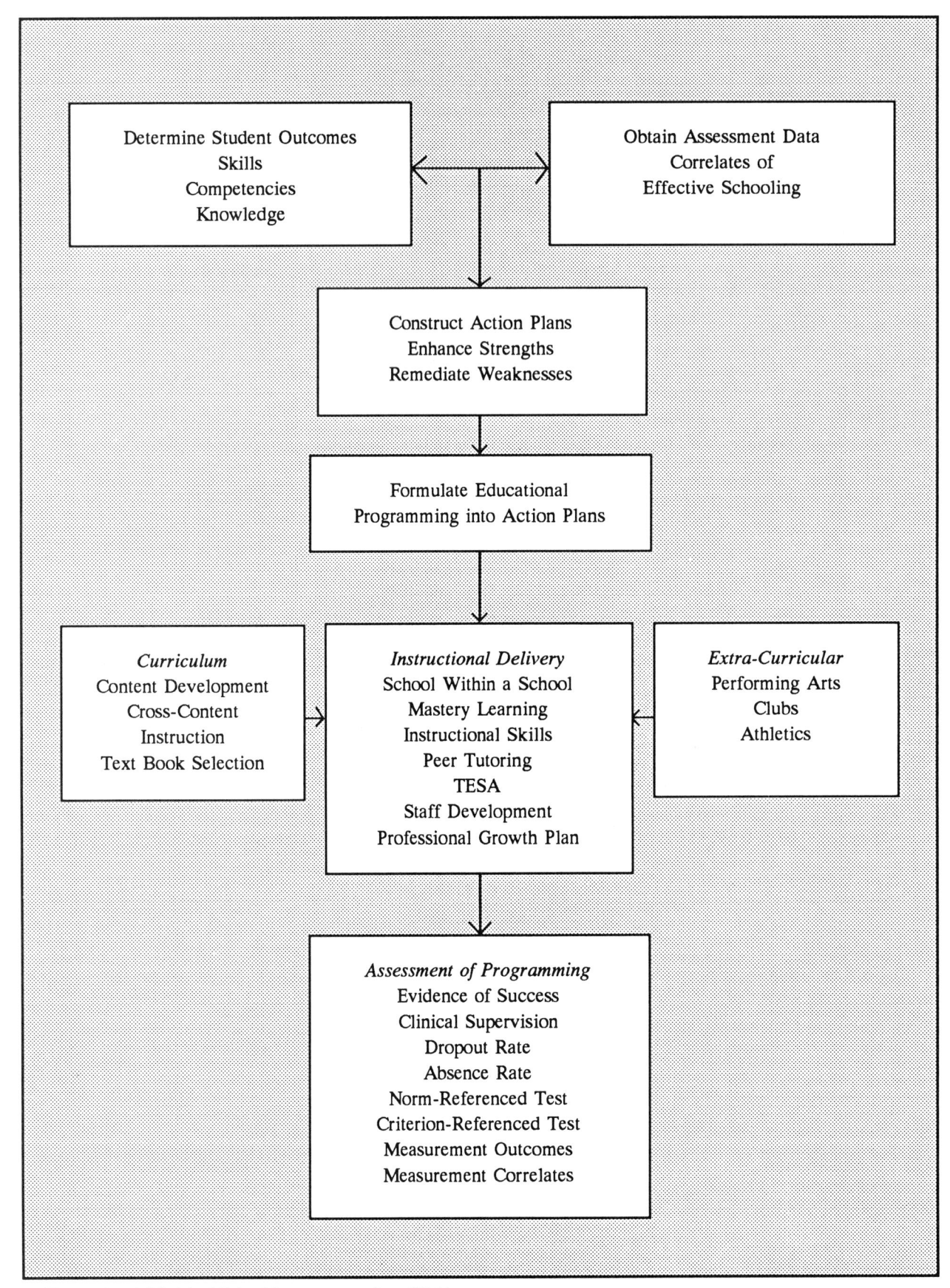

Figure 1. A Model of School Improvement from Within

School Effectiveness and Regional Accreditation

School effectiveness assessment, with its emphasis on student achievement and school functioning, is an ideal vehicle for school evaluation by regional accrediting agencies. In 1983, the district asked the North Central Association (NCA) for permission to replace the standard evaluation process with the Glendale Union Effective Schools model. Between 1984 and 1987, the North Central Association evaluated all of the district's nine high schools, using the Glendale Effective Schools model. On each campus the North Central visitation teams spent considerable time talking to faculty about the School Improvement Plan and student achievement. Team members studied school functioning in relation to the eight Effective Schools characteristics. Ultimately, the teams produced a series of specific recommendations which were incorporated into the School Improvement Plan.

The focus on Effective Schools in accreditation has great potential for school improvement. In the Glendale Union schools, NCA evaluators were able to transcend the traditionally used physical data (e.g., number of library books, semester hours, teacher transcripts) with meaningful analysis of student achievement and school operation. The success of GUHSD experience illustrates that the regional accrediting associations can become important vehicles for the future expansion of school effectiveness.

Problems and Issues Encountered in School Effectiveness

In the midst of a major school improvement effort, one stands on a higher hill than at the launching. From this improved lookout point, it is easy to see both ahead and behind—to confirm and celebrate some decisions; to regret, correct, and move beyond others. As practitioners do this, their reflections should have practical value to others. These final comments may help to guide other educators through the crucial early stages of implementation.

Looking Back

- No single resource has served Glendale Union's work in Effective Schools better than its mature program of valid and reliable criterion-referenced testing in core subjects. Good measures of student achievement are irreplaceable in an effort to document school improvement.

- No single decision has done more to enhance the professional climate of the district than the empowerment of local staff through school effectiveness teams. As school teams were given budgets of up to $5,000 for the achievement of school improvement goals, their decision making carried even more meaning.

- The introduction of school effectiveness teams into a system in which other leadership groups were functioning created some role ambiguity that should have been clarified. With the introduction of an Effective Schools plan, the span of authority of a school's various advisory committees should have been established.

- Because strong administrative leadership is vital to the entire school, it is especially important that a school effectiveness team maintain sharp focus on school management goals and translate goals into meaningful action. Maintaining team focus and limiting the activity of the team to assure high quality maximum input is a significant, continuous challenge to the principal and local leaders.

- A school's decision to focus on a few goals at one time, rather than work across the spectrum of Effective Schools issues, helps staff members develop understanding and commitment to key concepts.

- It is vital to school improvement that the Effective Schools plan be integrated into the deep structure of the school system. It cannot be managed as a "new program," hanging like an appendage to the main business of the school district. It must *become* the main business of the district.

- The decision to marry the district's work in school effectiveness with periodic assessment and evaluation by the regional accrediting association is an excellent method of (a) testing and improving district methodology through external review, (b) limiting the considerable work required of staff, (c) securing wide staff participation in the Effective Schools process and giving it tangible form.

Looking Ahead

With six high schools in the City of Phoenix and three in suburban Glendale, the Glendale Union District will experience dramatic population changes in some schools within the next ten years. The increasing urbanization of some communities within the district will call upon a strong belief system and tested methodology if schools are to continue to function at established high levels. Looking ahead together, district teachers and administrators see this challenge and share a commitment to deepen the culture of Effective Schools now—before significant changes in target populations occur.

References

Brookover, W. and Lezotte, L. (1979). *Changes in School Characteristics Coincident with Changes in Student Achievement.* East Lansing: Michigan State University. (ERIC Document Reproduction Service No. ED 181 005)

Curran, T. (1983, October). Characteristics of the Effective School—a Starting Point for Self-Evaluation. *NASSP Bulletin.* 71–73.

Edmonds, R. (1982, December). Programs of School Improvement: An Overview. Paper presented at the conference *The Implications of Research for Practices. Airlies, 40* (3).

Fredericksen, J. R. and Edmonds, R. R. (1981). *Identification of Instructionally Effective and Ineffective Schools.* Unpublished manuscript, Harvard University, Cambridge, MA.

School Improvement in Geary County Schools

Dr. Max O. Heim
Superintendent

Dr. David Flowers,
Assistant Superintendent

Mrs. Patricia Anderson
Director of Secondary Education

USD #475
Junction City, Kansas

Geary County, Kansas School District
Became involved in Effective Schools process in 1985

Community

Population
20,000 in Junction City
20,000 Fort Riley
 1,100 Grandview
 1,082 Milford

50 percent qualify for free-and-reduced price lunch

Junction City is in the middle of an agricultural area, yet is somewhat cosmopolitan due to the diverse population of Fort Riley. Because the U.S. government is the largest land owner, Geary County has one of the lowest assessed valuations in Kansas. Geary County has the highest birth and divorce rates, and the greatest rate of child abuse. The major employers are the United Telephone Company, the Geary County School District, and a few small industries. In general, demographic factors, including high mobility, high levels of poverty, and cultural diversity combine to increase the school district's concern with students at-risk.

School District

Enrollment
7,000

Ethnic Composition (percent)
African-American	33.1
American Indian	.3
Asian-American	4.8
Caucasian	54.6
Hispanic	7.2

Per Pupil Expenditure
1987–1988 $2,964.94
(general fund operating budget—capital outlay budget not included)

Percent bussed
17

Area (in square miles)
262

Schools
Elementary schools (K–6)	13
Junior high schools	2
High schools (10–12)	1
Other (alternative)	1

Number of Staff
Administrators	31
Certified teachers	464
Support staff	386

Student-Teacher Ratio
Elementary	25:1
Junior high	17:1
High school	16:1

Percent college-bound
65

Abstract

A tersely written case study, Geary County's report reflects the superintendent's, board of education's, and staff's firm intentions to run a solid organization. The setting of priorities, testing, and reports to all constituencies of information gathered in a systematic way has been the nature of change for Geary County from the beginning of its school improvement program. The superintendent believes quality, frequent communication, and shared decision-making are the primary factors in effective implementation of the program.

Attention is paid to ongoing staff development through Mid-continent Regional Education Laboratory (McREL) training and central office support through the Assistant Superintendent for Instruction and the Liaison for Effective Schools. Buildings take responsibility for determining their own staff development needs, and the results of these individual programs are shared between building staffs at the beginning of each year, along with other information that is pertinent to the school improvement effort. The collaborative, continuous staff development program is described in depth, with information on both content and process.

Brief Overview of the Effective Schools Program

Junction City, Kansas, with a population of approximately 20,000, is the principal city and county seat of Geary County. Nearby, Fort Riley, a military installation, has approximately 20,000 more inhabitants. The district is located 130 miles west of Kansas City. The nearly 7,000 students include those who reside on the Fort Riley Army Base, as well as residents of the community and surrounding rural areas.

Students represent multi-cultural backgrounds. The influence of active and retired military members of the community contributes to the global perspective of both students and patrons in the district. However, for many years, that same mobility was thought to be one of several excuses used to justify low student achievement. Fortunately, becoming involved in the Effective Schools process has emphasized instructional elements over which educators have control.

The district demographics are more descriptive of an urban setting than might be expected in rural Kansas. Over 50 percent of the students qualify for free-and-reduced price lunches, the district is poor in terms of assessed valuation and income, and 42 percent of the students are minority.

The Geary County School District first became aware of the Effective Schools process after Betty Kline, director of elementary education, attended an Effective Schools Conference with Larry Lezotte in Phoenix in January 1985. She insisted that others should be informed. In the summer of 1985 ten representatives of the district attended the Ron Edmonds Effective Schools Institute in East Lansing, Michigan. Those accompanying Superintendent Max O. Heim included three central office personnel, three building administrators, and three teacher leaders of the local NEA affiliate. One teacher, Pat Anderson, became the district's first liaison for Effective Schools in January of 1986. This group decided that the new knowledge available through Effective Schools Research was so exciting that more sharing should take place. Accordingly, Dr. Lezotte came to the district in August 1985 to explain the research and the process to another group of staff and to the members of the USD #475 Board of Education.

The commitment of the Board of Education came swiftly. The board authorized an agreement with the Mid-continent Regional Education Laboratory (McREL) in Kansas City, Missouri, a federally funded project which provides training and support to local districts in a seven-state area. For approximately $20,000, McREL agreed to train a panel of teachers from each of the district's sixteen buildings and to provide special sessions for administrators. Each month, from February through May of 1986, building panels, each including the principal, met for one full day of training with Susan Everson. McREL's request to limit participants to no more than 50 each day necessitated having two days of training back to back. Half-day administrative sessions preceded two panel days each month. Substitutes were secured for all teachers, an additional financial resource which demonstrated the commitment of the board of education.

The Geary County Board of Education substantially increased financial support as needs developed during and immediately after the McREL training of building panels. Teacher visits to Effective Schools in other districts helped to address doubts and fears about the change process and to verify positive outcomes. The board of education encouraged staff visits to Effective Schools in St. Louis, Missouri; East Cleveland, Ohio; Norfolk, Virginia; and Glendale, Arizona. All principals and their assistants were sent to an Effective Schools conference featuring Larry Lezotte in either Michigan or Arizona. The superintendent began to devote a regular portion of each monthly board of education meeting to reports, usually presented by teachers, about the Effective Schools process and specific instructional strategies. Dr. David Flowers, assistant superintendent for instruction, coordinated these informative presentations and provided district leadership in current staff development practices.

Commitments made by the board of education to fund necessary expenditures from the district budget were coupled with the support of building principals to plan more time for the staff to identify problems and collaborate in seeking solutions. Each building defined its own mission statement, and then set about scheduling time and resources with priorities stated in the district's mission.

Evidence That District Schools Are Improving

The primary monitoring process used to track students' academic achievement is the California Achievement Test (CAT) Form E/F, 1987, and the Kansas Minimum Competency Test, which is a criterion-referenced test administered by the state in reading and mathematics to all students in grades 2, 4, 6, 8, and 10. The intent in the district's achievement monitoring system is to assess quality and equity. At the same time, the district is moving forward with the development of criterion-referenced tests based upon locally determined teaching objectives. Curricular alignment has been accomplished in reading and mathematics.

Table 1
CAT Math and Reading: Combined Grades K–6.

	Percent of students scoring at or above the 50th percentile	
	Math %	Reading %
Boys	63.6	53.0
Girls	64.2	58.2
Free Lunch	54.2	46.3
Reduced Lunch	62.2	52.5
Paid Lunch	70.0	60.8
White	68.7	61.6
Black	53.5	45.6
Hispanic	67.5	53.8
Asian	81.4	62.4

Table 1 shows the total mathematics and total reading scores for the elementary grades. Each year the test results will be examined for evidence of improvement. The base-line data on the CAT indicate a clear gap between certain groups. The ongoing school improvement/Effective Schools process will focus on reducing these gaps. The good news is that in many instances even the traditionally lower achieving groups are at or above the 50th percentile on this norm-referenced test.

Students who took the second monitoring instrument, the Kansas Minimum Competency Test (KMCT), have shown dramatic improvements in achievement over the two years since the Effective Schools process was implemented in Geary County. The KMCT covers from 15 to 20 objectives in reading, and 15 to 20 objectives in mathematics, in grades 2, 4, 6, 8 and 10. The test has been given in Kansas each year since 1980, with the exception of 1983. Geary County Schools used to do rather poorly on the test. Although the stated intent of the test is to provide individual student data to districts so teachers can design remediation, each year the test has been the focus of considerable media attention. Districts are compared to one another. Geary County generally came up short compared to nearby districts and the state overall.

The revised, new edition of the California Achievement Test was administered in the spring of 1986–87. In this initial year the district piloted the test and analyzed it primarily on the basis of quality. During the second year, in the spring of 1987–88, the test was administered again and baseline data were established for a disaggregated analysis based on gender, race, and income. The criterion used to judge family income was whether the student participated in the free-and-reduced price lunch programs. Attempted use of the mother's level of education yielded unreliable disaggregated results due to inaccurate or reluctant reporting, particularly at the secondary level.

In the fall of 1986–87 each building designed an improvement plan to address achievement on the KMCT. Teachers were asked to help increase achievement on the KMCT and to monitor equity using a disaggregated analysis of the results. Principals monitored achievement on the KMCT objectives over the course of the year. A state practice test was administered in January each year before the actual test in March. The following graphs indicate dramatic improvement over a two-year period in reading and mathematics. Table 2 reports the actual percentages represented in the graphs.

Table 2
1986/1987/1988/1989 KMCT Achievement Results.

	Percent that met or exceeded standard									
Grades	2		4		6		8		10	
	R	M	R	M	R	M	R	M	R	M
1989	93.5	95.0	95.0	94.8	86.5	93.7	98.5	68.5	75.8	63.5
1988	98.4	99.5	91.6	97.7	87.9	93.6	89.6	74.3	82.9	55.8
1987	97.3	98.2	86.5	91.9	93.0	94.3	81.0	68.8	85.1	60.6
1986	81.3	93.5	71.5	72.1	74.7	77.8	79.2	58.9	77.2	66.0

Table 3
1987 District KMCT Disaggregation Report.

Grades	2		4		6		8		10		Totals	
	R	M	R	M	R	M	R	M	R	M	R	M
Total taking test	617	617	509	511	441	437	388	38	365	36	2320	2317
Total taking test whose mother has less than H.S. diploma	79	79	61	61	64	64	51	51	27	25	282	280
Percent passing	91	100	84	90	91	92	67	51	89	44	85	82

The KMCT results were also analyzed for equity after the first year using the mother's level of education. Table 3 shows the percentages of students passing the test whose mother had less than a high school diploma, compared to percentages passing the test from families in which the mother had a high school diploma or some college. These data indicate a relatively equitable distribution of achievement at the elementary level, and relatively high quality as well. At the secondary level the percentage of students passing the test was lower than desired. The important news is that a significant improvement in achievement seemed to be a direct result of the Effective Schools process.

Disaggregated results of the California Achievement Test (Forms E and F) for 1988 and 1989 illustrate one way in which the district monitors equity. The data in Table 4 clearly show a gap in the percentage of students from low socio-economic status families, and those from high SES families, in terms of the percentage of students scoring above the 50th percentile on the Total Battery score. For example, in 2nd grade in 1988, 52.3 percent of the students on free and reduced-price lunches scored above the 50th percentile, compared to 70.9 percent of the students who pay for their lunches. This is evidence of a lack of equity in achievement among students based on family income. What the district wants to see, however, is improvement over time as a result of the Effective Schools process. There is evidence of such improvement when we see a higher percentage of the students from low SES backgrounds scoring above the 50th percentile from one year to the next. This occurred between 1988 and 1989 in grades 2, 3, 4, 5, 8, and 12. There were declines in 6, 9, 10, and 11. The district will monitor this type of data each year to track progress in narrowing discrepancies between sub-populations.

An additional way that equity is monitored is to compare the percentage of students from a given sub-population, such as males, to the percentage of the total population represented by that subgroup in certain score ranges. The district has only begun to disaggregate data based on this method, thus the information in Table 5 represents baseline data. Where there are discrepancies, the district will look for improvements in subsequent years. For example, Table 5 demonstrates that there are not large gaps between the percentage of males and females in the total population, and the percentages that these sub-populations contribute to the scores above the 50th percentile. On the other hand, we see clear evidence of inequity in the ethnic data. For example, we note that 34.1 percent of the 4th graders are black, but only 27.7 percent of the students who scored above the 50th percentile were black. This pattern of inequity is repeated throughout the California Achievement Test results, and thus becomes a district-wide target for improvement. In subsequent years the district will expect the percentage of blacks scoring above the 50th percentile to be more in line with the percentage of blacks in the total population.

Table 4
Percent scoring above 50th percentile on CAT Total Battery

Grade	Low SES 1988	Low SES 1989	High SES 1988	High SES 1989
2	52.3	55.7	70.9	66.8
3	44.5	51.6	65.7	59.4
4	45.3	51.0	62.7	67.1
5	40.1	47.0	60.5	62.7
6	52.2	45.5	60.4	65.0
7	45.3	40.1	55.5	61.4
8	31.5	35.8	60.6	53.8
9	36.4	34.0	52.9	55.2
10	40.2	33.3	48.4	51.5
11	45.7	36.7	56.2	47.5
12	31.3	37.3	57.2	54.0

How the Effective Schools Process Influences Program Components

The Effective Schools process has been influential in focusing the curriculum on student outcomes and in reinforcing the need for a positive and professional climate for staff. The superintendent's goal to raise district test scores on the Kansas Minimum Competency Test (KMCT) quickly generated critical questions about the match between teaching and testing. Individual building plans included frequent monitoring of student progress, careful selection and design of materials to support the curriculum, and the increased sharing of successful teaching strategies among the staff. As test scores have improved, more teachers have come to enjoy their crucial role in formulating and teaching the intended curriculum.

The sense of empowerment is also stimulated by opportunities of staff at all levels to promote beneficial change. Pilot projects such as class-wide peer-tutoring, the whole language approach to reading and language arts, and an integrated library program have produced such successful results that teachers are becoming more enthusiastic and therefore more committed to the process each year.

Sharing these new efforts with visitors from other districts has strengthened the resolve of administrators and staff and led to more risk-taking and less fear of failure. News media in the community have provided information about school improvement activities in a positive and informative manner. The media have no doubt increased community interest and participation in the program of the district's schools. A recent example was the excellent coverage of parent-teacher-student conferences held for the first time prior to the start of school in the district's three secondary buildings.

How the Effective Schools Process Is Affecting Measurement of Student Data

Disaggregation of data sometimes confirms what has been feared. At other times it provides important information which could not have been anticipated apart from such analysis. For example, one elementary building noted that an unusually large percentage of students who fared poorly on the KMCT came from single-parent homes. Armed with those data, teachers sought help from research and experts in an effort to increase instructional effectiveness with these students from single-parent homes.

Another natural direction for measuring student data as part of the Effective Schools success is the development of criterion-referenced tests. Starting at the senior high level in the core subjects, teachers are identifying the essential outcomes in terms of student behaviors for particular classes and grade levels.

Changes in Staff Development Programs

The discrepancy model, which McREL encouraged as a basis for the school improvement process, examined current district practices and outcomes in a particular area, considering preferred outcomes and ex-

Table 5
CAT 1989. Percent in Subgroups Compared to Percent Scoring Above 50th Percentile—Total Battery

Subgroup	Grade 2 Percent in Subgroup	Grade 2 Percent above 50th	Grade 3 Percent in Subgroup	Grade 3 Percent above 50th	Grade 4 Percent in Subgroup	Grade 4 Percent above 50th	Grade 5 Percent in Subgroup	Grade 5 Percent above 50th	Grade 6 Percent in Subgroup	Grade 6 Percent above 50th
Males	49.3	48.9	51.9	51.0	46.6	42.3	48.5	43.7	51.6	48.9
Females	50.7	51.1	48.1	49.0	53.4	57.7	51.5	56.3	48.4	51.1
Whites	53.0	59.9	49.7	55.9	52.9	58.7	51.2	57.0	54.3	61.8
Blacks	33.3	25.4	37.1	29.8	34.1	27.7	34.6	28.3	33.0	26.0
Other Ethnic	13.2	14.1	13.2	13.5	12.8	13.5	14.3	14.7	12.5	12.2
High SES	40.8	45.1	45.4	49.0	41.9	48.7	45.6	53.0	50.7	59.5
Low SES	58.8	54.2	54.1	50.7	58.1	51.3	53.9	47.0	49.3	40.5
MLE < H.S.	6.7	3.8	8.5	7.2	9.7	4.2	6.9	3.6	9.1	7.6
MLE = H.S.	53.3	52.4	53.0	51.0	49.0	50.6	48.5	44.1	50.1	46.2
MLE > H.S.	29.1	33.2	27.4	32.4	30.2	35.8	31.9	42.3	28.5	33.2

amining the research to learn what practices might bring about the more desired outcomes.

This model has been applied also to district staff development. Prior to involvement in the Effective Schools process, staff development had consisted primarily of four days planned at the district level. Building staffs now take responsibility for determining their own needs and conducting three and one-half day development activities. The half day remaining on the calendar is used to begin the year with sharing information that is important to all district employees, information on AIDS, for example. The purpose of staff development at the district level is to provide research-based study to support individual needs. Because the district participates in the State Inservice Plan, teachers can recertify by participating in local staff development. The Geary County Board of Education also recognizes this recertification in determining teacher movement on the salary schedule. State and local support, along with a variety of research-based opportunities such as TESA, Thinking Skills, Class-wide Peer Tutoring, Cooperative Learning and Student Team Learning, have created a new awareness that staff development opportunities can lead to greater teacher efficacy.

The shift to building-based inservice programs ensures a more systematic, ongoing rather than a one-shot approach, to staff development. Building activities are linked directly to the school improvement plan of each site. Pat Anderson, as liaison for Effective Schools, encouraged consistency in the program by serving as a resource person for Effective Schools panels. Panel members draw from both formal and informal needs assessments in designing their school improvement plans and supportive inservice. Teachers also serve as the trainers for these programs.

Because training in Effective Schools Research and practice could not be provided to all staff initially, and because out-of-district conferences and school visitations could not include all teachers, a special staff development program was arranged during the spring semester of 1988. Thirty-five teachers, each representing a building, were invited to spend a day a month during February, March, and April attending the "Academy for Excellence." Organized by Pat Anderson, teachers were provided substitutes and spent each of the three days in comfortable meeting space offered by the local telephone company. Outstanding presenters included two University of Kansas professors, Drs. Nona Tollefson and Fred Rodriguez, Susan Everson of McREL, and several district teachers. The original 35 participants were so appreciative of this opportunity that these sessions will be continued.

Components of the Planning Process

The district level team which first attended the Effective Schools Conference with Larry Lezotte in 1985 was essentially disbanded after the decision was made to launch the school improvement process utilizing McREL as trainers for the district. In its place, each building Effective Schools panel has taken an important leadership role in planning and implementation of the Effective Schools process. Superintendent Heim and other central office staff have remained informed and supportive of differing needs and varied pacing while setting clear expectations for improvement.

Personnel Evaluation System Changes

As a result of the district's involvement with the Effective Schools process, emphasis in evaluating building administrators has moved beyond management functions to instructional leadership. Dr. Lezotte's words are significant with respect to personnel evaluation, "What gets measured, gets done."

Developments Related to the Effective Schools Process

The goals of the Instructional Division, now included as board of education policy, are also the correlates of Effective Schools. All instructional division activities support one of these targets.

The Effective Schools process has also generated a district slogan, decided upon by parents and school district staff. Every employee of the district has received a pin which conveys commitment and confidence in the words, "We Believe All Can Achieve." These words are included along with the Unified School District #475 logo on district documents and communications.

Visits to other districts have yielded important and useful ideas for consideration by the Geary County district. The position of instructional coordinator in the elementary school is one example. Four district elementary buildings are now served by a teacher who works full-time to assist the instructional improvement process under the guidance of the building principal. Long range plans call for the addition of this support role in all buildings, since the district and teachers believe this position is essential.

The Effective Schools process has focused attention upon the need for recognition and involvement of all staff. Accordingly, all district employees are eligible to receive The Shining Star Award, recognition presented quarterly to outstanding individuals. Also,

Superintendent Heim's emphasis on shared decision-making has been recognized throughout the state. Communications across the district are notably better because of the increased involvement of teachers and principals in deciding major issues pertaining to curriculum and instruction.

Concerns Related to the Effective Schools Process

Two concerns surfaced early in the process. The first concern was that emphasis on successful mastery of basic skills for all students would penalize faster learners. Test scores have revealed that concern to be groundless. Faster learners have improved along with those who need more time.

The second concern was how to find enough staff time to plan and prioritize tasks for doing the job right. The administration eliminated all weekly district meetings after school, thereby enabling building-level staff to hold meetings that day. Finding enough time will require constant monitoring and a large measure of creativity.

Advice to Other Districts

In retrospect, more widespread understanding of the change process would have helped. More staff should have been exposed to the process and should have discussed how they might be affected. The readiness phase was given too little attention.

Instead, the training provided by McREL focused primarily upon effective instruction, and although many teachers were excited about opportunities to examine research and to try new strategies, some questioned the need to alter long-standing practices. Specifically some wondered why willingness to behave differently appeared to identify them at once as being the problem and the solution. **Addressing change as a separate issue would have emphasized future empowerment rather than delineating any past lack of awareness.** The effective teaching research presented about instruction was appropriate content, but the process of change should have been provided as the principal framework for implementation. [Editors note: In the National Center's model, emphasis is placed on school/site restructuring, district planning and coordination, and team building skills **before** most of the effective teaching skills are addressed.]

The fact that more staff did not resist the Effective Schools process largely has to do with the outstanding teachers who were included in the initial training. Many were entirely comfortable in pursuing new strategies on their own. For example, some rethought their grouping practices and restructured their classrooms. Groups, as well as individuals, became involved in rethinking previous practices. One panel considered the research on beginning the school year more effectively. To accomplish this, several members elected to conduct summer parent-teacher conferences with their new families as soon as student enrollment had been completed. The fact that no mandates were issued by McREL or by principals enhanced many teachers' willingness to take risks. Certainly the necessity to allow for voluntary modifications was important with or without formal study of change, but perhaps more staff would have been willing to take risks earlier had they shared common insights into this rather stressful, but rewarding, opportunity.

Summary

Because the school improvement process is site-based, many of those whom James Lewis has referred to as "champions" have emerged in the district. Without being able to identify everyone, individuals representing particular segments of the organization deserve mention. Dr. Mary Devin, Deputy Superintendent, used her financial expertise and support of the Effective Schools process to provide the necessary budgetary resources to launch and continue the process. Teachers such as Nancy Hubbard, Jan McNeese, and Shelley Buchanan represent the many elementary staff who heard that reading groups were not the only useful strategy for teaching reading and designed a new classroom for their students. Lee Sharpe and Dr. Hazel Swarts are characteristic of district elementary principals who have dedicated their efforts to providing building climates conducive to teaching and learning. Dr. Larry Dixon, principal of Junction City Senior High School, exemplifies a secondary administrator whose enthusiasm for his staff and whose desire for success for students and teachers alike is unceasing.

Leadership at every level is crucial for success of the Effective Schools process. The superintendent's leadership is most critical. In this district clear goals have been shared, but dictates have been avoided. Trust is both the foundation and the by-product of the Effective Schools process. Empowerment, pride, and success are the governing goals for school improvement for all who come to teach and to learn in Geary County Unified Schools.

The Effective Schools Program in The East Detroit Public Schools

Joan Buffone
Reading, Language Arts Curriculum Coordinator

Emil Ciccoretti
Assistant Superintendent

East Detroit School District
Became involved in Effective Schools process in 1983

Community

Population
35,120

East Detroit, a city located in southeastern Michigan, was founded in 1830 by European immigrants. Though once a fairly affluent community, the population today is predominantly blue-collar, 85 percent middle class, 15 percent poor. The average income per capita is $11,726, slightly above the state average. Over the past 20 years the student population has decreased substantially.

Somewhat under half of East Detroit's residents, 16,500, are employed. Forty-four manufacturing firms, 41 wholesale firms, 281 retailers, and 281 service industries are located in East Detroit. A substantial number of other residents commute to nearby communities or work for the school system or the city.

School District

Enrollment
7,276

Ethnic Composition (percent)
Caucasian 98
Other 2

Per Pupil Expenditure
1987–1988 $3,718
1988–1989 3,614

Percent bussed
0 (except for special ed)

Area (in square miles)
4 plus

Schools
Elementary schools 8
Junior high schools 2
High school 1

Number of Staff
Administrators 28
Certified teachers 245
Support staff 31

Student-Teacher Ratio
Elementary 27:1
Junior high 27:1
High school 23:1

Percent college-bound
31

Abstract

East Detroit started (1983–85) with a pilot school and then expanded the Effective Schools process to the entire district in 1985. Although this district has only recently begun to see student standardized achievement scores increase at certain grade levels, it is building a solid foundation for future accomplishment. Student achievement scores are expected to continue to increase significantly in the next two years.

Curricular alignment and development and staff development are being integrated into a cyclical planning process at the district level. These systems are succinctly delineated in the following chapter. The process of setting up these mechanisms and making them operate to the satisfaction of the staff is described in several phases of development. Finally, the ongoing good relationship with the community of East Detroit produces increased millages in the tax base for schools and support for further school improvement.

Brief Overview of the Effective Schools Program in East Detroit

East Detroit, a suburban community of approximately four square miles bordering the city of Detroit, is a bedroom community that has few industries or commercial enterprises to increase the tax base. Little space is available for building new homes. Approximately 38,000 predominantly white, English speaking people live in East Detroit. The average education level of the adult residents is eleventh grade, with a population of approximately 85 percent middle class and 15 percent poor.

The public school enrollment in East Detroit has decreased from a high of 13,700 in the late 1960s to the current enrollment of 6,600. The school district now operates eight elementary schools, two junior high schools, and one high school. Three elementary schools and one junior high school were closed in the last decade. During this time the adult education enrollment has increased from 40 students to 600 students, bringing district enrollment up to 7,200 students.

Approximately 31 percent of the graduates of the East Detroit schools seek additional training at a two- or four-year college. The remaining 69 percent attempt to enter the job market, join the armed forces, or get married.

Educational research and Effective Schools literature suggest that improvements can be made even in the best of schools. Though administrators and teachers in the East Detroit public schools believe the system does a good job, they have always looked for ways to improve the instructional program to meet the changing needs of students and society.

In the early 1980s in response to nation-wide criticism of schools and in recognition that self-evaluation needs to be continuous, school leaders began to examine the literature on excellence in schools. The Effective Schools literature suggests that certain educational practices work better than others in developing a positive climate in schools, and that specific instructional practices can improve student successes. The literature also suggests that a normal curve need not be the standard of effectiveness. Ideas such as these motivated the leadership to introduce Effective Schools concepts to the administrative team.

Beginning in 1984–85 one elementary school piloted the Effective Schools process for two years as a result of principal and staff interest in the concept. The program focused on improving instruction through mastery learning. The staff of this pilot school found the process was very effective. This led to a district-wide effort to involve all schools.

In the spring of 1985 the assistant superintendent of instruction talked with the principals about the school improvement process, distributed literature, and discussed implementation. With the support of the principals, the board of education was informed of the program at a special session. The assistant superintendent also met with the president and chief negotiator of the teachers' union who subsequently endorsed the concept.

Key leaders in the Effective Schools program in East Detroit included the assistant superintendent of instruction and the building principals who were primarily responsible for developing and implementing the district plan. Dr. Lawrence Lezotte from Michigan State University provided the necessary consulting services. Other leaders included curriculum coordinators, volunteer teachers, union leaders, board of education members, and parents. The district Effective Schools/School Improvement Committee of 47 members developed the district plan. A steering committee of 20 members provided direction for the district committee.

The Effective Schools program in East Detroit has been funded with local funds, ECIA Chapter 2 funds, and state level Section 97 Professional Development funds. The latter, administered by a local staff development team, had support of the district school improvement plan as one of its objectives. Workshops that support the instructional process have included the Madeline Hunter model, Cooperative Learning, Mastery Learning, and Reality Therapy.

In addition to those Effective School projects sponsored at the district level, each school received $2,000 annually to support the work of the building improvement teams. In addition, during the first two years of the program, district funds supported half-day workshops for the building teams to meet with Dr. Lezotte. During these workshops, building teams read and discussed the literature on Effective Schools, gathered and examined data, and developed plans for meeting the needs of their individual buildings. These meetings were held during the school day at the elementary level and after school for the secondary and adult education levels.

During the second year of the program, teachers were paid a stipend of $400 to attend 15 days of workshops that focused on Outcome Based Instruction and the effective instruction characteristics of Effective Schools. The total cost of this program was $24,000. Eleven of the workshop days occurred during the summer and four were held in the evening or on Saturdays. Funding was also provided for staff from Johnson City Central Schools, Johnson City, New York, to be trainers at these workshops.

Building level teams of teachers and administrators visited outstanding school programs. Teams from four schools visited and observed Johnson City Central Schools. Two other teams visited the Glendale, Arizona program and one team attended a conference on Effective Schools and School Improvement in Glendale, Arizona. Such visitations provided staff members with valuable information and insights about how to develop a building level plan for Effective Schools and school improvement.

During this time, the East Detroit Public Schools also invested $6,800 of Chapter 2 Block Grant funds in teacher training for the Madeline Hunter approach to instruction and to send staff members to training that was offered by the Intermediate School District. Approximately 1/3 of the staff has participated in the Instructional Theory Into Practice (ITIP) workshops held during school, after school, or on Saturdays. Teachers were given the opportunity to participate in the workshops at a time that was convenient for them. At the same time, administrators participated in the ITIP and clinical supervision workshops. These strategies for instruction are believed to be consistent with the Effective Schools Research and supportive of the total school improvement program.

The East Detroit Public Schools has always supported staff development and professional growth experiences for administrators and staff members. In addition to support through funding, the Effective Schools/School Improvement Program has been supported symbolically by a leadership team that encourages attendance at professional conferences, workshops, curriculum development meetings, and visitations. Strong central administrative support, strong building-level administration support, along with board of education and parental support, have been important to the planning, implementation, and evaluation of the school improvement program.

What Evidence Does the District Have That the Schools are Improving?

As a result of the district involvement in the Effective Schools/School Improvement Program, teachers are expressing greater interest in developing a data-based instructional program. The purpose of gathering data on student achievement and specific outcomes is to assess whether improvement is taking place. Administration and staff believe that "all children can learn," and no longer accept the normal curve as a standard of effectiveness. As a result, there is a need to gather data to determine if all children are realizing quantitatively more success in school.

In the past, assessment tests were used to provide staff members with information about student achievement. While district data were gathered, no coordinated effort had been made to develop baseline data nor to examine growth over a period of time. As a result of the Effective Schools/School Improvement Program, an effort is now being made to develop district and building baseline data to provide information regarding improvement in student achievement over time.

Traditionally, norm-referenced assessment tests have been used in the East Detroit schools to provide data on the achievement of the students in East Detroit as compared to students throughout the United States. In general, students in East Detroit have performed at or slightly above the normal distribution or curve. The IOWA Test of Basic Skills has been used to determine growth at the third, fifth, and eighth grade levels. The Gates-MacGinitie Reading Test has been used to assess general reading ability for students in grades six through ten.

Presently, baseline data are being gathered for all of the testing programs. While slight but steady progress is seen in some areas, student performance in general has been stable. As the curriculum in all of the schools is revised, and as staff development and school improvement programs are implemented, it is expected that student achievement will improve. At this time, the direct influence on curriculum and instructional practices is just beginning.

The Michigan Educational Assessment Program (MEAP), a criterion-referenced test, currently assesses achievement in reading and mathematics. Baseline data on the performance on the MEAP reading test shows that results are stable with 81.2 percent of fourth grade students performing in the fourth quartile in 1987. This is a small improvement from 80.6 percent in 1986 and 81.6 percent in 1985. Greater improvement has been seen at the seventh grade level with 86.2 percent of students performing in the fourth quartile in 1987, an increase from 82.4 percent in 1986 and 79.8 percent in 1985. At the tenth grade level, a slight decline in performance was seen in 1987 with 79 percent of students performing in the fourth quartile, a decrease from 82.4 percent in 1986 and 81.9 percent in 1985.

In the area of mathematics, 89.4 percent of fourth grade students performed in the fourth quartile, a slight increase from 88.4 percent in 1986 and 85.9 percent in 1985. At the seventh grade level, 79.8 percent of students performed in the fourth quartile, a significant increase over the 71.3 percent in 1986 and 64 percent in 1985. At the tenth grade level, scores again increased from 76.1 percent of students performing in the fourth quartile in 1987, an increase from 70.1 percent in 1986 and 66.6 percent in 1985. While these scores may appear to be low, it is interesting to note that they are above the state and county averages at the 4th grade level, and well above the state and county levels for 1987 in grades seven and ten.

The computer management programs for both reading and mathematics basal programs have enhanced the district's ability to examine student progress more specifically in the reading and mathematics curriculum. Students in grades 3 through 6 use the computer management programs when taking unit and summary tests.

After two years of using the computer management program that accompanies the basal reading program, baseline data reveal that students are mastering an average of 84 percent or more of the reading objectives district-wide. At one elementary school, third and fourth graders who are using a mastery learning approach to reading instruction have mastered an average of 96 percent of the reading objectives. Fifth and sixth grade students in the same school but not exposed to the mastery approach averaged 83 percent. Though there may not be any direct causal relationship, it will be interesting to observe whether the outstanding performance of the current third and fourth grade students continues.

In mathematics, the data show that an average of 85.5 percent of third grade students, 81.5 percent of fourth grade students, 74.7 percent of fifth grade students, and 77 percent of sixth grade students are mastering the essential mathematics objectives of the curriculum Again, it is interesting to note that in the school that participated in the mastery learning approach, an average of 89 percent of third grade students, 84.4 percent of fourth grade students, 85.9 percent of fifth grade students, and 68.7 percent of sixth grade students mastered the objectives. Their performance is consistently better than the district-wide average.

To both administrators and staff members, the need for additional indicators of school effectiveness has become apparent. While achievement test data are valuable, many other indicators of improvement can be examined. Efforts are being made to document improved attendance at all grade levels. Information regarding suspensions, grading, retentions, and graduation rates is being gathered through a district computerized data-base program called OSIRIS.

Participation in staff development has been growing. One hundred percent of all elementary staff members have had inservice training in "outcome-based education." One-third of all staff members have taken ITIP (Instructional Theory Into Practice) training. Staff members throughout the district are also learning about and incorporating concepts such as team teaching and Cooperative Learning in addition to the correlates of Effective Schools.

Finally, over the past three to four years surveys regarding the attitudes of staff, students, and parents have been developed and conducted as a result of individual school improvement plans. These informal indicators can often provide the most valuable insights into how well schools have met the individual needs of staff, students, and parents. Such qualitative data are valued by the administration and staff of East Detroit.

How Has the Effective School Process Influenced the Following Program Components?

The Effective Schools process has had a significant influence on people, programs, and the instructional process in the East Detroit schools. Most importantly, the process has affected how both administrators and teachers discuss program and attempt to resolve problems. A greater emphasis is placed on professionalism at all levels and the need to use research-based information in making decisions.

To resolve questions related to the district's mission and program components, East Detroit used the Outcome Driven Developmental Model (ODDM) Problem Solving Model developed by the Johnson City schools in New York. The ODDM Problem Solving Model requires that five important questions be asked when addressing concerns:

1. What do we want?
2. What do we know (research)?
3. What do we believe?
4. What do we do?
5. What do we want to become?

In answering these questions, the staff is able to review concerns and needs, and make quality decisions regarding curriculum, instruction, and the many difficult problems related to the learning environment in general.

The Curriculum

In response to the question, "What do we want?" the initial Effective Schools/School Improvement Plan adopted by the East Detroit Board of Education in January of 1986 included an ambitious plan for a K–12 curriculum review in all of the major subject areas. The assistant superintendent along with two K–12 curriculum coordinators and three secondary level curriculum coordinators are leading efforts to improve the curriculum. The general purpose of all curriculum committees is to involve the staff in the effort to provide continuity and consistency in programming across and between grade levels. District-wide adoption of curriculum materials is promoted in all areas. Between 1984 and 1988 adoptions included textbooks for reading, English, mathematics, science, and social studies. Numerous adoptions of secondary level textbooks for specialized courses were also completed.

Throughout the process of curriculum development in all major content areas, committees work to develop curriculum guides. Because of the Effective Schools process and the ODDM Problem Solving Model, the curriculum guides reflect much more than a scope and sequence of skills to be mastered. Teachers give more attention to the total instruction and assessment program in each content area, and guidelines include objectives, materials, instructional strategies, corrective and enrichment ideas, and suggestions for assessment. The complex process of curricular alignment is seen in the many drafts and revisions of curriculum guides as committees work to define and refine the instructional program.

Throughout the process of reviewing the K–12 curriculum, the instructional staff has identified areas in which new units and courses need to be developed. The curriculum review process has led to the identification of significant gaps in instruction, and to greater continuity in the K–12 program. At the junior high school level, staff members are developing an exploratory program that reflects the needs of adolescents and a program for at-risk students. At the secondary level, the tracking of students has been reexamined and is being systematically abandoned.

Program Implementation

In implementing instructional programs, the staff of the East Detroit schools has made a commitment to being "intentional" about identifying instructional objectives and employing good instructional strategies. Such planning is focused on helping each learner to achieve the desired outcomes for the grade and course of instruction. Emphasis is placed on providing high quality instruction to whole groups while providing corrective and enrichment support to those who need it.

A concurrent step is providing inservice for staff on the instructional process. From 1984 through 1988 numerous opportunities for inservice in the Madeline Hunter ITIP have been offered to the staff; approximately one third of the staff has participated. As the staff has become trained in ITIP procedures, curriculum guides, unit guides, and lesson guides have begun to reflect the ITIP instructional process.

The administration recognizes that "change is a process and not an event." Thus, successful implementation of new curriculum will occur over time. Teacher commitment to the curriculum development and implementation process is essential, thus teacher input is essential at every stage of the change process.

Team planning is promoted in a variety of ways depending on staff and building needs. Experiments in whole group instruction are being promoted, as well as teaming for teaching of specific units or content areas. Grade level teaming or cross-grade grouping may be used to create whole group instruction while meeting the needs of developmental differences in specific subject areas.

Teachers are also encouraged to make classroom visitations to learn from each other. The staff provides a wealth of knowledge to be modeled and shared. One of the most successful events has been a mini-conference in reading strategies in which teachers explained and modeled instructional strategies.

Program Evaluation

Existing instructional programs and programs to improve the learning environment need to be evaluated continuously through informal and formal measures. In asking "What do we want?" the staff of East Detroit also asks, "Is what we're doing helping us to get what we want?" The question is applied to curriculum, as well as concerns about discipline, building climate, and instructional strategies. More formal evaluations are outlined in school improvement plans of individual buildings and include staff surveys, parent surveys, development of data bases using standardized and criterion-referenced testing, and disaggregated analyses of the performance of subgroups of the school population such as gender and mother's education.

While the administration and staff values such studies of student performance, the current emphasis of the Effective Schools process is on program improvement. Until the program improvements are firmly in place, such data will provide baseline information for examining future successes.

Staff Evaluation

Communication, the hallmark of the Effective Schools process, includes staff evaluation of the question, "How are we doing?" Continuous dialogue is promoted, and more formal surveys of staff needs are conducted frequently. While individual buildings evaluate their own progress, district committees continuously evaluate the needs of the district as a whole.

All staff development activities are evaluated and, when appropriate, results shared with staff.

Community Attitudes

East Detroit has enjoyed the reputation of having excellent schools with few of the problems that could plague a district bordering a major urban area. The innovative programming is recognized in the county, and businesses are renewing their interest in the schools. A number of school-business partnerships have been established. Civic groups have been asking for presentations on school improvement. The elementary schools report good attendance at parent conferences and school activities. Parent support groups work to support the school programs and to pass needed tax millages.

As a result of the Effective Schools program, parent groups are focusing their attention on the efforts to improve curriculum and the total school program. The board of education and parent groups have participated in workshops on topics such as the instructional process and "reality therapy."

The Effective Schools process has influenced many policies, procedures, and practices. Most changes that have occurred reflect the district-wide effort to provide consistency in policies and procedures and to communicate more effectively to both students and parents.

Student handbooks have been revised at all levels and reflect the district-wide school mission and all relevant policies, procedures, and practices. Efforts to explain policies to the students and community are offered at all levels through parent-teacher organization meetings, conferences, and school programs.

How Does the Effective Schools Process Affect the Way Student Achievement Is Measured?

The leadership is aware of the dilemma created by the ability to test and measure how well students are learning the curriculum, and the problem of measuring what is truly valued in the curriculum. Nevertheless, assessment information provides data on whether children are learning in general and whether specific subgroups of children are learning as well as other subgroups in the course of finding out how well specific subject matter is being mastered.

School personnel have analyzed student learning by conducting disaggregated analyses. Subsets of the student population have been compared by parent education groups and by gender. Where disparities existed, school improvement plans have outlined efforts to assure that causes are not related to inadequacies in instructional practices or programs.

Curriculum-based testing is the product of curriculum development in the major subject areas. As curriculum guides and unit guides are developed, testing will be further aligned with instruction. Assessment of prerequisite skills is being included in unit development in many areas. In addition, formative and summative tests are being developed.

Several instructional programs include criterion-referenced tests. The elementary reading and mathematics programs include computer managed assessment programs that provide the teachers with convenient and efficient measures of student learning. Such programs are providing the administration and teaching staff with information for evaluating the curriculum, program, and needs of students. In addition, the state assessment tests provide criterion-referenced data on student performance in the areas of reading, mathematics, and science in grades four, seven, and ten.

Standardized tests are used to compare the general progress of students in the East Detroit schools with a nationally normed population. The administration and staff realize that such data allow evaluation of how students are progressing. Standardized reading tests are given district-wide in grades six through ten. The IOWA Test of Basic Skills is used to assess a broader range of student learning. Baseline data from these tests are being gathered for longevity studies of the effects of the Effective Schools/School Improvement Program on learning in general.

While the Effective Schools process has raised awareness of the need to examine how well children are learning and "How are we doing?" it has also led to questions of whether tests measure what is valued in the curriculum. The focus of many tests on isolated subskills or knowledge level information is being challenged across the curriculum. Leading educators are questioning the effects of testing on teachers' sense of professional competence and their ability to make or influence important decisions about educating children.

Curriculum committees are evaluating assessment-of-learning instruments, and making recommendations for modifications in commercial programs. Methods of evaluating student performance may include surveys of student attitudes, surveys of teacher observations, and surveys of parent perceptions. Behavior inventories in such areas as reading readiness may be used in conjunction with commercial assessments that accompany readiness programs. Other inventories may be used to assess higher-order thinking in content areas. Portfolios representing student performance are being considered. Such data will be examined along with norm-referenced and criterion-referenced test results. Disaggregated analyses will continue to be used to assess whether the schools are equitably serving all subsets of the student population.

Conclusion

In general, the Effective Schools process has brought focus and structure to the efforts of all in the district. It has revitalized the communication among the entire staff and has released creativity in developing plans for continued school improvement at the building and district levels. The Effective Schools process has forced examination of the practices that are known and believed to be most effective. Staff have questioned and in some cases discarded those that were judged to be less effective. This has allowed East Detroit to agree that its schools may be good, but "things can be better."

Most importantly, the Effective Schools process has resulted in the district-wide mission statement that "all children can learn." In East Detroit, it is clear that the students are the beneficiaries of the Effective Schools process. Every effort is made not to select and sort children and to ensure that programs are inclusive rather than exclusive. All children are offered a "rich" curriculum, as opposed to reserving enrichment for a select few. The former "gifted" program has been restructured into an enrichment program available to all students through the regular classroom and through after-school opportunities.

In most discussions, the most critical question regarding policy and program asks, "Is this good for kids?" The district-wide statement of outcomes includes the goal of promoting the self-esteem of each student as a learner and as a person. Instruction is success-oriented and recognition of achievement in academic and non-academic tasks is recognized and rewarded. Building mottos and mission statements are posted in hallways and in classrooms. Bulletin boards and display cases feature students with smiling faces and examples of student achievement. Student work is displayed in hallways and in classrooms. There is clearly a more intentional effort by staff to be positive and to promote pride in self and the school experience.

Reflections

The East Detroit Public Schools effort to improve schools is typical of the many districts involved in such programs. Change brings many frustrations, yet it also creates many challenges that can revitalize a district.

This review of one district's efforts to improve its schools establishes that change is a process, not an event. One would like to prescribe the perfect school improvement plan, the perfect "event." Yet that is likely to be impossible. While districts and schools must identify their unique needs and establish their own plans, some of the problems might be allayed by *providing for the following.*

Awareness for All Staff Members

It is essential that all staff members be included in the early awareness sessions that introduce the Effective Schools Research and the concept of school improvement. It is important to gain the interest and commitment of all staff members before conducting surveys, identifying building teams, and developing plans. When a district does not introduce all staff members to the process, there is greater risk of the school improvement process being viewed as a top-down administrative effort to have staff improve their performance.

When awareness is provided to all staff members, an understanding of many of the issues surrounding school improvement in general can be developed, and the more likely result will be district-wide commitment to the process.

Needs Assessment Surveys

It is necessary to preview and adapt the respected school improvement needs assessment surveys so that they use language that is appropriate to the district. For example, titles of administrators or references to types of programs that may be appropriate for one district may cause great confusion and frustration to staff members in another. It is necessary to review the needs assessment surveys carefully and make appropriate adjustments before distributing to staff members.

Establish District Goals and Focus

The school improvement goals of the district must be clearly listed and should provide the focus that is needed to help all schools and staff members move toward achieving the goals. The seven correlates of Effective Schools provide perhaps too broad a range of areas of concern. A district SIP plan can address long range (3–5 years) and short range (1 year) goals. This would help to provide focus for the district-wide efforts to inform staff about Effective Schools Research and ongoing school improvement programs within the district.

Communication Networks Need to Be Established

Both formal and informal communication networks on a district level and building level need to be established. Reading lengthy newsletters is unrealistic; but brief research summaries, announcements, or stories about school improvement can become part of a communication network to disseminate information about SIP progress.

Limit Committees—Focus Activities

A district-wide school improvement program might consist of a district steering committee, building committees, and teams of staff members engaged in special but temporary projects. The charge of the committee needs to be clearly established and time lines developed. It is easy to establish new committees to address needs as they arise (discipline policy, grading and reporting, etc.), yet too many committees or task forces can cause the program to appear to lack direction and purpose.

Develop Base-Line Data

The existing data on student performance may provide the base-line data that are needed to establish whether schools are improving. It is important that an organized and systematic method be established to coordinate the gathering and analysis of data. Appropriate graphs and charts need to be developed and put on computer so they can be easily adapted each year. Each district needs to identify what information needs to be collected and develop a method for easy input and retrieval of information in the form that is most understandable (graphs, charts).

Mishawaka Moves to Improve

R. Steven Mills
Assistant Superintendent
School City of Mishawaka

Mishawaka School District
Became involved in Effective Schools process in 1985

Community

Population
40,000

East of South Bend, Indiana in the northern part of St. Joseph County; the economy is based on services and industry; major employers include Uniroyal, Miles Laboratories, Nyloncraft, and Liberty Mutual Life Insurance.

About 22 percent of all students receive free-and-reduced price lunches; half the mothers attended college.

School District

Enrollment	5,300
Ethnic Composition (percent)	
Caucasian	97
Per Pupil Expenditure	
1987–1988	$2,420
Percent bussed	
0 (neighborhood schools)	

Area (in square miles)	8.5
Schools	
Elementary schools	8
Junior high schools	2
High school	1
Number of Staff	
Administrators	35
Certified teachers	292.5
Support staff	181
Student-Teacher Ratio	
Elementary	15.3:1
Junior high	18.7:1
High school	17.8:1
Percent college-bound	30

Abstract

The School City of Mishawaka's case study delineates specific steps taken, the sequence of these steps, and the general reactions of constituent groups. The SWEAT (System-wide Effective Action Team) is the primary district coordinating vehicle for the school improvement program. From their deliberations an orderly planning process fans out to building-level teams (BLTs). Building plans are "reviewed, revised, and approved" in the schools before they are submitted to the board of education for final approval. The plans, three-year projections, are updated every year.

Because the Effective Schools process for school improvement has been in effect only one year (1987–88), achievement scores have not measurably increased. The district switched from the Iowa Test of Basic Skills to the California Achievement Test in the spring of 1988) and so new base-line data have been gathered. Disaggregation of student scores along socioeconomic status categories has been performed since the beginning of the program. Because tests are given only at the third, sixth, eighth, and tenth grade levels, and there are no district-wide criterion-referenced tests, Mishawaka's student monitoring system is not yet developed enough to be useful for school improvement based on Effective Schools Research.

However this is one of the best cases in this monograph to demonstrate the complexity of "starting-up" procedures. Quotations from a personnel questionnaire bring alive the personal and professional concerns of staff, central office administrators, and principals.

An extensive Appendix to this case study is an example of a truly comprehensive approach to school improvement based on Effective Schools Research. Mishawaka was fortunate to begin their process when more was known about the importance of strong supportive district relationships with schools. Some of the forerunners, like Jackson, Mississippi; Norfolk, Virginia; Spencerport, New York; and others cited in this monograph had already designed reporting systems, and other feed-back and coordinating structures to carry the school improvement process forward. Mishawaka is a good example of what works when leadership, commitment, and quality staff development programs are added to the fundamental Effective Schools Research model.

The City of Mishawaka

Mishawaka, a city of approximately 40,000 people, is located just east of South Bend in the northern part of St. Joseph County, Indiana. Mishawaka's economy is based on services and industry. Major employers include Uniroyal, Inc., Nyloncraft, Liberty Mutual Insurance Company, Miles Laboratories, Inc., School City of Mishawaka, and Civil City of Mishawaka. Currently the community is "shifting" from a highly industrial base to a service-based economy.

School City of Mishawaka (SCM) covers 8.5 square miles and serves 85 percent of its resident children. The remaining children attend school in neighboring districts and parochial schools. The Mishawaka Municipal Common Council appoints a five-member board of school trustees to govern the school district. Operating funds come from state support (approximately 50 percent), local taxes (approximately 45 percent) and other sources (approximately 5 percent). The local school tax level is $5.81 per $100.00 of assessed valuation. The annual expenditure per student in 1987–88 was $2,420.

Over 5,300 students attend the eight elementary schools (grades K–6), two junior highs (grades 7–8), and one senior high school (9–12) within the Mishawaka School Corporation. The system is staffed by 34 administrators, 318 teachers, and 142 support staff. Pupil-teacher ratios average 20–1 and are unsurpassed by most public schools in the area. Great pride is taken in maintaining facilities in such a way as to provide a safe and orderly school climate conducive to teaching and learning. The Mishawaka Administrative Center houses the business and instructional administrative offices, the Hannah Lindahl Children's Museum, and the "Survive Alive House" (fire safety program).

The corporation's commitment to the "neighborhood school concept" encourages personal contact between parents and school personnel. This close relationship permits ongoing communication and close supervision of each child's school-related activities through the Mishawaka system. Elementary students reside within walking distance of the school they attend. Transportation is provided only for special education students who need programs outside their normal attendance areas.

The following statistics describe the student population:

	Percent
Socioeconomic status	
Single parent homes	23.7
Mothers with less than high school degree	21.0
Mothers with college education	50.78
Free lunch program	16.50
Reduced lunch program	5.44
Ethnic background	
White	97.03
Black	.97
Hispanic	.875
Asian	.746
Other backgrounds	.136
Language spoken in home	
Only English	98.95
Second languages	.796
Non-English	.220

Motivation for Launching the Effective Schools Process

In June of 1985, at the invitation of the superintendent of a neighboring school district, the entire administrative staff and teacher association leaders of the Mishawaka schools, along with like members of the neighboring district, participated in an intensive two-day workshop on Effective Schools Research. As a result of this persuasive, logical approach, the Mishawaka district decided to study and review the entire instructional program during the 1985–86 school year.

Although the over-all consensus was that the school district had an admirable "track record" of educating the youth of Mishawaka, participants in the workshop concluded that the implementation of the Effective Schools process should be encouraged.

- Certain practices have been proven to be more effective than others in the teaching and learning process. School leaders wanted to be certain that these proven practices were being followed in every classroom.
- The socio-economic status of Mishawaka students is changing. The challenges of negative societal factors needed to be addressed with new, proven practices and procedures.
- The dynamic nature of education itself mandates the need for constant efforts to improve.
- Self-renewal efforts in purposeful cycles must be implemented for schools to continue to be successful and effective.
- Citizens and legislators are demanding public school improvement and accountability.

A History of Launching SCM's Programs

School City's commitment to a process of school improvement based on Effective Schools Research began in June of 1985, when administrators from the school corporation attended two Effective Schools workshops. On August 26, 1985, the entire staff attended a meeting at which Superintendent Richard Brainerd presented the Effective Schools model for improving the quality of education for all students in the Mishawaka School System.

From November 1985 until April 1986, teams of administrators and teachers presented the correlates of Effective Schools to every instructional staff member in the school corporation. During this time, administrators and selected teachers attended institutes presented by researchers and practitioners of Effective Schools Research. On May 5 and 6, 1986, Lawrence Lezotte met with administrators and selected teachers from each school in the system to provide suggestions and to outline actions to start the Effective Schools process.

June 10, 1986, the board of school trustees directed the administration to prepare a district plan for proceeding with the Effective Schools process. During June and July 1986, administrators and teachers developed a three-year plan. In August the board gave its approval. During this time, staff members attended a variety of workshops which related to skills needed to implement the plan. (See Appendix to this Case Study.)

The Key Leaders... "SWEAT"

Dr. Lezotte met with the entire staff on October 29, 1986 to share his expertise on the Effective Schools process to all 494 employees. That afternoon all employees completed a survey that was designed to help identify both strengths and areas needing strengthening in Mishawaka schools.

In December 1986, the System-wide Effective Action Team (SWEAT) was formed. Led by Assistant Superintendent Steve Mills, this team of representatives (principals and teachers) from each of the ten schools were given specific tasks to take back to their buildings.

The assistant superintendent for personnel; the assistant superintendent for curriculum evaluation and secondary education; the directors of gifted and talented programs, computer education, the joint services of health, physical education, and safety; and the school psychologist made up the representatives from the district office. The Mishawaka Educational Association president, Bruce Shannon, was also a member of the SWEAT team.

March 27, 1987 marked the culmination of one and one-half years of research, study, and preparatory work. On that day, the entire school corporation staff met in their individual buildings for "Staff Development Day." During these meetings, each school discussed the preliminary draft for school improvement, and the response was overwhelmingly enthusiastic.

At each building, a building-level team (BLT) was formed, composed of the building's SWEAT representative, a central office administrator, the school principal, and both certified and support staff members. Each school-level team wrote, then reviewed, revised, and approved a final written school improvement plan for its individual school. These plans were submitted to the school board on June 9 and 11, 1987, and were approved at the June 23, 1987 meeting of the board.

In September 1987, all schools selected community representatives to serve on their building-level teams. These representatives included school parents, business leaders, and senior citizens.

SWEAT-ers met one day a month during the school year; teacher reps were given release-time for that day. The building-level teams met at least once a month, generally prior to the SWEAT meeting. While most of the original SWEAT will be back for the 1988–89 school year, several chose to name replacements chosen from those teachers attending the last two meetings of the SWEAT. The high school requested additional teacher representatives, so that they now have three teachers on the 1988–89 team.

Individual School Teams

Each school has a building-level team composed of the school principal, the SWEAT representative from the building, a central office administrator, various teaching support staff members and representatives from the community. Every building has a three-year plan, which is updated yearly.

Funding the Process

Funding required to meet the goals established by all schools for the 1987–88 school year required a $43,000 appropriation by the school board. A budget of approximately $40,000 to fund the projects for the 1988–89 school year is expected to be approved by the school board.

Sources of Program Support

The board allocated monies from the general fund and uses state funds to support school improvements. Indiana's "A+ Program" has many provisions which support some of the Effective Schools projects. A $12,000 Teacher Quality Grant from the state will provide 22 teachers with Essential Elements of Instruction training this summer. A Phi Delta Kappa

Teacher Training Grant provided for two teachers to undergo similar training.

Symbolically, the board and superintendent have made the Effective Schools process an obvious "Number One" priority. The board has called special meetings to hear from all building-level teams. The board has approved system-wide guidelines for policies submitted by the SWEAT. At these meetings, the board expressed delight in the progress being made. For the first time ever, the district held a "Teacher Recognition" Banquet on May 23, 1988. Every board member and all SCM administrators were present to congratulate and recognize the system's teachers. Prior to the banquet, the board proclaimed a "Teacher Recognition Day." Superintendent Brainerd went to every school on that day and personally presented every teacher with an enameled apple pin with "I made the difference" engraved on it.

Numerous staff development inservices were held at each building and system-wide during the year. The chances for personal-professional development were supported at every level. A teacher mentor program was officially launched at the end of the school year, with 26 volunteers responding.

Measured Student Outcomes

At this juncture, School City of Mishawaka can provide no hard evidence that schools are improving. During the 1986–87 school year, all schools in the district used a disaggregated analysis of student scores in reading and mathematics on the Iowa Test of Basic Skills to establish baseline data for use with the building-level needs assessments. Students were categorized for this purpose based on the educational level of the mother. Three test score categories (students whose mothers had not graduated from high school, students whose mothers had a high school diploma, and students whose mothers had a college degree) were established for this purpose. Student scores were plotted graphically so that the three categories of students could be compared for equity and achievement at the 40th and 80th percentiles of achievement. A great shortcoming of this process, beyond the fact that the district was not using criterion-referenced testing, was that the district had tested children only at the third, sixth, eighth, and tenth grade levels, thus making it impossible to follow the progress of specific students continuously from one grade to the next.

During the spring of 1987–88, School City of Mishawaka changed from the Iowa Test of Basic Skills to the California Achievement Test, and is now testing at all grade levels annually. Currently the system is in the process of performing a disaggregated analysis of these test results to once again establish a baseline for measuring improvement. This process will be conducted yearly and will form a basis for measuring growth in student achievement.

Documented Changes Related to the Correlates

Since the implementation of School City's Effective Schools program is only one year old, documented facts and figures are not available at this time. Responses to a survey given to teacher, central office administrator, and principal representatives on the System-Wide Effective Action Team are condensed here.

Teachers: Improved communication within and among school buildings has contributed positively to almost every Effective Schools correlate. A system-wide grading scale, retention policy, and homework policy have made a statement to the school community and the community at large as to what we want to accomplish with the students in our schools.

Administrators: People are not beginning to equate or relate test scores to instruction and ultimately to teacher behaviors.

Principals: The strength and presence of the correlates of Effective Schools are documented in a system-wide assessment, training for principals in instructional areas, school and system mission statements, the existence of collected demographic data in all our schools, an awareness of SES groups and related student achievement, and the functioning task committees and building-level teams at each school.

Other Organizational or Personnel-Related Improvement Data

Teachers: Broad-based decision-making has resulted in decisions that reflect staff feelings and ideas. The availability of programs to improve instruction have improved skills and teacher self-concept. Enthusiasm is visible in school buildings. Teachers are talking about improved schools resulting from changes initiated by needs identified by staff members.

Administrators: Needs have been assessed. Plans are in place for improvement. People are actively thinking about how to get better.

Principals: Increased communication among staff; increased awareness of effective instruction; increased awareness of the value of current research . . . the Effective Schools process provides the structure for change Inservice sessions devoted to building-level concerns . . . gym schedules built around instructional needs! A shift from climate to personal improvement and development.

Battell School principal Dan Wilson uses words like "excellent" and "very important" when he describes what has been doing on at Battell School since last January. "When BEAT, the Battell Effective Action Team, first met to discuss the steps our total school staff should take to prepare for a three-year plan for school improvement, there was some skepticism as to whether such a monumental task could be accomplished," stated Wilson. "But," he continued, "as the process evolved, it was met with a lot of excitement and enthusiasm when results from the individual study groups started to form." The total staff at Battell School spent months gathering data, studying the results of a school survey, and learning what Effective Schools Research had to offer.

Professional and General Staff Development Programs

Staff development programs are seen in a more positive light since the implementation of the Effective Schools program. Since many of the programs are building-based, the contents of the programs meet the needs and interests of the staff and students much better than previous efforts. Current development programs are geared more to the improvement of instruction than in the past.

The 1987–88 Young Junior High School Staff Inservice Calendar was as follows:

August 24, 1987	Effective Schools Agenda and Computer Training
October 13, 1987	Inservice on Middle School Concepts
November 10, 1987	Inservice on Test Construction
December 9, 1987	Follow-up on Test Construction
December 14, 1987	Inservice on Creativity and Motivational Thinking
January 6–7, 1988	Great Book Northern Indiana Regional Workshop
January 15, 1988	Inservice on Interdisciplinary Teams and Middle School Conference Sharing
February 2, 3, 4, and March 29, 30, 31, 1988	Staff Writing Workshops
February 5, 1988	MGAP and CSPAN News Access Presentations
March 14, 1988	Dr. Joel Milgram, Inservice on Understanding Transescents

Currently, a system-wide staff development program based on Effective Schools Research is being compiled. Specific components include:

Teachers: Staff development programs have improved; they are more useful in regard to more effective instruction. Attendance at other programs is also encouraged. Staff morale has improved. Changes have resulted or will result from needs as they are identified by staff.

Administrators: Staff development is much more focused now; the Effective Schools process provides a basis for making staff development plans—not just whatever comes along.

Principals: Staff development now centers on building-identified needs and has a specific purpose. The focus on improving the schools has provided structure for identifying needs; this same structure will provide direction for years to come. Efforts are more focused now. The clearer focus created by this process has allowed the staff to also maintain that clear mission.

Curriculum

Teachers: Specific statements and objectives make curriculum easier to implement and tell exactly what is expected. Changes are taking place in response to needs identified by teachers.

Administrators: People understand the need and concept of a unified curriculum that teaches what we test and vice versa.

Principals: The curriculum model is in place. One principal, who is co-chairing School City's reading adoption committee says that this year's committee is unlike any previous adoption committees. First, they began their search for a text by developing a statement of direction. The committee is functioning much like the building-level teams. They have also used outside consultants to give two-day inservice workshops on selecting a reading textbook.

Program Implementation

Teachers: Timelines and guidelines tie all schools together. Teachers are able to attend programs and inservice sessions designed to improve instruction. Involving staff members in planning for decision-making has decentralized the implementation of programs that needed change. Leadership is spread throughout the system's schools.

Principals: The presence of the "Essential Elements of Instruction" inservice programs for administrators, principals, and staff.

Program Evaluation

Teachers: System-Wide Effective Action Teams bring viewpoints from the schools to the administration. This increases the amount of staff input; it is more representative of total staff views.

Principals: Program evaluation is now a part of the curriculum model. It provides a systematic way to use test data that will be used to measure any progress.

Staff Evaluation

Principals: Stresses helpful suggestions to make each instructor more valuable to students. Avoids criticisms that destroy teacher self-concept. Has provided for increased awareness of the need for change in our present system. TESA and Essential Elements of Instruction inservice sessions, together with other workshops designed for principals in the area of staff evaluation, have made them feel much more comfortable with the process.

Historically, personnel evaluation has been used in our system as a means of determining whether or not an employee remained an employee of our school system. As a result of the Effective Schools program, evaluation has become much more of a formative process between the employee and the administrator. All administrators within the school system have received and are continuing to receive training in the areas of the essential elements of instruction and the formative evaluation process. All staff members are to be observed annually and pre and post conferences will be held between the staff member and the administrator to mutually determine areas of growth. This process, along with the results of the building-level needs assessments and subsequent staff development plans for each building, are being utilized to strengthen the instructional skills of both administrators and teaching staff.

Community Attitudes

Teachers: Publicity and public relations efforts have increased awareness of what makes schools effective. Building teams have included community representatives to foster this involvement and to communicate results.

Administrators: The community is much more aware of the instruction-related activities in the schools since the introduction of the Effective Schools program.

Principals: Introduction of a weekly parent visitation program; improving of community attitudes since we are publicizing more instruction-related items. Parent interest and involvement in the schools has increased dramatically.

Service and Funding Agencies

Teachers: Many sources are available that were unknown to us before. Suggestions on funding are now networked among schools through the System-Wide Effective Action Team; many good ideas are generated.

Recognition of the Instructional Process

Teachers: Staff members are asking for information instead of being told that they need to increase skills and knowledge. "Their" school corporation has become "our" school corporation.

Principals: Emphasis put on instruction has never been greater, and has a very positive effect. Introduction of Essential Elements of Instruction inservice training and the annual teacher recognition program reinforces this.

Disaggregated Data

Student test data from the system's norm-referenced testing is currently being disaggregated and used to check for equity and excellence in achievement. This is being done on a grade-by-grade basis in the areas of reading and mathematics. The 40th and 80th percentiles have been established as cut-off points for this purpose. Student test scores in these areas will be disaggregated, analyzed, and graphed on an annual basis to measure equity and growth.

Development of Curriculum-Based Testing/Criterion-Reference Tests

A total revision of the student curriculum is underway within the school system so that the total curriculum will be stated in outcome-based terms. This alignment has been accomplished in the areas of science and mathematics at the elementary level. The reading curriculum will soon be completed. At the secondary level, this has been accomplished in all areas. The goal is to establish criterion-referenced testing at all grade levels in all curricular areas.

Development of Policies and Procedures at District and School Level

A system-wide homework and promotion-retention policy have been written by SWEAT and approved by the board of education. Individual schools will then set their own policies using the system-wide policies as a guide.

Teachers believe that this system-wide approach has established a vehicle for developing school-based procedures. Building-level teams and faculties develop written building procedures regarding routine matters, supplies, discipline, referrals, and scheduling. Regular team meetings help facilitate this process.

Instructional and classroom practices are changing because teachers recognize the opportunity for making suggestions and seeing them discussed. Practices "that work" can become systematized and coordinated rather than "shotgun" and this change pleases administrators.

It was important to take the first two years for district and school staff orientation, awareness, and planning (1985–86, 1986–87). During the planning year, too many deadlines were set, however, and frequent meetings led many school staffs to feel "harried" by June (1987). One teacher remarked,

I would not be in such a hurry to try to do everything in year one! I think the anxiousness showed. It would be good to begin the first-year needs assessment and evaluation of findings earlier in the school year in order to spread the tasks over a longer time frame.

Principals agreed that decentralization made the central office more aware of the many budget decisions that can best be made at the building level. However, district restrictions in the first-year plan did not allow the building to complete plans for the many (too many) areas identified for attention. They agreed with their teachers it was better to concentrate on one or two important areas than try to do everything at once.

Administrators regretted not getting involved in the process early on. One district staff member remarked, "It is the most exciting and rewarding educational experience of my 24 years in education." Administrators also felt a different needs assessment survey and procedure should be used. They would have made curriculum alignment an important priority from the beginning.

Summary

During the 1988-89 school year, School City of Mishawaka will be entering into its second full year of operation utilizing system-wide and building-level school improvement plans based on Effective Schools Research, as its vision and guide in a quest for excellence. Those affiliated with the corporation sincerely desire to provide Mishawaka students with a quality and equitable education which will offer them more choices and opportunities when they graduate from Mishawaka High School.

Many things vital to the continuing educational growth of our school system have been accomplished during the past three years. These accomplishments have been outlined in previous sections. Many areas remain to be addressed before our schools can truly qualify as "effective" schools, including valid measurement of our progress. Most importantly, however, we have taken the first step, in committing ourselves to excellence. We have even taken the second step by putting that commitment into an organized plan for achieving excellence. In the third step, we actually began implementation of that plan. We are a vital, healthy, enthusiastic corporation; Mishawaka is an exciting place to be . . . with "miles to go, before we sleep."

APPENDIX TO MISHAWAKA CASE STUDY
EFFECTIVE SCHOOLS: The Mishawaka Plan, August, 1986

School City of Mishawaka Board of School Trustees

Emery S. Petko, President
Dale E. Emmons, Vice President
Marilyn J. Schroyer, Secretary
Virginia H. Currey, Member
Thomas L. Klaer, Member

Richard L. Brainerd, Superintendent

School Improvement Planning Committee

Mary Ann Bogucki
Chris Currey
Terry Grass
R. Steven Mills
Dr. M. Kay Novotny
Norma Pangrac

Jerry Seese
Robert D. Smith
Doris Speicher
Steve VanBruaene
Pamela von Rahl

Introduction

This plan for school improvement in the School City of Mishawaka, based on Effective Schools Research, was developed by a steering committee composed of central office administrators, building-level teachers, and principals. Each received extensive training through study and exposure to nationally recognized researchers and practitioners of the effective schools' model. It was approved and adopted by the Mishawaka Board of School Trustees on August 19, 1988, for implementation in all schools of the district.

The plan is based on belief in and value of the merits of Effective Schools practices and theories. If implemented, the plan will cause significant and measurable improvement in the Mishawaka schools. The steering committee believes that improvement centered at each building level with support from the district level is essential. The employees in each school are quite capable, and will accept the responsibility for improvement both in quality and equity in all areas of school programs. Therefore, the committee believes the district has the people and resources required to successfully implement this project.

The plan is directed to professional staff at the building level as to broad guidelines, expectations, and actions over the next three school years—1986–87, 1987–88, and 1988–89. It is intended to be purposeful, reasonable, and attainable. Materials for communicating with support staff, students, patrons, and the community as to their involvement in school improvement will be developed.

Information and data based on research, experience, or practice are presented in the following areas in order to support the plan ingredients, and to give direction to those implementing the plan:

- Background on Mishawaka
- Why School Improvement is Necessary
- What is Known about School Improvement
- Characteristics of Effective Schools
- Definition of an Effective School
- Mission of the Mishawaka Schools

The three-year plan is intended to be broad and general. It is expected that revision and updating will occur each year.

1985–86 Background on Effective Schools Research and School Improvement in Mishawaka

In June of 1985, at the invitation of the superintendent of a neighboring school district, the entire administrative staff of the Mishawaka schools, along with like members of the neighboring district, participated in an intensive two-day workshop on Effective Schools. Also, teacher association leaders from each school system were participants. The content of the workshop was based on research of the late Ron Edmonds, a pioneer in effective schools research, as to the characteristics of effective schools and the school improvement process. It was decided that this persuasive, logical approach was worthy of study and review by the entire instructional staff during the 1985–86 school year.

Subsequently, teams of teachers and administrators prepared and presented five two-hour sessions on the subject to the professional staff over the course of the year. One of Edmond's five "correlates," or characteristics, was reviewed, described, and analyzed during each session. The process of school improvement based on effective schools' research and practices was stressed to develop awareness, understanding, and interest of the staff. At the same time, extensive research on the concepts, beliefs, and values of effective schools was accomplished by the members of each presentation team. Each staff member received descriptive materials throughout the year for staff review, including the Effective School Report, a publication of the Kelwynn Group.

The System-wide Instructional Improvement Council met five times throughout the year to discuss the correlates and the improvement process. In order to further familiarize key leaders with the effective schools improvement model, ten administrators and two teachers also attended institutes presented by researchers and practitioners describing successful implementation practices and significant data.

All these efforts were intended to initiate, train, and commit Mishawaka instructional staff to school improvement based on Effective Schools Research. Substantial numbers of teachers and administrators have expressed strong interest and desire to proceed with implementation processes.

With this as an objective, Dr. Lawrence Lezotte, a nationally recognized leader in the Effective Schools movement and associate of Ron Edmonds, met with all administrators and selected teachers from each building on May 5 and 6, 1986. Dr. Lezotte provided valuable insights and suggestions, and outlined possible actions to start the process, for implementation of a school improvement project in all the Mishawaka schools.

Finally, on June 10, 1986, the board of school trustees determined that an effective schools project would have merit for the school corporation, and directed the administration to prepare a district plan for proceeding with such practices and concepts in all schools. This is that district plan.

DISTRICT PLAN FOR MISHAWAKA SCHOOLS
Why School Improvement Is Necessary

The schools in Mishawaka have a long standing reputation and tradition of strong educational programs. Intense community pride is readily apparent to visitors and newcomers in the city. This pride stems, in part, from the stability and success of school programs. Conditions and characteristics now exist that are usually associated with quality schools. Citizens in the area, and particularly in the Mishawaka community, have been supportive of good schooling and have expected delivery of positive programs in their public schools. The Mishawaka schools experience active parental involvement, experience low turnover of certified and classified personnel, have strong building-level administrators, practice collaborative and collegial decision-making, and are financially sound, but not wealthy. Most importantly, most students generally express interest in learning, and demonstrate reasonable behavior and attitudes. In fact, those with contact in other districts as well as Mishawaka schools—parents and pupils who have transferred into the district, substitute teachers, and those in higher education—testify to the quality, atmosphere, and offerings in Mishawaka schools. The synergistic effect of these positive factors has developed a sense of confidence on the part of the community in operation of the schools. The questions logically might be asked: Why is there interest or need to embark on an effective schools/school improvement project? With such a heritage and seeming indicators of success, if things aren't broken, why fix them? Do we have to be sick to get better?

There are several answers to such queries:

1. A growing body of research and current literature strongly indicates a general consensus is emerging about the elements of effective schooling. Certain practices are more effective than others in the teaching and learning process, and should be sought in classrooms, in schools, and in school districts. Hundreds of schools across the nation have successfully instituted such practices. Although the Mishawaka schools incorporate many of these practices now, others may be lacking.
2. Although most Mishawaka youngsters have positive attitudes and behaviors and achieve well over national standards, increasing numbers do not. The impact of negative societal factors, drugs and alcohol, lack of interest and motivation, poor basic skills, poor achievement, assertions that school is boring—all are factors that challenge schools to do something different or something better. Attempts to overcome these factors have met with limited success. If we continue to do the same things, it's reasonable to assume that we'll get the same results. Thus, we may need to abandon some practices and procedures, as well as change others.
3. Organizations are dynamic, not static, and thus, the assumption is made that schools either decline or improve in their attempts to adapt to societal and organizational changes—there is no constant state. Our schools should improve.
4. Successful organizations plan and implement continuing self-renewal in purposeful cycles in order to remain successful and effective. Schools should, too.
5. Public schools in the nation have been criticized in recent years by various commissions and reports. There is a public and legislative demand for public school improvement and accountability.

School personnel and the board of school trustees recognize the legitimacy of these concerns, wish to continue the tradition of the district in pursuing excellence, and desire to respond in a forthright and responsible manner. Thus, the decision has been made to adopt a school improvement plan based on Effective Schools Research.

What Is Known About School Improvement

Research on educational change has clarified and specified some of the ingredients necessary for school improvement. "Change is a process, not an event," according to Michael Fullan, sociologist. The interactive phases of the process are described as adoption, implementation, and continuation or institutionalization. For the purpose of bringing together the research findings of the school improvement literature, the following propositions are offered:

Proposition 1

Public schools, individual classrooms, and school systems can and do improve, and the factors facilitating school improvement are neither so exotic, unusual, or expensive that they are beyond the grasp of extraordinary leaders in ordinary situations.

Proposition 2

People matter most in school improvement programs:

A. Teachers can and will implement new practices and programs, given active leadership from building and central office administrators, a chance for planning the implementation process, appropriate training, opportunities for interaction, breathing space to try and fail, and continuous assistance and support.
B. Building-level administrators make a difference in school improvement programs by establishing a climate of expectations that teachers will successfully improve practice and by providing on-site coordination, communication, assistance, and support.
C. District-level administrators affect school improvement programs by exhibiting active backing in the form of communicated expectations for success, psychological support, needed resources, and local facilitation assistance.
D. External assisters are most effective at the school level by providing concrete and practical assistance on implementation issues, such as planning, scheduling, problem-solving, and follow-through.

Proposition 3

An innovation is more likely to be adopted and implemented if it is perceived as having relative advantage, compatibility, simplicity, and legitimacy. Implementation is more effective when the innovation focuses on a specific need and demonstrates clarity in purpose and techniques.

Proposition 4

Specific resources are necessary to support effective school improvement programs.

A. Staff development programs that are task-specific and provide ongoing, continuous assistance and support; and
B. Monetary resources that are adequate to provide the people, materials, and time needed in the program.

Characteristics of Effective Schools

Several school researchers have identified those characteristics that distinguish the effective from the less effective schools. The number of characteristics may vary from study to study, because of the research design or the way in which the characteristics are subdivided or grouped, rather than from any real conflicts in the research findings. Three factors emerge in the school effectiveness research on characteristics:

1. School effectiveness encompasses the total school organization and culture as well as classroom management and teaching.
2. The characteristics can be defined and assessed individually, but the research indicates that all must be in place, at least to some degree, to maximize a school's effectiveness.
3. The interaction of the characteristics creates a critical atmosphere in a school which results in an impact that is greater than if the characteristics were applied individually.

The School City of Mishawaka will use the five characteristics (correlates) of effective schools as identified by Ron Edmonds. These were used for study and review by the entire instructional staff during the 1985–86 school year and are familiar to the staff. The following characteristics, or correlates, will be used to guide decisions, planning, and implementation of the school improvement project:

1. Positive School Climate
   There is a safe, orderly, and purposeful environment which is conducive to teaching and learning. The atmosphere reflects a focus on student achievement and the accomplishment of the school's mission. Staff and students share confidence in the students' ability to learn. Staff and students consistently accept responsibility for the established standards of behaviors and respect the school as a place of learning.
2. Clear and Focused School Mission
   The major focus of the school is clearly identified as instructional. A standard district curriculum is established and instructional goals are clearly defined. There is a shared staff understanding of, commitment to, and responsibility for clearly articulated goals, objectives, priorities, and assessment procedures.
3. Strong Instructional Leadership
   The principal acts as the instructional leader who effectively communicates the mission of the school to staff, parents, and students. The principal understands and applies the characteristics of instructional effectiveness in the management of the instructional program of the school. Staff members are involved in decision-making and share a leadership role in the improvement of instructional effectiveness.
4. Teacher Behaviors Which Convey High Expectations
   The staff shares the belief that all students can learn. Staff behaviors convey to students the expectation that all students have the ability and will master, at least to a minimum standard, the essential learning outcomes of the specified curriculum. Students will be engaged in planned learning activities for a high percentage of the allocated time and effective classroom management establishes a productive, work-oriented environment.
5. Frequent Monitoring of Student Progress
   Feedback on student achievement progress is frequently obtained. Multiple assessment methods, such as teacher-made tests, samples of student's work, mastery skills checklists, criterion-referenced tests, and norm-referenced tests are used. The results of assessment are used to improve individual student performance, and also to improve the instructional program.

Definition of an Effective School

If effective schools commonly possess the characteristics identified, how then is an effective school defined. The steering committee proposes the following definition:

An effective school is one in which all students learn the specified curriculum, regardless of factors in their background which have ordinarily been identified as those which prevent such learning.

The definition of an effective school rests on four assumptions:

The first assumption is that the primary purpose of schooling in our society is teaching and learning. Although schools have other competing alternative functions, such as providing custodial care for the community and providing evaluative data to future employers and to institutions of higher education, these responsibilities must not sublimate the primary mission.

The second assumption is that the degree of a school's effectiveness must be judged in terms of student output data, primarily student achievement measures. Through various accreditation processes, schools are often judged by the number of books in the library, the availability of curriculum guides, the certification of its teachers, or the quality of its teachers. Certainly, these are important areas; however, ultimately the effectiveness must be judged on measurable student outputs. Today's public is not satisfied with "Our school is doing a good job." They want schools to be accountable and to have proof of that accountability.

The third assumption is that an Effective School is one which demonstrates both quality and equity in its student outputs. The determination of quality is associated with the overall high level achievement of students. Equity is based on the belief that all students can demonstrate school success, especially when success is defined as mastery of the essential curriculum. The determination of equity is associated with the analysis of pupil achievement to ensure equitable distribution of that achievement across student subgroups.

The fourth assumption is that there are many things over which the school has control that can significantly influence student achievement. A school cannot alter the educational level of parents, the socioeconomic status (SES), nor the intelligence quotient of a child. However, working together, the school staff and community can unite to influence such factors as school climate, expectations, schoolwide emphasis on academics, instructional leadership, and frequent monitoring of pupils and programs. All of these factors, research shows, correlate with high student achievement.

As the late Ron Edmonds so eloquently stated: "We can, whenever and wherever we choose, successfully teach all children whose schooling is of interest to us. We already know more than we need in order to do this. Whether we do it must finally depend on how we feel about the fact that we haven't done it so far."

Mission of the Mishawaka Schools

According to Dr. Lawrence Lezotte of Michigan State University, straightforward answers to the following two questions should be embraced in the school's mission statement or concomitant curricular goals and priorities:

1. "What do we want our students to know and be able to do when they complete their K–12 schooling?" and,
2. "How many students do we expect to learn what it is that we want them to know and be able to do?"

These questions, and acceptance of the following propositions as both reasonable and possible, form the framework for the mission statement of the School City of Mishawaka and its curricular priorities:

Proposition 1

The primary **goal** of public education is to empower students with choices. Restated, the goal of K–12 schooling is to give as many students as possible as many options as possible for choosing what they might do after the twelfth grade.

Proposition 2

The primary **function** of schools is teaching and learning. The empowering of choices is assumed to derive from what students are taught and what students learn. Therefore, the centering focus of the school derives from its program of curriculum and instruction.

Proposition 3

The primary **evidence** for establishing the effectiveness of a school is to be found in its student outcomes. It's essential to provide solid evidence which verifies that students, in fact, are learning what it is we want them to know and be able to do. These outcome indicators should be observable and measurable to assure pupils, teachers, parents, or the community that students are mastering the essential curriculum.

Proposition 4

In the final analysis, the effective school is a school that is successful in **teaching all** of its students the **essential skills** they need to know or to be able to do. The focus of each effective school is on quality **and** equity. The outcome indicators selected to demonstrate student achievement should reflect with accuracy the curriculum being taught. In addition, the outcome results should be examined in such a way that educators can be certain that no major subset of the student population is left behind.

These propositions form the basis for the following mission statement for schools in the School City of Mishawaka.

The School City of Mishawaka believes that all students can learn mastery of basic skills and that it is the responsibility of school employees to teach all students the specified curriculum at each grade level. The mission of the School City of Mishawaka, therefore, is to educate all students to their highest level of academic performance, while fostering positive development of their health, their attitudes, and their behaviors, so that each individual student may make a positive contribution to our democratic society.

IN MISHAWAKA, ALL STUDENTS WILL LEARN
SCHOOL CITY OF MISHAWAKA

SCHOOL IMPROVEMENT PLAN
—1986–87 YEAR ONE—

September

- Data completed for each student for disaggregated analysis of test scores by September 26, in order to encode for standardized tests administered to selected grade levels in late September and early October.

October

- October 29, 1986—Development Day with students dismissed.
- Staff surveys of effective schools characteristics conducted for each school and address by Dr. Lawrence Lezotte to entire professional staff.

November

- Assessment questionnaire completed by noncertified staff, selected parents, and selected students.

December

- Building-level improvement team formed in each school prior to December 19, and names reported to superintendent.
- One member of each school-level improvement team designated by the team to be its representative to the systemwide improvement team, and name reported to superintendent by December 19.

January-February

- Orientation and training of building-level improvement teams.
- Profile of each school developed based on surveys and standardized testing.
- District-level team meets to determine roles and responsibilities.

March

- Development of preliminary draft of school improvement plan for each school.
- March 27, 1987—Staff Development Day with students dismissed.
- Discussion of preliminary draft for school improvement in each school.

April

- Refinement of each building-level plan and discussion of possible action plans.
- District-level team meets to begin preliminary planning for updating district improvement plan for 1989–90 year.

May

- Each faculty reviews, revised, and approves final written school improvement plan for submittal to superintendent on or prior to June 1, 1987. Each plan should include indicators for measuring outcomes, cost estimates, time required and/or staff development requests.
- District-level team meets to make final district improvement plan for year four, 1989–90.

June

- Each building submits its final plan to superintendent for approval. Superintendent reviews and submits to the school board, with accompanying summarized cost and time estimates, for its approval.

—1987-88 YEAR TWO—

- Implementation of year one building-level plan in individual buildings with continued support and encouragement from central office.
- Complete update of disaggregated analysis of standardized test scores.
- Continue utilizing district and building-level teams to support implementation of building-level plans.
- Implement staff development programs necessary to support accomplishment of building-level plans.
- Continue curriculum cycle to develop aligned curriculum.
- Utilize disaggregated analysis of test results to plot student achievement and monitor building growth toward equitable learning environment.
- Complete evaluation of building plan, analyze test results, and re-evaluate building-level needs assessment to develop updated building-level plans for the coming school year.
- Develop new building-level plan for approval by the superintendent and board of school trustees for implementation during the school year 1988-89.

—1988-89 YEAR THREE—

- Implementation of year two building-level plan in individual buildings with continued support and encouragement from central office.
- Complete update of disaggregated analysis of standardized test scores.
- Continue utilizing district and building-level teams to support implementation of building-level plans.
- Implement staff development programs necessary to support accomplishment of building-level plans.
- Continue curriculum cycle to develop aligned curriculum.
- Utilize disaggregated analysis of test results to plot student achievement and monitor building growth toward equitable learning environment.
- Conduct new needs assessment, analyze test results, and evaluate results of building-level plan in order to generate data related to current school needs.
- Develop new building-level plan for approval by the superintendent and board of school trustees for implementation during the school year 1989-90.

San Pasqual Union School District: Working Towards School Effectiveness

Janet Chrispeels
Mary Beall

San Diego County Office of Education
San Diego, California
August 1988

San Pasqual Union School District
Became involved in Effective Schools process in 1986

Community

Population
500 registered voters

San Pasqual, located 30 miles northeast of San Diego. San Pasqual Valley is largely agricultural.

The residents are predominantly middle class, with 65–70 percent of the children coming from families that are professional, semi-skilled or skilled; the rest come from mostly unskilled families engaged in agriculture. Only 1 percent receive Aid to Dependent Children. The school district is in San Diego County, which shares a border with Mexico.

School District

Enrollment
217

Ethnic Composition (percent)
Asian-American 9
Caucasian 66
Hispanic 35

Per Pupil Expenditure
1988–1989 $3,105

Percent bussed
100

Area (in square miles)
30

Schools
Elementary school (K–8) 1

Number of Staff
Administrators 1
Certified teachers 10
Support staff 7

Student-Teacher Ratio
Elementary 24:1
Middle/junior high 26:1

Percent college-bound
NA

Abstract

San Pasqual Union School District is the only one-school district represented in this collection of case studies. Largely because of the less complex nature of a one-school district, San Pasqual's planning and implementation of the Effective Schools process has proceeded more smoothly than most larger districts. The district has also made good use of the San Diego County Office of Education's consultants and facilitators over the two years of implementation.

As a result of learning well the Effective Schools process for school improvement, San Pasqual has integrated a school-wide staff development program with the student monitoring system. Teachers plan for their training and focus on workshops which will help them understand the connection between the district mission statement and instructional decisions.

Because of the confusion which existed in the district (school) about teaching objectives, many teachers were not certain of what was actually included as core objectives for instruction. The curricular alignment process which followed, in which teachers collaborated to discuss tests and then formed the continuum of teaching objectives, is detailed in this case study. The subsequent process of curricular development, especially in the area of mathematics, is also described.

The strengths and limitations of a small one-school district are described, and strategies are offered to meet the demands of implementing the Effective Schools process consistently.

Brief Look at San Pasqual[1]

San Pasqual Union School District is located in north San Diego County about 30 miles northeast of the city of San Diego. The small K–8 school sits on the north side of the San Pasqual Valley, an agricultural reserve and site of the only California battle fought in the Mexican-American War. The original two-room school was built in 1918. These two rooms served the valley until 1970 when the current facility was built. The school still shares its site with an Indian graveyard. This peaceful rural valley, however, now abuts the rapidly growing city of Escondido. Approximately 30 percent of the school's 217 students, in fact, attend San Pasqual on interdistrict transfer permits. The school's population is 30–35 percent Hispanic in origin, coming mostly from semi-skilled and unskilled families who work on nearby farms. The other 65–70 percent of the student population comes from middle income, professional, semi-professional, or skilled families who work in a variety of professional and white collar jobs. A few families farm in the valley. Only one percent of the families receive Aid to Families with Dependent Children.

The enrollment of the school has steadily increased over the last few years so that there is now one class and one teacher per grade level. The staff consists of teachers, a retired teacher who serves as the librarian, an eighth grade algebra teacher, the school's PE teacher, and three classroom aides hired with Chapter 1 and State of California School Improvement funds. The kindergarten teacher works as a reading specialist in the afternoon.

Motivation for Launching the Effective Schools Program

The school has undergone some difficult personnel transitions in the last few years. In 1986 the Board of Education terminated the contract of the superintendent-principal; however, this person was retained as the kindergarten teacher and business manager, and still held the title of principal for the duration of the year. One board member resigned from the board and applied for the position. He was hired as the new superintendent-principal in the spring of 1986. This course of events caused considerable tension and confusion among staff members, even though the new superintendent displayed considerable diplomatic skills, and all were trying to make the best of an awkward situation.

The new superintendent-principal decided the time was ripe to take stock of school programs, solicit views of students, staff, and community, and to assess student achievement. He contacted the San Diego County Effective Schools Program, which offered an appropriate vehicle for helping the principal in this task of assessment. The county's program consists of the following components: data collection, data analysis, development of an improvement plan, implementation, and reassessment. The data collection involves information collected through the following means: San Diego County Effective Schools Surveys for staff, parents, and students; an Effective Schools interview for staff members; the Association for Supervision and Curriculum Development Organizational Health Descriptive Questionnaire; classroom time-on-task audits; and a disaggregated analysis of test scores.

After the county office shared all of the elements of the Effective Schools program with the principal, he was eager to begin. The next step was to conduct an orientation for the staff and allow them time to discuss the merits of launching an Effective Schools assessment and improvement program. Several staff members were reluctant. They were uncertain how the information would be interpreted by the former principal. Also they thought they did not know the current principal sufficiently well to complete the surveys. However, it was pointed out that there was a "don't know" response that they could use in completing the survey to address those areas where information was lacking. The principal was able to persuade the staff that he genuinely wanted their views and that he wanted a good data base to guide their improvement efforts. In December 1986 the Organizational Health and Effective Schools staff surveys were administered, and the interviews conducted. In January 1987 the parent and student (upper grades only) surveys were completed. Also, the teachers were trained to conduct the time-on-task audits. Although they had enjoyed the visits to each others' classrooms during the training sessions, the staff decided not to do the audits themselves. Thus, county office staff assisted in this part of the assessment as well. The school staff was not functioning as a team yet, and previous tensions were too near the surface to risk observing each others' classrooms in a formal way with data being recorded.

---

[1] The authors wish to thank J. Gordon Christensen, Superintendent-Principal of San Pasqual Union School District and the teachers—Bryce Bacher, Wynona Behling, Patricia Gammie, Karalee Gorham, Marydee Hinrichs, Diana Kirby, Patricia Matson, John Mayo, Jane Trussel, Victoria Young—and the staff of the school—Steve Bostrom, Candi Gates, Linda Govatos, Bob Johnson, Dee Petinak, Lidia Quiroz, and Lola Rosas—for allowing us to tell the story of their improvement efforts. All of them are dedicated educators who have worked especially hard in the last two years to strengthen the quality of the educational program for all children at San Pasqual.

At the end of January, once all the data had been collected, an all-day planning day was organized for the staff. The staff spent the morning working in small groups, with each group analyzing all the data for two different correlates. Each team identified strengths and targets for improvement by doing item analyses and comparisons from the different surveys. They also disaggregated test data from the California Assessment Program (CAP).

Some of the data are summarized in Graphs 1–4. Graph 1 presents the responses to the Effective Schools Surveys from teachers, principal, and classified staff. This graph shows that the views of the teachers and classified staff are not as positive as the principal's, especially in the areas of instructional leadership, clear school mission, and frequent monitoring. On the whole the responses of the classified staff are much less positive. An item analysis revealed that for many items, respondents marked "don't know." In discussing the data, a critical question for the staff was (1) what do they need to know and (2) how can they be kept better informed.

Graph 2 presents the responses of parents and students, which show good support for the school. The students, however, view the school less positively. Graph 3 depicts the composite results of the time-on-task audits. This snapshot of audits revealed a relatively high time-on-task percentage of 87 percent and a higher than average interactive time allocation of 55 percent. Graph 4 shows some of the disaggregated test data that were shared with the staff. This graph shows that students whose first language is not English do not do as well as English-only students.

In the afternoon the staff turned their attention to developing a school-wide discipline plan since this was one of their top priorities based on the needs assessment data. Dr. Sammie McCormack from the San Diego County Office of Education assisted them in developing a school-wide positive discipline plan. By the end of the day the staff had a good understanding of the Effective Schools data, had outlined a school-wide discipline plan, and had decided that one of the next tasks would be to develop a mission statement for the school. Table 1 is a sample page from the San Pasqual Effective Schools Assessment Summary Report that presents data on the clear school mission correlate. It illustrates how strengths and targets for improvement are identified and why formulating a clear school mission was chosen as one of the areas for attention.

The staff morale soared at the conclusion of this day. Many commented that it was gratifying and rewarding to be focusing on school programs and students. They reported that they had not worked together like this as a staff for a long time. The Effective Schools process proved to be a healing one,

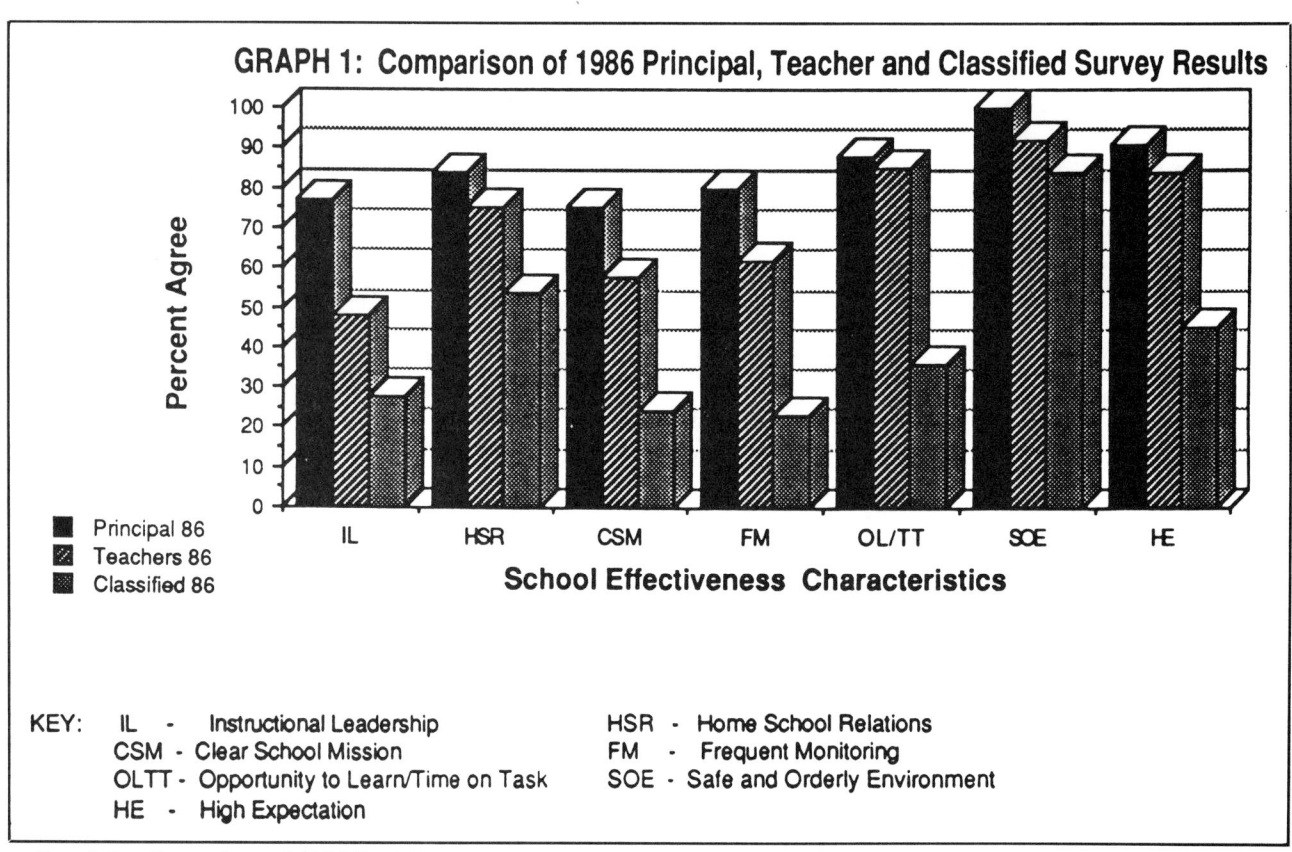

Graph 1. Comparison of 1986 Total Results

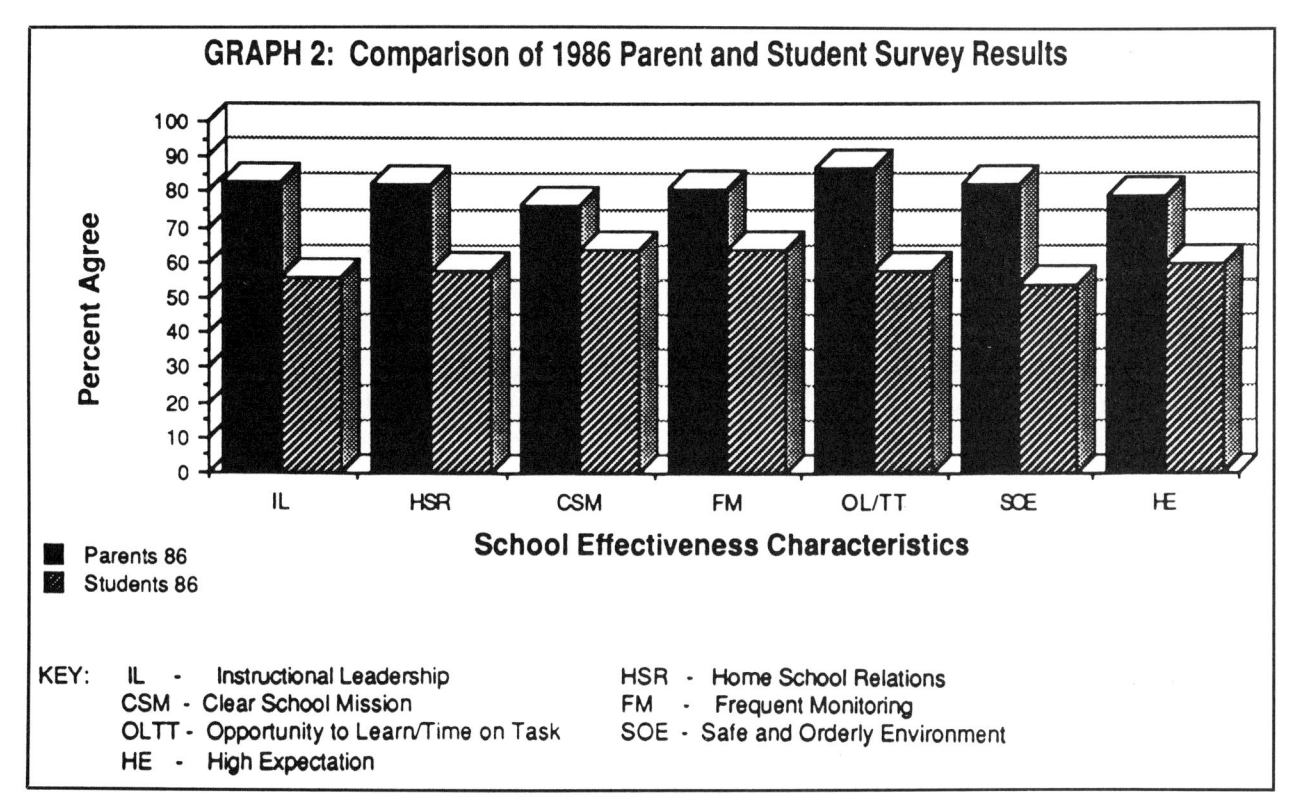

GRAPH 2: Comparison of 1986 Parent and Student Survey Results

KEY:
- IL - Instructional Leadership
- HSR - Home School Relations
- CSM - Clear School Mission
- FM - Frequent Monitoring
- OLTT - Opportunity to Learn/Time on Task
- SOE - Safe and Orderly Environment
- HE - High Expectation

Graph 2. Comparison of 1986 Parent & Student Results

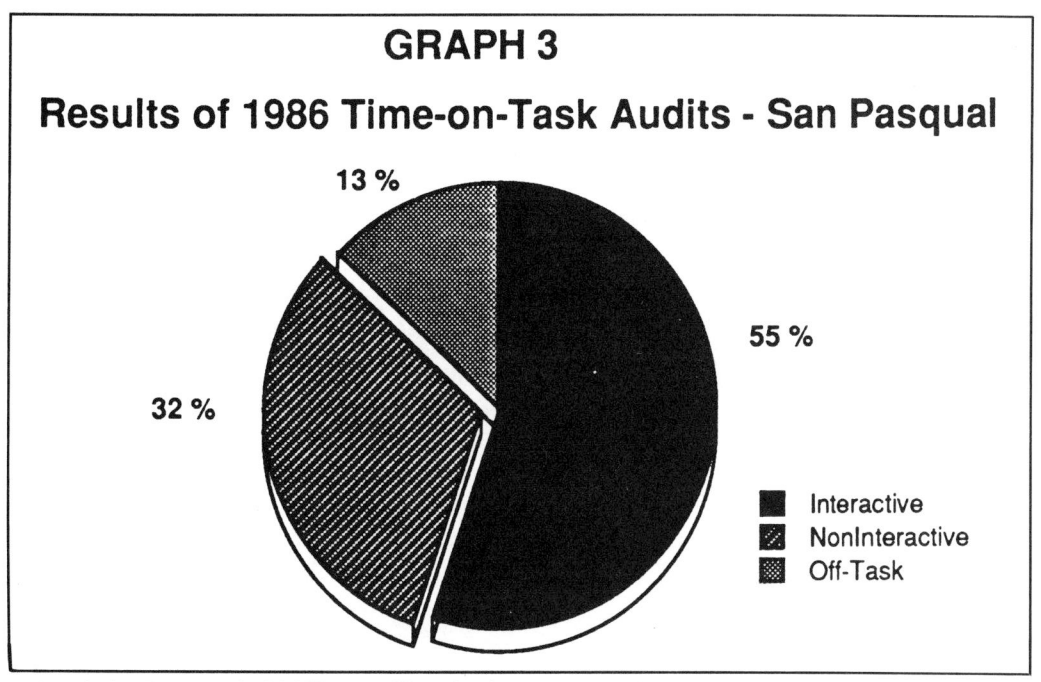

GRAPH 3

Results of 1986 Time-on-Task Audits - San Pasqual

- Interactive: 55%
- NonInteractive: 32%
- Off-Task: 13%

Graph 3. Results of 1986 Time-on-Task Audits

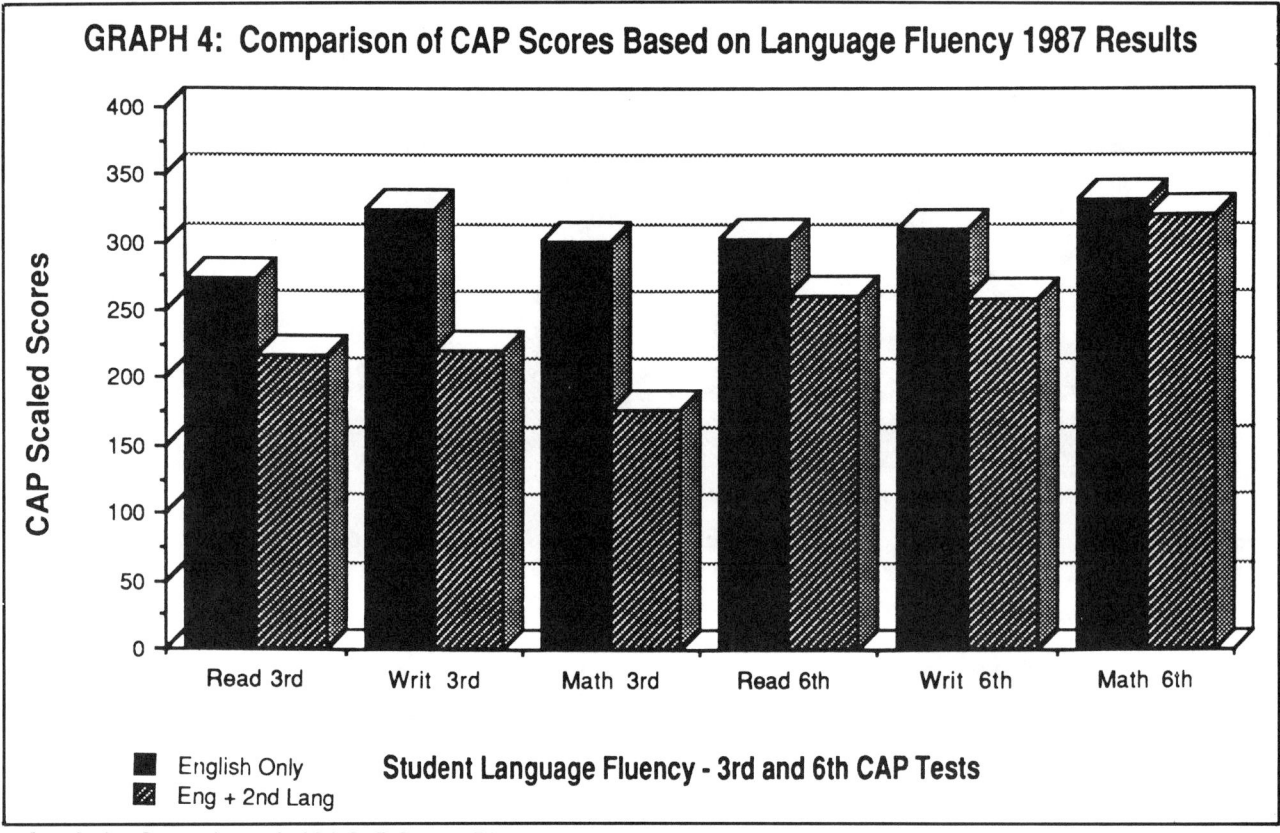

Graph 4. Comparison of 1986 CAP Scores: Disaggregated Analysis

enabling the staff to overcome previous divisions and mistrust.

In February the superintendent-principal, a board member, and a staff member attended the county's Effective Schools Conference where they heard Larry Lezotte and Robert Fortenberry. They also learned strategies first hand from other San Diego County principals and staff members who were implementing school effectiveness programs. Participating in this conference helped the staff to understand more clearly school effectiveness goals and processes. Later that spring McCormack reviewed and refined the positive discipline plan with the staff and conducted an evening workshop for about 50 parents to explain the discipline plan and give parents tips for positive interactions at home. Several staff members attended. By late spring the principal and staff had developed a mission statement.

Funding

The Effective Schools assessment and assistance services are provided free to San Diego County Schools. The estimated cost of the personnel time and services is approximately $1,500 to $2,000 per school per year. General fund monies provided the release time for the staff to learn to conduct time-on-task audits, attend the Effective Schools Conference, and other selected inservice activities. The staff inservice day and several staff meetings were devoted to school improvement.

In the second year of the school improvement efforts some funds were allocated to achieve the school's goal of improving their mathematics program. Funds, including contributions from the Parent-Teacher League, have been spent for math materials, a staff development consultant in math, and attendance at math conferences by staff members. The allocation, however, did not exceed $2,500. State textbook funds were used this past year to acquire a new math textbook. The San Diego County Office of Education again provided free ongoing support and consultant services. The principal has actively and symbolically supported the program by his allocation of time to classroom observations, attention at faculty meetings to instructional issues, and follow through to see that the goals set by the staff are carried out.

For the past two years the school has participated in the California School Improvement Program and received $6,000 in state funds. Most of the entitlement money funds classroom aides, with a small portion going toward instructional supplies. The school-based improvement program permits the staff to hold a staff inservice day and collect Average Daily Attendance funds generated as though the students were in attendance. Though it is customary to develop a writ-

Table 1
Clear School Mission

Relative Strengths

- 100 percent of the teachers surveyed agreed or strongly agreed that academic achievement is stressed as the highest priority in the school.
- 92 percent of the parents surveyed indicated that their children understand that essential academic skills is the main goal of education.
- 88 percent of the parents surveyed agreed or strongly agreed with the overall purpose and goals of San Pasqual elementary school.
- 98 percent of the parents surveyed indicated that the school provides the necessary textbooks and materials to support the school's instructional program.
- 74 percent of the students surveyed indicated that teachers explain what they will learn in each of the courses.

Targets of Improvement: Strategies for Improvement

- 26 percent of the teachers surveyed indicated that the school has a written statement of purpose that focuses on student learning and achievement.
- 88 percent of the teachers interviewed strongly disagreed that there is a written statement of purpose that guides instructional decisions.
- Up to 50 percent of the teaching staff were uncertain as to whether written standards of expected student achievement exist in all major content areas.
- 38 percent of the teachers surveyed disagreed that students must achieve identified standards in all subjects.

ten plan, the school in these first two years has used the Effective Schools data to guide its improvement efforts.

Evidence of Improvement

The school administers two norm-referenced tests, the California Assessment Program (CAP) given to third, sixth, and eighth grade students in the spring of each year, and the Comprehensive Test of Basic Skills (CTBS) given at each grade level each spring. In 1988 was the first time that eighth grade students also took the direct assessment of the writing portion of the CAP. Individual teachers use chapter tests to assess mastery of class work, and a minimum competencies/proficiency tests are given at fourth, sixth, and eighth grade. The proficiency tests were developed by the district. No comprehensive criterion-referenced tests are given.

With such small sizes, the CAP, a matrix sampling test, presents some problems in providing valid data. The state test is useful, however, because test data are disaggregated by family income and language proficiency. The language proficiency data provides a reasonably accurate measure because there are sufficient numbers of students in each subgroup. The CTBS is taken by every child, but the data are not reported to the school in a disaggregated form. The school had previously not disaggregated these results. In 1987 the disaggregated eighth grade CAP test results show that there are considerable inequalities in achievement between the Hispanic and English-only students in reading, written language and mathematics. Graph 5 illustrates these disparities.

As described in the previous paragraph, in the second year of the improvement program, the staff's focus has been on improving math instruction and achievement. The 1988 CAP and CTBS results indicate that the goal was achieved. Graph 6 shows the CTBS math results for 1987 and 1988. Gains were made at all but two grade levels. Graph 7 shows the comparison of 1986–1987 and 1987–1988 in all areas tested by CAP at the third and sixth grade levels. Gains were made in math at both third and sixth grade. The disaggregated results are encouraging for sixth, but less so for third, as shown in Graph 8. Graph 9 shows that when the CTBS math results are disaggregated by quartile, the second, sixth, seventh, and eighth grade results are very positive for the low-income Hispanic students. At the 7th and 8th grade levels no students scored in the bottom quartile and only a few in the second quartile. Unfortunately the disaggregated results are less encouraging at some of the earlier grades. One explanation for this, based on other studies of schools serving limited-English proficient students[2] is that it takes until fifth or sixth grade for the students' English to be sufficient for them to show gains more equivalent to English-only students.

The language arts portion of CTBS and CAP showed promising gains both in overall achievement and in disaggregated results. However, in reading

---

[2] Pollack, S., Chrispeels, J., and Watson, D. (1987). *A Description of Factors and Implementation Strategies used by Schools in Becoming Effective for All Students.* Paper presented at the Annual Meeting of the American Educational Research Association Meeting, Washington, D.C. April 1987.

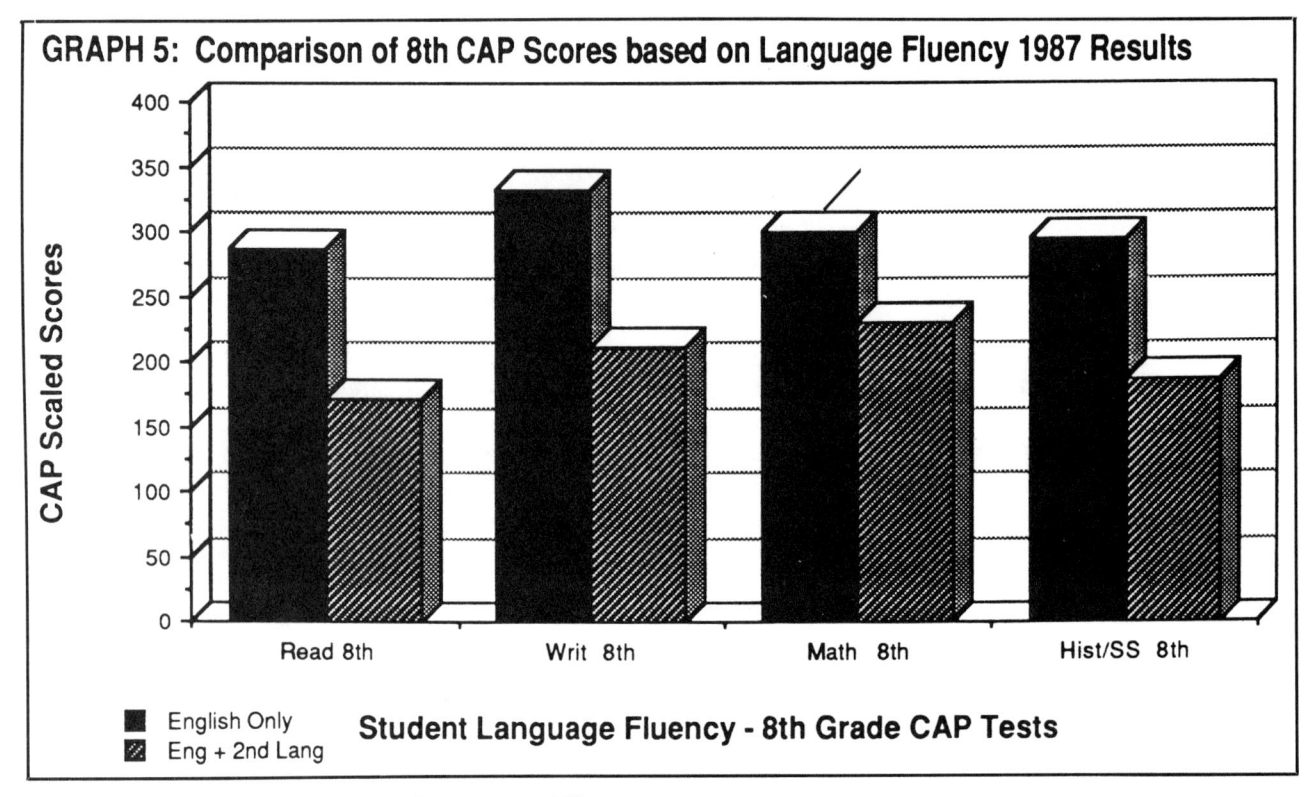

GRAPH 5: Comparison of 8th CAP Scores based on Language Fluency 1987 Results

Student Language Fluency - 8th Grade CAP Tests (English Only vs. Eng + 2nd Lang, across Read 8th, Writ 8th, Math 8th, Hist/SS 8th)

Graph 5. Comparison of 8th Grade CAP Scores, 1987

considerable inequality of results exists between subgroups of white and Hispanic students.

The school has three aides, and this past year, a part-time reading specialist, who assist students with the greatest need. However, according to the Effective Schools Research, the pullout programs are disruptive to the regular program. Furthermore, the school does not have a bilingual teacher or a bilingual program for its Hispanic students. Next year's improvement target will be in the area of reading and language arts with plans to implement a home reading program and to reevaluate the pullout programs.

In addition to test score data, the School Effectiveness Survey represents another measure of change. The survey for the staff was readministered in June of 1988. Graph 10 compares the results of principals and teachers in 1986 with those of 1988.

One should note two important changes in the school. First, the principal and the teachers have moved closer together in their views about the school. Second, substantial improvements have been made in three of the correlates: instructional leadership, clear school mission, and frequent monitoring. Also, there has been a small gain in the area of high expectations. In the recent survey, the staff results reflected less uncertainty and greater approval of the principal's leadership. For example, the 1986 survey results show that 75 percent of the teachers were uncertain and 25 percent disagreed that the principal provided clear, strong, and central instructional leadership. In 1988 the survey results showed only 22 percent of the staff members were uncertain and 11 percent disagreed regarding the principal's leadership. Clear school mission has been enhanced by the development of a mission statement for the school that focuses on enabling all students to develop skills, goals, and dreams. In the area of frequent monitoring, an item analysis of the surveys shows that changes have occurred in regard to using test results to plan for making reteaching and remediation an important part of instruction. These three correlates have received the most attention, and they reflect the greatest gains in terms of a positive opinion shift.

Graph 11, a comparison of the classified staff's views in 1986 and 1988, shows a shift in attitudes. The parents and students were not resurveyed in 1988 and no comparative data are available.

Influence of Effective Schools Process on Program Components: Curriculum Alignment

The Effective Schools correlates gave the focus needed to continue San Pasqual's school improvement process into the second year. With the staff believing that the school is a major determinant of achievement, they formulated a plan to implement interventions in

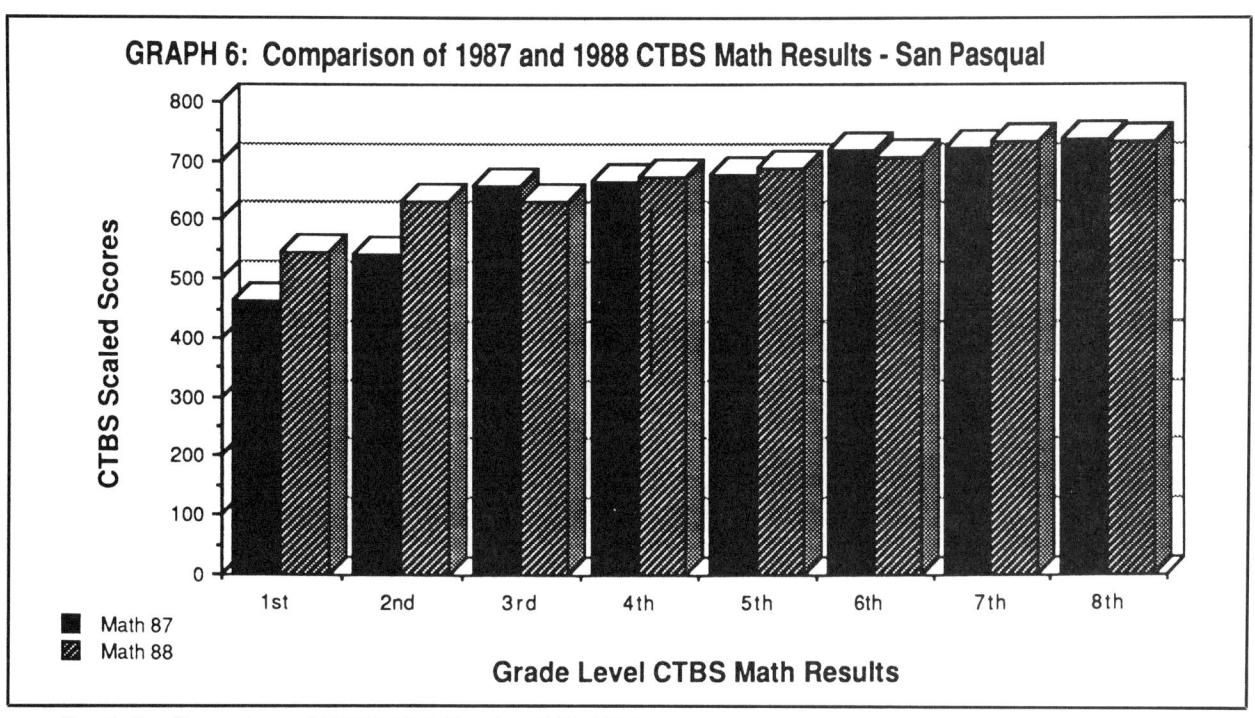

Graph 6. Comparison of CTBS Math Results, 1987, 1988

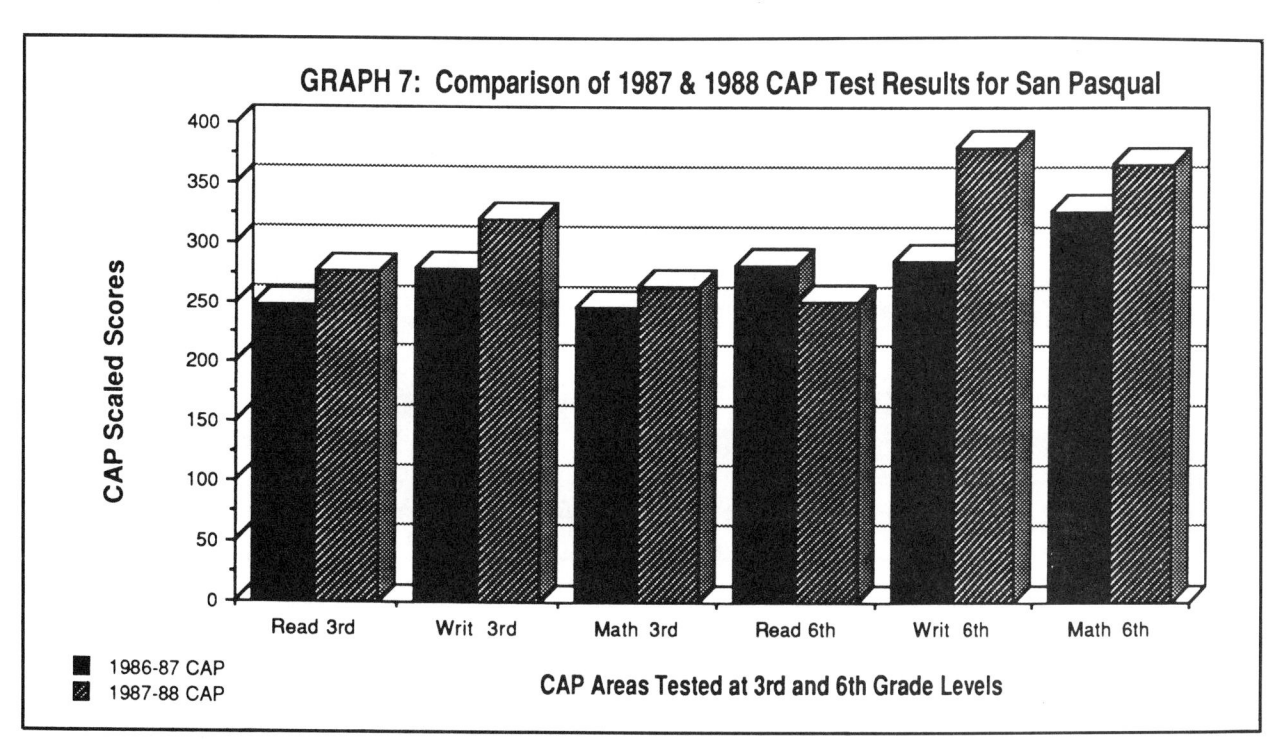

Graph 7. Comparison of CAP Test Results, 1986–1987 and 1987–1988

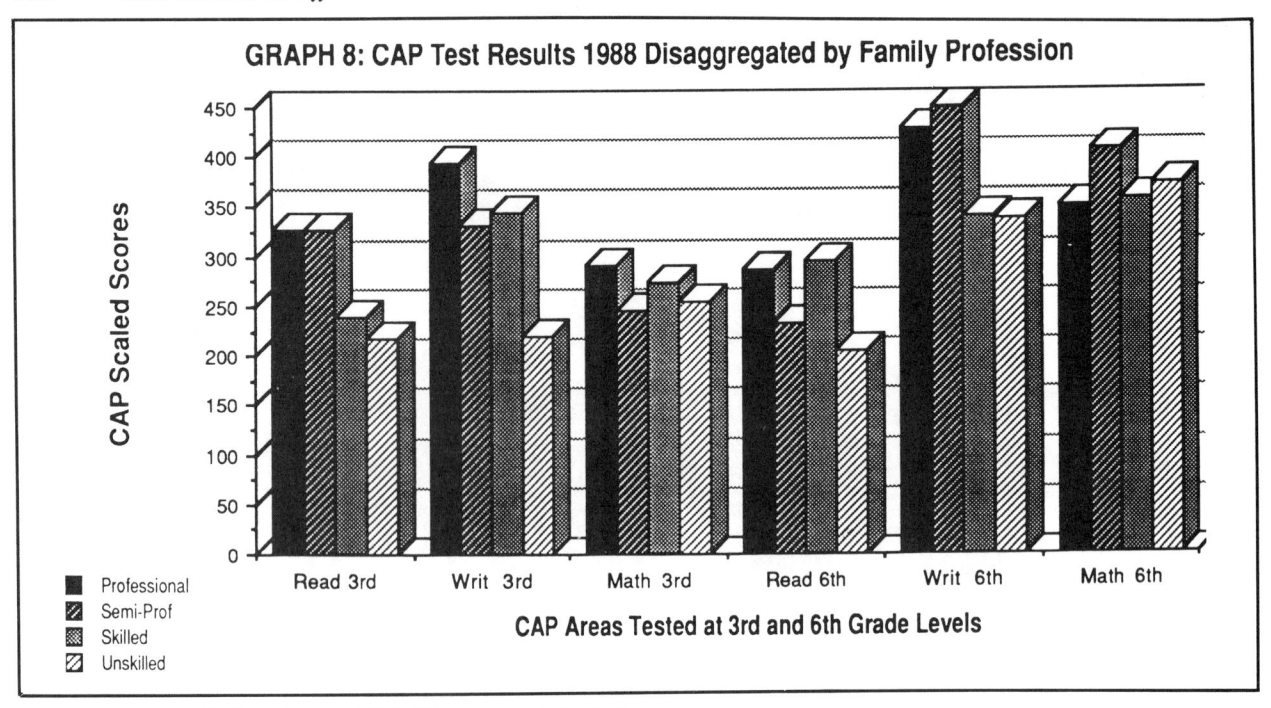

GRAPH 8: CAP Test Results 1988 Disaggregated by Family Profession

Graph 8. CAP Test Results 1988, Disaggregated Analysis

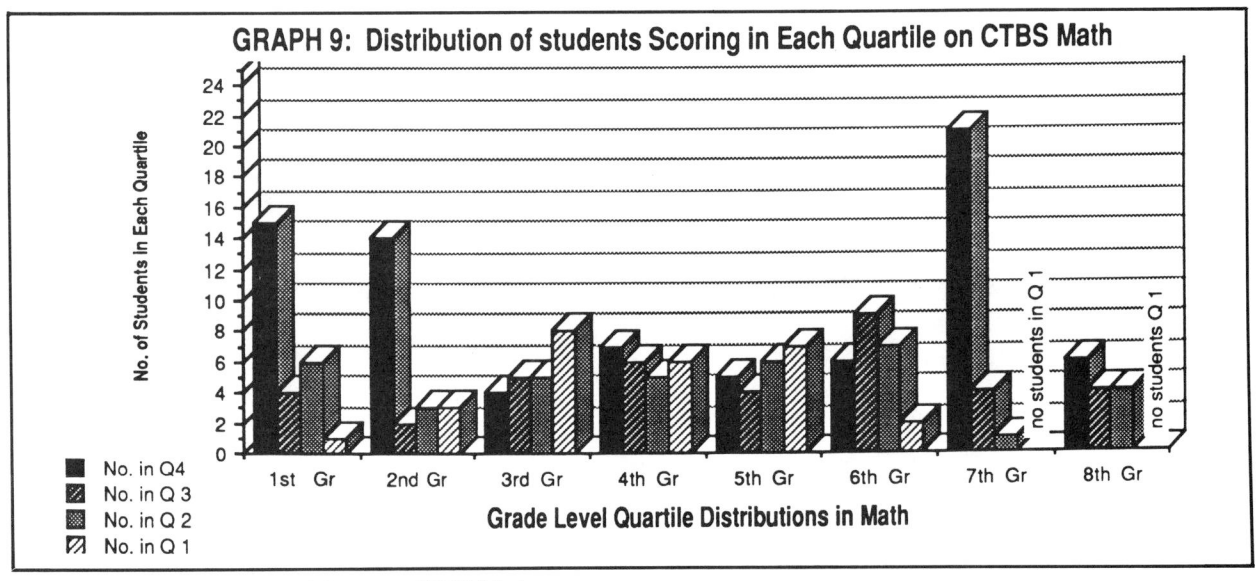

GRAPH 9: Distribution of students Scoring in Each Quartile on CTBS Math

Graph 9. Distribution of Students, CTBS Math

the curriculum. Curriculum alignment in mathematics was targeted as a need because of the adoption of a new textbook series. The survey data also indicated not all staff members were in agreement that instructional objectives were in place and that written standards of expected student achievement existed.

The school staff spend two afternoons looking at all the variables that make a difference in student learning, i.e., what teachers choose to teach (instructional objectives); how it is taught (instructional methodology); and the order in which things are taught (sequencing and timing). To strengthen the K–8 mathematics program, the following steps were carried out:

Step 1: Review the Objectives and Benefits of Curriculum Alignment

The curriculum alignment process focuses on defining the core set of teaching objectives that all stu-

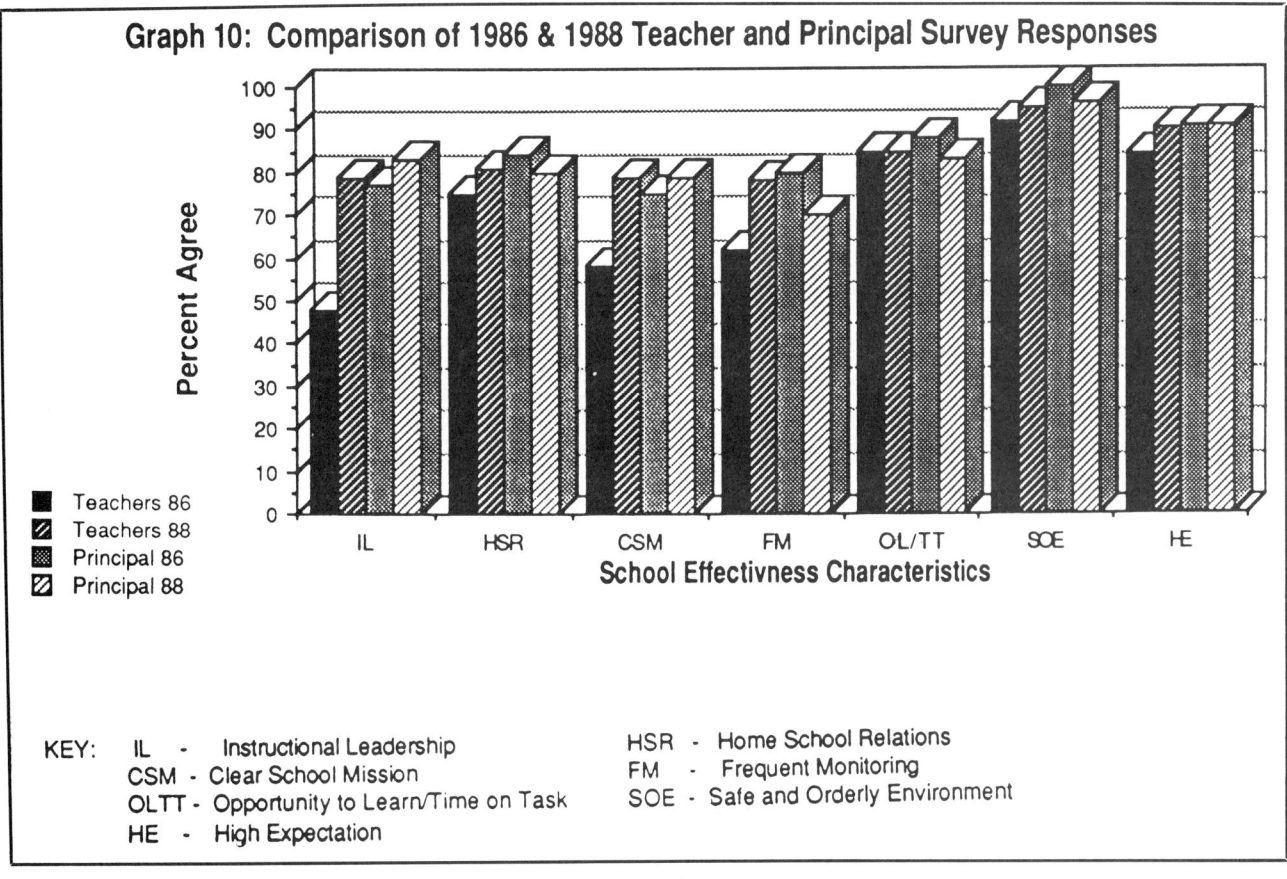

Graph 10. Comparison of 1986–1988 Principal's and Teachers' Responses

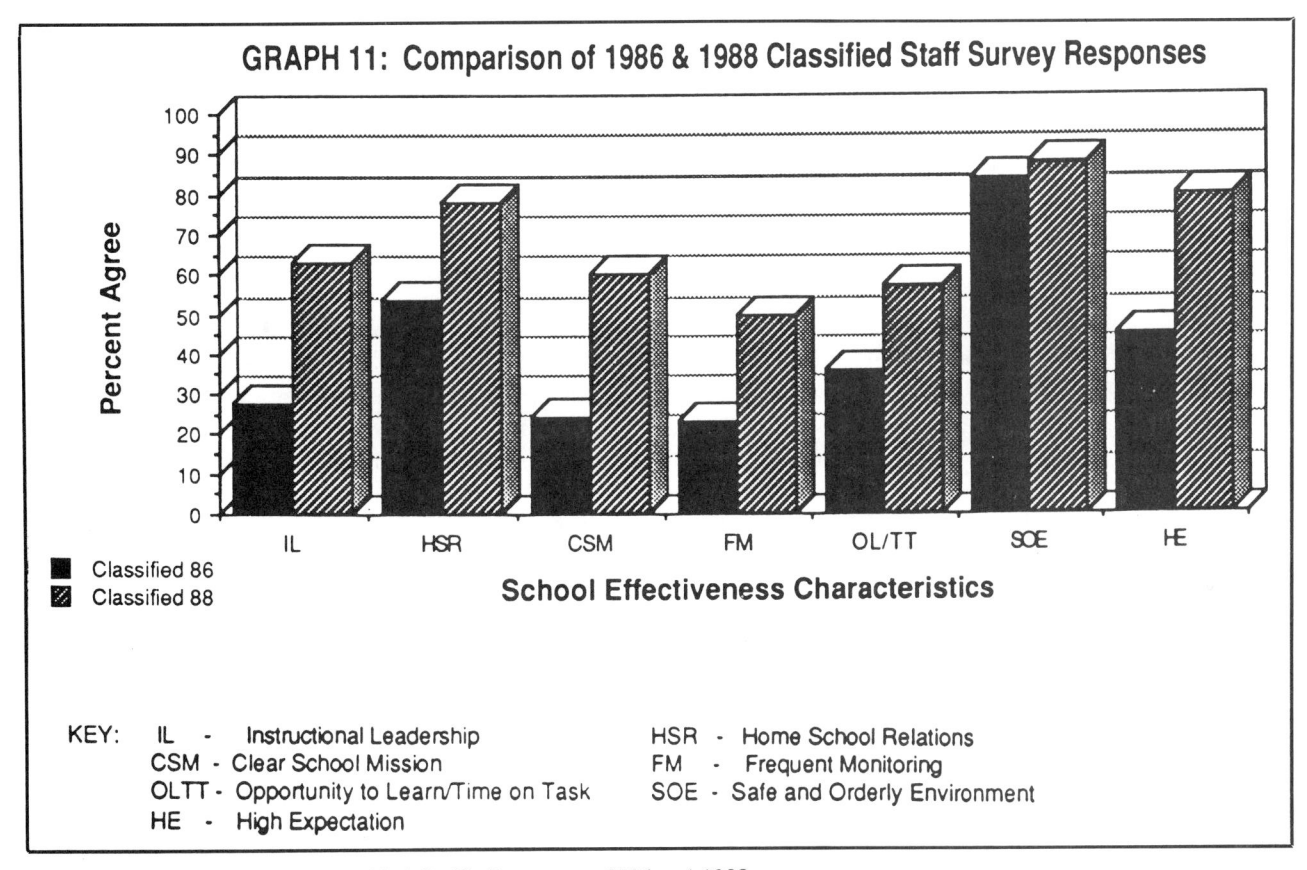

Graph 11. Comparison of Classified Staff's Responses, 1986 and 1988

dents are expected to master, selecting appropriate materials and strategies that will insure mastery, and using appropriate tests to measure the level of student mastery. The teachers examined reports and statistics which indicated that the current mathematics textbooks had voids in providing lessons that prepared students for all test questions. Teachers noted that some questions asked on the norm-referenced tests covered material that was not presented in the texts until after the tests. In addition, they discovered that the format and appearance of problems in the textbook were quite different from the way the problems were presented on the tests. Teachers agreed that the material in the textbook could not be adequately covered in the school year. They discussed the need to make informed decisions about what would or would not be covered.

Step 2: Clarify the Objectives of the Instructional Program

Primary, middle, and upper grade teachers grouped to examine a set of core objectives by grade level that were matched to the tests given to their students. All teachers had an opportunity to discuss the appropriateness of the objective, decide if it was important, and if they should teach it. Next they decided whether the objective should be to master by the year's end, and what percent of the students should achieve mastery. Several of the teachers concluded that they were not thoroughly aware of what was being tested. They also thought they were covering other objectives of equal importance that were not covered on the tests. However, they recognized that not all students were mastering the core objectives and that this presented a challenge. A core curriculum in mathematics was developed for the school.

Step 3: Establish the Top Instructional Priorities in Mathematics

Teachers identified the top priorities of the instructional program by performing an item analysis of the mathematics portion of the CTBS test. They identified the essential skills that every student needs to have and then established priorities for teaching and learning.

Step 4: Develop an Effective Instructional Plan for Teaching the Mathematics Objectives

The teachers realized that they needed to plan the year's activities so that the objectives for the year are fully covered and mastered. The teachers recognized the need to schedule some lessons that appeared in the back of the textbook earlier in the school year before testing occurred. For example, one teacher observed that ration, proportion, and percent are not presented until the end of the textbook, and that 25 percent of the test items focused on this area. The teachers recognized that they were in charge and the textbook did not have to dictate sequencing and presentation of the objectives.

Step 5: Increase Math Competencies and Check Progress

The staff adopted Bellworks, a set of sponge activities, that follows the formatting, vocabulary, and sequencing of the test items for which students are being held accountable.

Step 6: Increase Instructional Skills of Teachers in Mathematics

The staff scheduled a day-long inservice with Leigh Childs, county office mathematics consultant, and Merilyn Beck, mathematics consultant for the Encinitas School District (Encinitas, CA). The consultants taught the staff cooperative learning strategies and higher level thinking mathematics lessons that would provide the instructional strategies to best support the core set of objectives adopted by the staff. All teachers committed themselves to trying out three new lessons in the classroom that supported the objectives and the new state Mathematics Framework.

Impact of Effective School Process on Disaggregated Student Achievement Data

As mentioned previously, the CAP program does provide disaggregated student achievement data. However, this information is infrequently used by schools, and especially by the classroom teacher. The school effectiveness process has helped the staff to highlight the value of the data contained in the CAP report to the school. In addition, San Diego County Office of Education staff members have worked with the principal to disaggregate the results by Hispanic and white subgroups from the CTBS. This information gives the school a clearer picture of student needs.

The school does not have a system of criterion-referenced tests, except for their proficiency tests. The smallness of the district and the lack of auxiliary staff preclude the district developing its own criterion tests. However, the superintendent-principal is planning to visit a neighboring district, Escondido Union Elementary District, which does have a complete criterion-

and norm-referenced testing program. If there is sufficient alignment between the texts and objectives of the two districts, the district may be able to use their criterion testing system.

The Effective Schools surveys reveal that the district needs to devote more attention to the objectives and mastery standards expected in each subject and at each grade level. Attention has been given to mathematics this year. Language arts and reading are likely to be the focus next year. As the staff sets its learning objectives and aligns its curriculum, it will be in a better position to find appropriate criterion-referenced tests.

Staff Development Programs

As a result of the Effective Schools program, staff development is now viewed as one vehicle for implementing the improvement plan. Previously San Pasqual had no school-wide staff development. The one day set aside for staff development had consisted of teachers selecting a school or class they wanted to visit and spending a day there. Since San Pasqual had no needs assessment process, little data were available to guide the planning of a staff development program. Now with data from the school effectiveness surveys and data from analyzing the test results, the school has information to guide its staff development.

Two important staff development changes have been implemented. First, staff members now have opportunities to attend workshops and conferences linked to the improvement goals. For example, this year a staff member and the principal attended the Greater San Diego Math Conference to support the school's efforts in math. Second, two school-wide staff development days were arranged. The first year's focused on reviewing the school effectiveness data and developing a discipline plan; the second year's focused on mathematics, e.g., learning how to use manipulative, problem-solving, and cooperative learning strategies. In addition, a day was devoted to aligning the math curriculum.

The principal has also made a substantial commitment to strengthening his own skills by participating in the California School Leadership Academy. This program provides 15 days annually of staff development for principals in such areas as vision, mission and goals, analyzing test data, curriculum and instruction, school climate, planning staff development, evaluating staff, and home-school partnerships. The principal will participate in the second year of the program during the 1988–89 school year. This leadership program fully integrates the research on Effective Schools and thus complements and supports the principal in his efforts to improve the school.

Comparisons of the responses from the Effective Schools survey conducted in December 1986 with the results of the survey completed in June 1988 show that attitudes regarding staff development have changed. Some items reflect the changes that are summarized in Table 2.

The School Improvement Process

San Pasqual Union has only nine teachers and a librarian/resource/physical education teacher; therefore, the whole staff served as the planning team. The board of education has been fully supportive of the school's efforts. The principal has given periodic reports to the board regarding the school's progress and improvement plan. They have expressed their support by renewing the superintendent-principal's contract. The parents have been involved through input on the Effective Schools surveys. In general their views of the school are very positive. In the first year of the improvement program, parents were also involved in a workshop on assertive discipline. The parent group usually raises funds as one of its primary functions. However, as a result of the improvement efforts, they are being brought in more fully as partners. For example, next year one parent, who has a background in children's literature, will coordinate the school's literature program. She will be spending three hours a week at the school reading stories to the students and assisting them in selecting reading materials. Other volunteers will be solicited for this program as well as for other purposes.

In the fall of 1988 the school staff and parents began preparing for the California State Program Quality Review which was conducted in the spring of 1989. The review required a self-study conducted by staff and parents. The school effectiveness surveys and data formed the foundation for the self-study. In addition, the school staff examined in-depth curriculum and instructional practices. They compared the school's curriculum and instruction with the state's challenging quality criteria in six curricula and six school-wide areas. The criteria fully incorporate research from the Effective Schools and effective teaching literature.

After the staff completed the self-study, an outside review team of two administrators from other nearby districts and a county office staff member spent three days at the school observing classrooms, interviewing staff and parents, and comparing their own findings with the school's self-study. The Program Quality Review (PQR) culminated in a Report of Findings. On

Table 2
Change in Attitudes Regarding Staff Development

Survey Item	Year	% Disagree	% Don't Know	% Agree
Principal emphasizes participation in staff development activities?	1986	0	13	87
	1988	0	0	100
Principal and staff plan staff development activities?	1986	25	0	73
	1988	11	0	88
Primary focus of staff development is increase knowledge of topic?	1986	0	50	
	1988	0	0	100
Primary focus of staff development is acquisition of new skills?	1986	13	63	26
	1988	22	0	88
Primary focus of staff development is application of knowledge and skills?	1986	13	38	50
	1988	0	22	77
Principal provides follow-up assistance for skills learned in staff development activities?	1986	0	38	63
	1988	0	11	89
Is there a staff development program based on school goals?	1986	13	75	13
	1988	11	11	78
Is staff development evaluated on evidence of use in the classroom?	1986	0	88	13
	1988	22	56	22

the afternoon of the third day of the review, the PQR team and staff met to develop an action plan. Three major improvement targets were set: language arts, visual and performing arts, and the special needs of students covered by state and federal programs such as low achieving students, limited-English proficient students, and gifted and talented students. The action plan details who, what, when and how the improvements in each of these critical areas will be made.

The PQR team found that the school had made good progress in many areas, and they identified as strengths the Effective Schools process, the positive school climate, the alignment of the math curriculum, the clear school mission that focused on learning, and the leadership of the principal. The three year improvement plan indicates that learning objectives need to be developed in language arts and in the visual and performing arts. Staff from the San Diego County Office of Education will again assist the school staff in developing these curriculum objectives and engaging in curriculum alignment as they had done for math. The plan also states that the staff will need to work toward a literature-based reading and language arts program and to modify grouping practices, moving away from traditional reading groups organized around a basal reader.

To better meet the needs of its limited English-speaking students, the review team recommended that the school focus future inservices on the acquisition of second language skills, visit schools implementing the English for Limited-English Proficient Students Program (ELEPS), adopt and implement the ELEPS program, and attend conferences on the writing process.

The review process confirmed the gains the school had made during the previous two years and commended the staff for their efforts. The self-study and review also set some clear targets for future growth, thus keeping the school effectiveness and improvement momentum going.

Personnel Evaluation System

In California, the personnel evaluation system is spelled out in state law. The number of formal observations is specified as one every other year. The law also defines the procedures to be followed. Each year teachers write two to three objectives on which they will be evaluated and state what evidence will be collected to demonstrate accomplishment of the objectives. At San Pasqual, the principal does not make formal observations other than those specified by California law. Teachers are uncertain whether or not the principal plans with teachers what will be observed and adequately discusses the observations in a post-observation conference. However, the staff agrees (100 percent) that the principal makes frequent contacts with students and teachers, is highly visible throughout the school, and is accessible to discuss instructional matters. Another change since the implementation of the Effective Schools program is that faculty meetings frequently focus on instructional issues; 78 percent agree and 22 percent are uncertain. Previously 38 percent had said instructional issues **were not a focus** and 50 percent said they did not know.

The principal reported that he has changed personnel evaluation practices in two ways. First, when he is observing classrooms, he now looks for much more than just an orderly, neat classroom with attractive bulletin boards. He is more alert to how time is used in the classroom. He observes instructional practices more carefully. He is on the lookout for equality of treatment by the teacher among all students. Second, the principal said that now when he has the opportunity to select new staff members, he is looking for different skills, and for teachers that have some knowledge of the Effective Schools literature and practices.

Problems, Issues, and Concerns Encountered

Once the initial concerns of the staff were addressed, the school effectiveness efforts have met few obstacles at San Pasqual. However, the small size of San Pasqual contributes both strengths and limits as the district tries to implement its Effective Schools program. One asset of smallness is that it facilitates communication. Once a direction has been set, communication about the direction and monitoring are relatively easy tasks. Involvement of the whole staff is possible thereby greatly increasing ownership of the plan and speeding implementation. The small number of teachers means that it is easier to plan and coordinate a K–8 curriculum. On the open-ended comments of the school effectiveness surveys, the small size was mentioned by many parents and staff as a strength of the school.

However, the small size poses some problems as well. Few extra staff members are available to take on additional work. In particular San Pasqual has no specialists in the district who can assist the staff. They must rely on the outside assistance of the county office staff or other consultants. The superintendent-principal must do all of the school paperwork as well as attend to the district administrative tasks. Resources, both staff and budget, are limited for meeting the needs of the limited-English proficient students. Currently the district allocates only one staff development day a year. This provides very little planning, training, and implementation time for staff. The school plans to expand its staff development time next year by increasing the school day by 15 minutes. The time will be devoted to sustained silent reading. The extra minutes generated will allow the staff to have two additional minimum days for staff development.

Advice for Others Implementing a School Improvement Process

In guiding others in carrying out a school improvement process, the superintendent-principal advised securing the full support of the board of education. He found this support had a positive impact on the successful implementation of the school effectiveness efforts.

His second recommendation is, "Focus on a doable objective that everyone can rally behind." Given the fact that there were tensions and confusion among staff members when the process was started, it was important to undertake an objective that would bring the staff together and have some immediate effects. The success of implementing the school-wide discipline plan laid the groundwork for addressing curriculum and instructional issues in the second year.

The third, engage the staff in an analysis of learning objectives in a particular curriculum area and to spend time seeing that these objectives are covered in their materials. Analyzing test items also proved extremely useful for the staff. In larger school districts, it is more likely that this curriculum alignment activity would be done by district staff. In San Pasqual, the school staff is the district staff. The exercise proved to be a valuable one and should not be overlooked by others as a helpful learning activity for the entire staff.

Fourth, involve as many of the staff members as possible. If a small planning group had been in charge of the improvement program, the impact would not have been nearly as great. The size of San Pasqual made it ideal for involving the whole staff. Larger schools need to find strategies, like task forces or subcommittees, that insure that every staff member has some responsibility for meeting the improvement objectives.

Fifth, utilize the resources of outside consultants who can offer an impartial voice and help guide the improvement efforts. The county office services were particularly helpful in San Pasqual's case. An important role of the consultant, in addition to bringing resources and information, is to be a sounding board for the principal or other staff members.

Summary

In the past two years, San Pasqual has made great progress in implementing its school effectiveness program. The board of education, the superintendent, the teachers, and the parents seem to be in agreement regarding the goals of the school and district. The initial resistance by the staff has yielded and all are pulling in the same direction. The staff has seen the payoff from its efforts in terms of higher overall achievement for students in mathematics and language arts, and important gains for its Hispanic students. With knowledge of these gains, the staff completed the 1987–88 school year in high spirits. The challenge for the school next year is to carefully examine strategies for teaching reading and to explore ways to be more effective in teaching reading so that all students master the basic skills.

The school effectiveness process has shown the staff the importance of data and the value of using data to plan improvement objectives. The process has helped to target resources—people, material, funds, and staff development. Once resources and objectives are targeted, teachers will increase opportunities for student learning.

The staff of San Pasqual now realizes that school improvement is an ongoing process. They can celebrate how far they have come as well as work on the challenges that remain. The challenges are ones they know they can achieve. With careful planning and staff development the teachers know they can raise the achievement level of **all** students.

Effective Schools Do Make a Difference in Jackson, Mississippi

Carol R. Adams
Principal, Wingfield High School

Henriette L. Allen
Administrative Assistant to the Superintendent

Robert N. Fortenberry
Superintendent of Schools

Jackson, Mississippi School District
Became involved in Effective Schools process in 1980

Community

Population
210,000 (school district) Greater Jackson area 400,000

Urban. Major employers include the public school district, state government, the University of Mississippi medical and dental schools, four large hospitals, and two large shopping centers. Jackson has many smaller industries, including electronics companies. The Jackson Chamber of Commerce actively supports the school district through a foundation trust and the PRIDE program for recognizing scholastic achievement.

Half of the students live in one-parent households; 75 percent can be classified as having low SES.

School District

Enrollment
33,100

Ethnic Composition (percent)
African-American	71.00
American Indian	< .05
Asian-American	1.00
Caucasian	21.00
Hispanic	1.00

Per Pupil Expenditure
Year 1987–1988	$3,377
1988–1989	3,670

Percent bussed
60

Area (in square miles)
105

Schools
Elementary school	37
Junior high schools	11
High schools	8

Number of Staff
Administrators	162
Certified teachers	1,775
Support staff	2,151

Student-Teacher Ratio
Elementary	*
Junior high	22:1
High school	21:1

Percent college-bound
69

Abstract

From the beginning the superintendent and board of education gave leadership to and supported the school improvement process in Jackson, Mississippi. In the late seventies the Jackson Public Schools had completed a program which, over the previous decade, had attempted both desegregation and the unification of all school districts into one system. In 1980, the superintendent was seeking a process for school improvement built on a quality education and equity for all students, and asked Ron Edmonds to speak to teachers at a retreat. "The result of that conversation continues" through the present day.

All district and school staff were trained to have a good understanding of the Effective Schools correlates, with components of shared decision-making (school-based management), and administrators were given an Executive Training Program. Jackson was implementing the Effective Schools process at a district level well before the model had developed to include district relationships. (The early Effective Schools model was primarily Planned Change for individual schools. A "Shared Governance Liaison Committee" was put in place in Jackson to coordinate district decision-making, especially with regard to development of a unified curriculum.)

In 1982 Jackson rewrote the personnel evaluation system (for teachers and for administrators) to focus on the correlates, especially issues relating to instructional leadership. In 1985 an instructional management system (IMS) was installed. After performing curricular alignment, teachers had written criterion-referenced tests for the district. Together with personnel from the research and evaluation department, computer software was developed to assure fast grading and turn-around in grading these tests, so that the teachers had timely and accurate data to plan for reteaching and emphasis in future lessons. Jackson considers this system central to the improvement process, as they attempt to teach a uniform curriculum to all students. "All teachers are expected to follow the curriculum and are monitored by their principals. One of the areas in which the teachers are directly evaluated is implementation of the curriculum. Thus, failure to teach the curriculum is insubordination, not just disagreement with administrative guidelines." (From the Case Study, p. 152)

Jackson Public School District is a district committed to teaching all of its students. The Effective Schools process promoted ownership of the new process by teachers with district support for risk-taking and innovation in teaching-learning strategies.

---

*State Department accreditation Standards:

Kindergarten — Standard 81: 22:1
27:1 with teacher aide
Grades 1–4 — Standard 83: 27:1
5–6 — Standard 84: 30:1 (self-contained)
5–6 — Standard 85: 33:1 (departmentalized)

Making a Difference in Jackson, Mississippi

Jackson, Mississippi, a city of more than 200,000, has a heritage of public education. Now Jackson is moving forward to excellence in education. The Jackson Public School District educates approximately 33,100 students in grades K–12, with approximately 78 percent minority and 22 percent non-minority. About half of the students live in one-parent households and close to 75 percent can be classified as students from low socioeconomic backgrounds.

A five-member board of trustees appointed by the city council makes policy in the district which contains 37 elementary, 11 junior high and 8 senior high schools. In addition to these regular schools are four special schools: Alternative Elementary School, Alternative Secondary School, Career Development Center, and the Academic and Performing Arts Complex. The school board oversees a budget of $100 million—51 percent from local taxes and 49 percent from state taxes.

The struggle for excellence has not been without anguish. The late 1960s and early 1970s were fraught with desegregation and the unification of racially isolated districts into one school district. Making the change was painful, but it went smoothly. In the late 1970s a serious, demanding examination of the district's instructional program began. By 1980 the superintendent was seeking, quietly and unobtrusively, an answer to the question, "Can all children learn?"

The question, "Can all children learn?" was asked of everyone involved in the educational process. The responses in most instances were a resounding yes, but in a few cases the answer was yes with some reservations. School district leaders invited Ron Edmonds to speak at a retreat for two teachers from every school who were elected by their peers. The result of that "conversation" continues through 1988.

An instructional council comprised of a majority of teachers, elementary and secondary principals, and the instructional management team members, led by Robert N. Fortenberry, butted the Jackson educational reform movement. They worked together on several fronts.

The district was fortunate in having a biracial board of trustees that endorsed the belief that all children can learn. These same board members, under the leadership of board chairman Rowan Taylor, when apprised of the correlates of Effective Schools, supported this philosophy without reservation and urged the district administration to move forward. This endorsement allowed the relocation of funds to implement programs needed to support the correlates. School board leadership and support have made an important difference in what the district has been able to achieve. This support has come through testimonials, personnel assignments, and financial commitments. Local tax increases and prudent budget allocations and expenditures have financed the Effective Schools process.

Several programs that support the correlates were implemented and are presently ongoing. The first of these programs was **Shared Governance,** a collaborative decision-making process involving teachers, students, administrators, and parents. This involvement—whereby decisions are the result of extensive participation by those affected—is not the final answer to all problems, but it enables the district to keep as its primary focus the welfare of all children.

Teachers restructured the curriculum. They identified what students need to learn in every subject and established a base-line curriculum. For grades one through six, teachers identified essential objectives each student must achieve to be promoted to the next grade. After one implementation and the gathering of much information, the teachers revised and realigned the curriculum. The district is now in a five-year review process which allows every subject to be studied, reviewed, and revised within a period of five years.

The Jackson Staff Development Program is being given greater emphasis. During the first year of Effective Schools implementation, every person in the district became familiar with the Effective Schools correlates. Prior to their employment all new employees, especially new teachers, are trained in the philosophy and practices of the school district. The establishment of a common vocabulary and belief system keeps the focus on the teaching and achievement of all students. This is further carried out with an executive training program that provides special training for administrative candidates.

The best indicator that change has taken place in the district is undoubtedly the data the district has collected. California Achievement Test (CAT) scores have increased, attendance is up, and the dropout rate is down—all during a time when the district was increasing the standards. The disaggregation of data has provided the best indicator that all students are learning. (See Figure 8)

Figure 1 reveals at all levels a general decline in the number of students leaving school before completing diploma requirements. Figure 2 shows a dramatic decline in grade 12 enrollment loss from 1979 through 1986. In 1979 almost eight percent of seniors left school before the end of the year, while in 1987 only slightly more than three percent did.

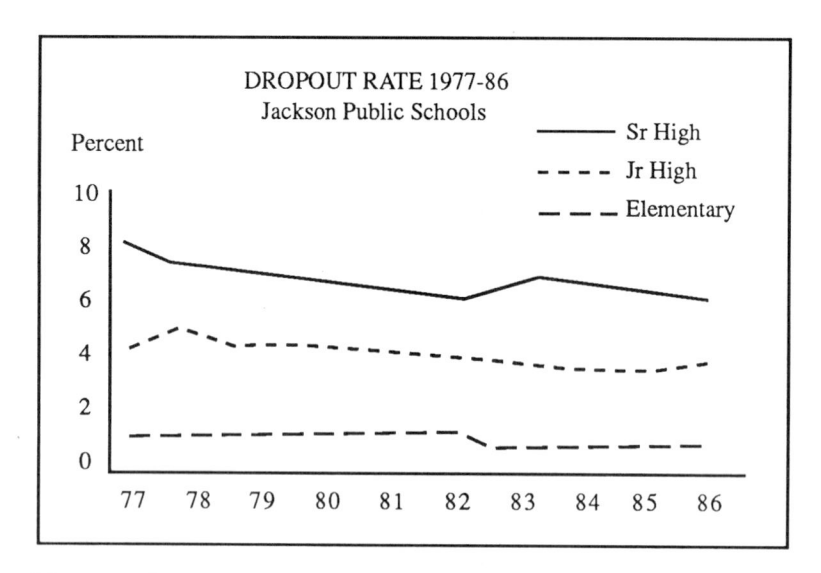

Figure 1. Dropout Rate

District attendance information for the last four years is detailed in Figure 3 (percent average daily attendance or ADA). Highest attendance was registered at 95.3 percent average daily attendance in 1986, the year in which a very restrictive attendance policy was implemented, and the district-wide attendance has consistently remained over 94 percent each year.

The CAT is the principal norm-referenced assessment instrument used by the district. Steady increases in CAT scores have occurred in the district. Figure 4 reveals fourth grade CAT results from 1975–1985 and shows an increase in scores from the 26th percentile in 1975 to the 67th percentile in 1985. The greatest increases have occurred since 1980, the first year discussion of the Effective Schools correlates began. The average percentile score on the total battery has risen from 41 to 67 during the six year period from 1980 through 1985.

A look at eighth grade CAT results for the same period of time (Figure 5) also reveals steady increases in average percentile total battery scores. From 1980 to 1985, scores increased from the 38th to the 51st percentile.

Figure 6 details increases in CAT percentile scores for grades 4, 6, and 8 at five-year intervals. The greatest increases in scores occurred at grade 6 with movement from the 28th to the 51st percentile, while fourth grade scores showed increases from the 26th to 42nd percentile. Progress was also registered in eighth grade scores as they advanced to the 42nd percentile from the 28th percentile in 1975.

In 1986 a renormed California Achievement Test was used in the district and scores declined somewhat on the renormed test. However, in 1987, it became apparent that educational progress was continuing. Figure 7 (CAT Scores: Grades 4, 6, 7, and 8) reveals results for grades 4, 6, 7, and 8. Seventh grade percentile scores showed the largest increases moving from 38.7 to 44.9 while increases for sixth graders ranked second as they advanced from percentile scores of 50.5 to 64.6. At all grade levels, scores continued to move forward. In addition, the number of students achieving at the upper percentiles also increased. In 1987, 770 students scored in the 90–99 percentile range as compared to 538 in 1986.

The Effective Schools correlates permeate every area of the district and every facet of its operations. The leadership of the district has become committed to the philosophy that all children can learn and has placed the ultimate responsibility for student learning on the schools. The school board has amended district policies to bring them into alignment with the correlates, reallocated funds to implement necessary programs, placed great emphasis on the training of certified and classified personnel to insure a common knowledge base, and altered the personnel evaluation system to make certain that the behavior of every employee will reflect the district's philosophy. Further evidence of the presence of the correlates can be seen in the development of and adherence to the district's five-year plan and the school improvement plan for individual buildings, both of which are constructed around the Effective Schools correlates. In looking at the correlate of safe and orderly climate, for instance, it is gratifying to note that 91 percent of the district students committed zero discipline offenses for the school year 1986–1987, while six percent committed only one offense.

During that same year graduates of the district received more than $6.4 million in scholarship offers from such national prestigious schools as the U.S. Air Force Academy, Harvard, Yale, Duke, and Baylor.

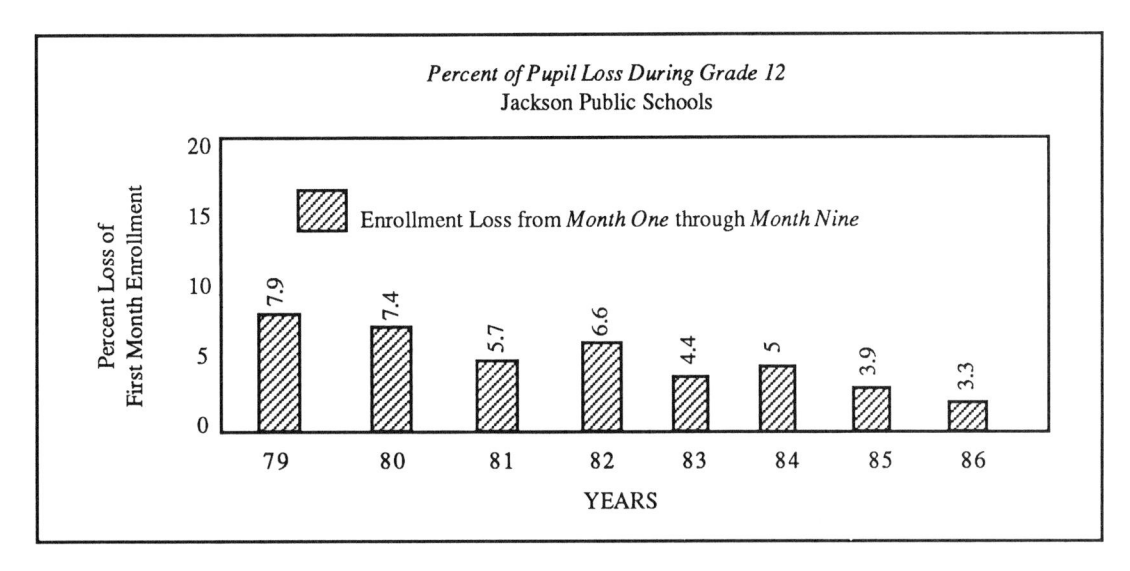

Figure 2. Percent of Pupil Loss, Grade 12

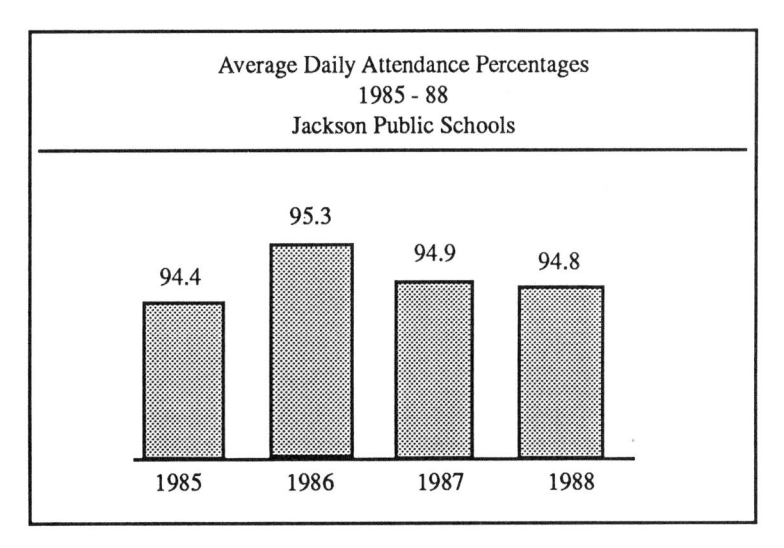

Figure 3. Average Daily Attendance

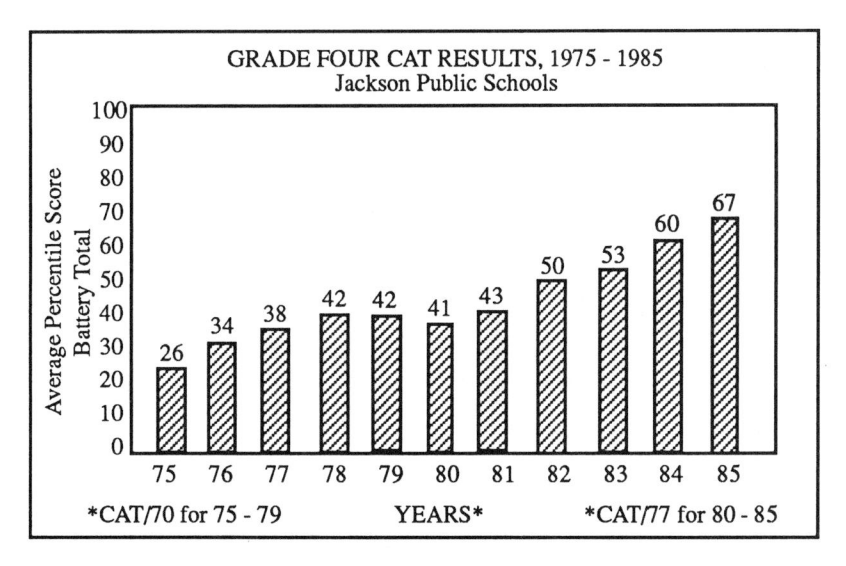

Figure 4. Grade 4 CAT Results

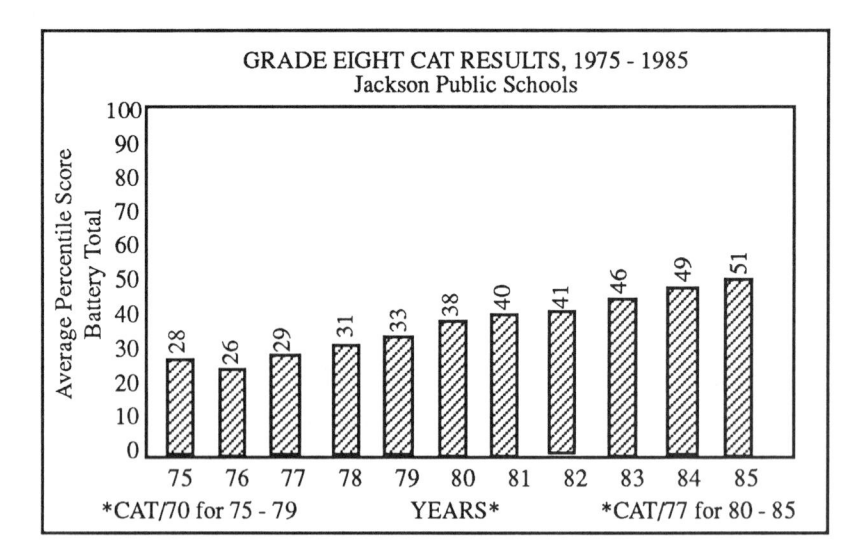

Figure 5. Grade 8 CAT Results

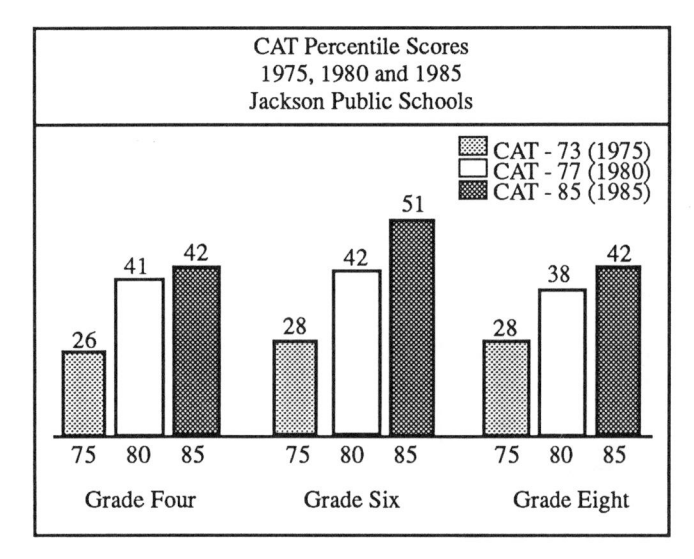

Figure 6. CAT Percentile Scores

Seventeen seniors were named National Merit or National Achievement scholarship winners and almost 81 percent of the spring graduates pursued advanced study.

District programs received national recognition for excellence. The Jackson Public School Five-year Plan received the Award for Excellence from the American Educational Research Association. A Golden Achievement Award was presented to the office of Community Relations/Public Information by the National School Public Relations Association for its efforts in building community support for public schools. U.S. Secretary of Education William Bennett named the district Chapter I program one of 95 exemplary programs in the nation. And because of his strong leadership, Dr. Robert N. Fortenberry, superintendent, received the Executive Educators Top Administrators in America Award for a second time in 1985.

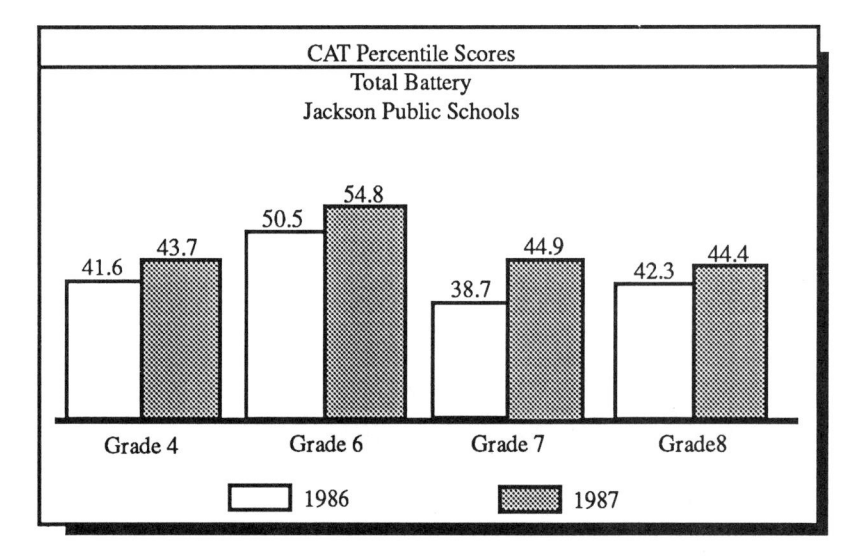

Figure 7. CAT Percentile Scores—Total

Importance of Student Testing and Monitoring System to Jackson Public Schools Success

The influence of the Effective Schools process has been largely responsible for the non-optional, objective-based curriculum and the criterion-referenced unit tests developed by the district. The leaders of the district wanted to ensure that all students, no matter what school they attend, would receive instruction measurable by uniform standards. Implementation of the curriculum and tests were enhanced by the addition of the instructional management system which grades tests, calculates attainment or non-attainment of mastery, and reports results to teachers, principals, and their superiors. In this way evaluation of the instructional processes can be monitored by subject, teacher, and school.

The district continues to examine test results to determine the effectiveness of its programs. After developing a uniform objective-based curriculum, preparation of curriculum-based tests began. Next, within the district both reliability and validity studies were conducted on the tests. Disaggregated analyses of norm-referenced and criterion-referenced test results have identified the student population the district is having the greatest success in educating as well as those students toward whom the district must direct more effort. Figure 8, for example, shows sixth grade CAT scores disaggregated by socioeconomic class, race, and gender. Upper SES, non-minority females and males showed the highest levels of success on the test while low SES, minority males were least successful followed closely by low SES, non-minority males. Dialogue is continuing and plans are being made toward improving delivery of services to the less successful student population.

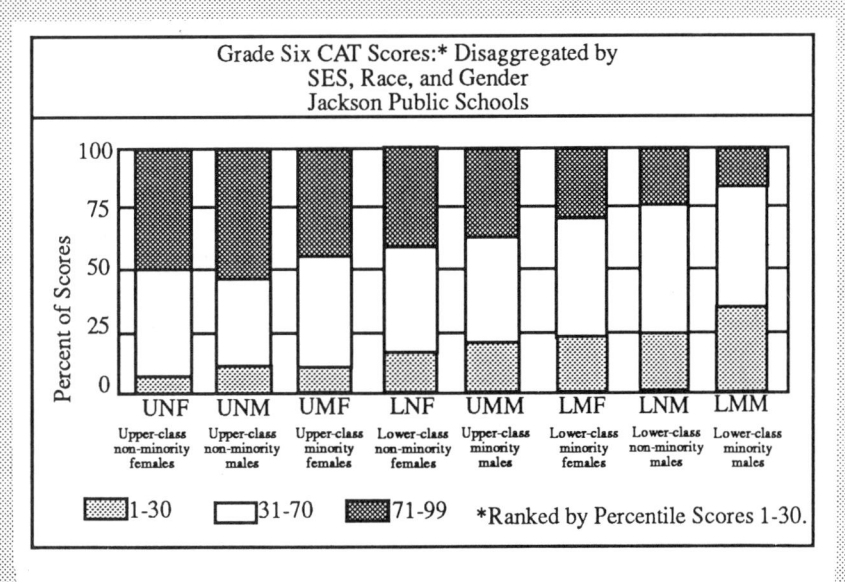

Figure 8. Grade 6 CAT Scores, 1988

Instructional Management System

The grading system is directly tied to the mastery of the curriculum. District-made unit tests are used to measure student outcomes; the tests compose 70 percent of the student's grades each grading period. Students who do not pass the unit tests the first time are retaught the material and are retested. Students who pass the tests but fail to master some objectives are also retaught and are expected to provide evidence of mastery of essential objectives.

To assist the teachers with grading tests and record keeping, an instructional management system (IMS) has been put in place. Objective tests are graded using a scanner, and a print-out is provided for the teacher showing the test grade as well as mastery or non-mastery of each objective for each student. At the end of each term the system computes term grades and at the end of the year, final grades. The way in which grades are reported was also changed. Report cards were given a new format to show not only the numerical and letter grade, but also the number of objectives taught and the number mastered.

Importance of Staff Development System

The thrust of the district's staff development programs has focused on the correlates of Effective Schools and related concepts since the district began implementation in 1981. All employees of the district—both certified and classified—have been actively engaged in staff development programs.

The initial intent of the inservice programs was to educate all employees in the philosophy of the Effective Schools movement to the extent that all staff members would become convinced of the educability of all students. Initially 13 training modules were created to detail school effects research, the characteristics of an Effective School, and the development of a school improvement plan. Later the original set of 13 modules was revised and consolidated into 4 modules requiring only 8 hours of training rather than 40. Thus, the training of employees new to the district could be accomplished more quickly and efficiently. Subsequent to the development of modules in Effective Schools concepts, the district developed additional material on effective instruction, teaching competencies, time management, learning styles, and multicultural education.

District leaders deliberately decided to involve classified employees in the district training in Effective Schools concepts. Since over half of the district personnel are non-certified employees, their beliefs and behaviors have an impact on the individual school and district climate. Classified personnel attended inservice sessions with their various groups to ensure that they understand the focus of the district and the importance of their role in the district's mission.

A small cadre of trainers—using modules that employed a videotape, overhead transparencies of the main points, a workbook of activities, and an objective and process evaluation—learned to train others. These trainers instructed central office personnel, building principals, and a teacher from each school. The principal and a teacher then conducted staff development sessions at individual schools. At the conclusion of each session participants were tested on the material that had been presented. Each school retained the videotape and related materials of the modules for future review and reinforcement.

Preparation for implementing Effective Schools Research began in January 1980. The superintendent met with teacher representatives from each school in the district during a weekend retreat to discuss the focus of the district. At that work session the teachers and the superintendents decided on two vital components of the Effective Schools movement in Jackson: **shared governance and a unified curriculum.**

The Jackson Shared Governance Liaison Committee emerged as the district-level coordinating committee for Effective Schools planning. Shared governance is a district decision-making process. Although all sides of issues are debated and discussed, voting on outcomes is not allowed. All final decisions and subsequent reports detailing those decisions must be reached by consensus.

Shared governance consists of three types of committees: (1) liaison committees, (2) ad hoc committees, and (3) local school committees. The liaison committee, chaired by the superintendent, is composed of elected representatives of central office personnel, building administrators, teachers, and parents. The committee addresses issues vital to the district and through ad hoc committees studies issues and offers suggested solutions and plans which are subject to approval by the school board. Ad hoc committees, composed of elected representatives from each school group, are established by the liaison committee for a limited time to study a single issue. Ad hoc committees have provided direction in a number of important areas such as the certified evaluation system, grading system, attendance policy, and extracurricular activities policy, to name a few.

The local school shared governance committees consist of the principal and elected representatives of teachers, classified employees, parents, and, at the secondary level, students. Local committees usually develop the annual school improvement plan for the school, although the principal may establish a separate committee to write the school improvement plan.

The writing of the school improvement plan is based upon a review of the school's needs assessment and school profile. The needs assessment identifies areas in the school the faculty and staff wish to improve. The school profile is a compilation of statistical information about the school including such areas as pupil enrollment, average daily attendance, disaggregated standardized test results, course grades, pupil discipline, and dropout information.

The school improvement plan committee addresses each of the correlates of Effective Schools as it writes the plan and includes a mission statement, school goals and objectives, problem areas, activities designed to improve the problem areas, methods of evaluating the attainment of objectives, and assignment of responsibility for each activity. Once the plans are implemented, they are monitored throughout the school year by the building principal.

While the individual schools develop annual improvement plans, the district develops a five-year plan as prescribed by the 1982 Mississippi Education Reform Act. In annually updating the five-year plan, committees that represent various groups address the Effective Schools correlates.

School Board Alignment of Policies to Correspond to Improvement Initiatives

Personnel at all levels show total commitment to implementing Effective Schools Research and practices. The school board, which has the ultimate authority to suggest, study, evaluate, and approve all matters, has provided support to the superintendent in his effort to ensure learning for all students. The superintendent has provided the vision, direction, and willingness to involve every individual in the improvement process and to share with them the power of decision-making. Central office administrators have provided the necessary leadership and expertise in their respective areas and have aided in the analysis and evaluation of the results. Principals, teachers, parents, and students have brought their own unique insights to the problems at hand and have worked together to make decisions and give support to those decisions.

Another outgrowth of the Effective Schools process has been the adoption of a stringent attendance policy. The school board recognizes a direct relationship between time spent in class and learning. Thus the attendance policy was amended to state that a student may not miss more than five days of school per term without forfeiture of grades for the term. Principals may exercise discretionary judgment in hardship cases. The policy has resulted in increased school attendance as well as in less time needed in individual classrooms for reteaching and retesting.

The extracurricular activities policy is also a direct outgrowth of effective schooling. Since the primary function of the school is the education of children, mastery of coursework takes precedence over extracurricular activities. Students must pass five courses each year with a minimum grade of 70 in each course to be eligible for participation in out-of-the-classroom activities. Grades are checked each semester and the student must maintain a 70 average to remain eligible for participation.

A tuition-free, extended-time summer school program for students in all grades has been implemented for students who have not mastered the curriculum objectives needed at the next grade level. Designed to provide for different rates of student learning, the summer program includes such subjects as English, math, social studies, science, and reading. High school students have the opportunity to earn two Carnegie units of credit. Elementary and junior high students can be promoted to the next grade level upon successful completion of the summer program. Students are grouped for instruction based on mastery of objectives.

Jackson's overall retention rate at the elementary level is 9.9 percent (out of an enrollment of 16,000). After summer school that figure is reduced to 4 percent; about 60 percent pass their summer classes and stay with their class. Of the 60 percent, only 3.5 percent, on average, will need to attend summer sessions the next summer.

At the middle and high school levels summer sessions enable additional students to remain with their classes. The success rate is improving.

Personnel Evaluation System

The personnel evaluation system for both teachers and administrators was rewritten during the summer of 1982 by a shared governance ad hoc committee and subsequently adopted by the school board to become school policy. The old evaluation document proved to be too cumbersome. The new system requires evaluation in only 16 areas and emphasizes the implementation of Effective School correlates and the district curriculum. Teachers and administrators are now evaluated mostly on research-based items.

Formative evaluation of teachers occurs a minimum of twice yearly following a pre-observation conference, observation, and a post-observation conference. Summative evaluation results are discussed with teachers each spring prior to contract renewal. Administrators are also evaluated formatively twice a year and summatively once a year by their immediate superiors. The school board evaluates the superintendent annually.

Many practices and procedures initially followed to implement the Effective Schools process have been adopted as policy by the school board. A number of examples in personnel evaluation may serve to illustrate this fact. One direct outgrowth of improving education for the students was the development of a uniform curriculum. All teachers are expected to follow the curriculum and are monitored by their principals. One area in which teachers are directly evaluated is implementation of the curriculum. Thus, failure to teach the curriculum is considered insubordination, not just disagreement with administrative guidelines.

Staff development and formative evaluation procedures have been and continue to be the primary means of communicating to employees the district's commitment to the educability of all children as well as the means by which teachers' skills are improved. The major problem encountered as a result of implementing Effective Schools policies was resistance to change. Teachers had to be convinced not only that all children are capable of learning, but that they, the teachers, possess the skills necessary to teach them effectively. Teacher and student mind-sets had to be altered from "I can't" to "I can."

Resistance to change diminished with (1) increased involvement of teachers and administrators and (2) more staff development related to school improvement. Programs, procedures, and policies were developed with input from all levels of employees, parents, and community supporters.

Principals have become the primary change agents. Their role in the school and in the entire educational process has expanded greatly. They were challenged to change their own ways of thinking, to convince teachers of the value of the direction in which the district was moving, to involve teachers in the process, and to train them through staff development in addition to monitoring and evaluating them.

What We Would Do Differently

At the time Jackson Public Schools began implementing Effective Schools Research, few models were around to follow. In retrospect, the one area that stands out as possibly needing a different approach was the development of a district curriculum which would ensure minimum mastery for all students and provide a systematic method of assessing student achievement.

When the superintendent realized that a non-optional, uniform, objective-based curriculum was essential for the improvement of education in the district, he moved forward with its construction as quickly as possible. First, all teachers were asked to write down what they considered to be the necessary units and objectives for their courses. Second, a group of teachers, working daily after school and into the early evening, began to develop the curriculum.

It soon became evident that this procedure would not provide a finished curriculum quickly enough. Therefore, a group of the best teachers were taken from their classrooms for a six-week period to write the district's first uniform curriculum. Substitute teachers taught in their classrooms. Though the curriculum was largely completed during that time, the regular teachers had a difficult time because they were not only writing the new curriculum, but they were also overseeing lesson plans, grading assignments, and providing tests for their classrooms.

Also, the newly developed curriculum and grading system, based on mastery of objectives, would force the district to find a better way to keep up with student records. Teachers just could not manage the additional information they were required to keep using the grade book format. The district, therefore, had to explore available technology and determine how best to utilize that technology.

To support these new programs, additional resources were needed. The district requested and received from the school board approval to increase local support through taxes. At this time the district is almost at the maximum level allowed for local tax support.

Therefore, if the district were to begin again, the curriculum would still be teacher-written, but it would be developed over the summer months to avoid disrupting instructional processes. Furthermore, the initial curriculum contained too much material to be covered in a school year. Other districts may need to keep in mind that the curriculum should include only those units and objectives deemed essential for minimum mastery and that the writing of a curriculum is never completed for it requires constant reexamination and revision.

Summary

Figure 9 summarizes the components of the Effective Schools movement in the Jackson district. At the heart of the movement have been the five correlates implemented simultaneously with zeal. Central to suc-

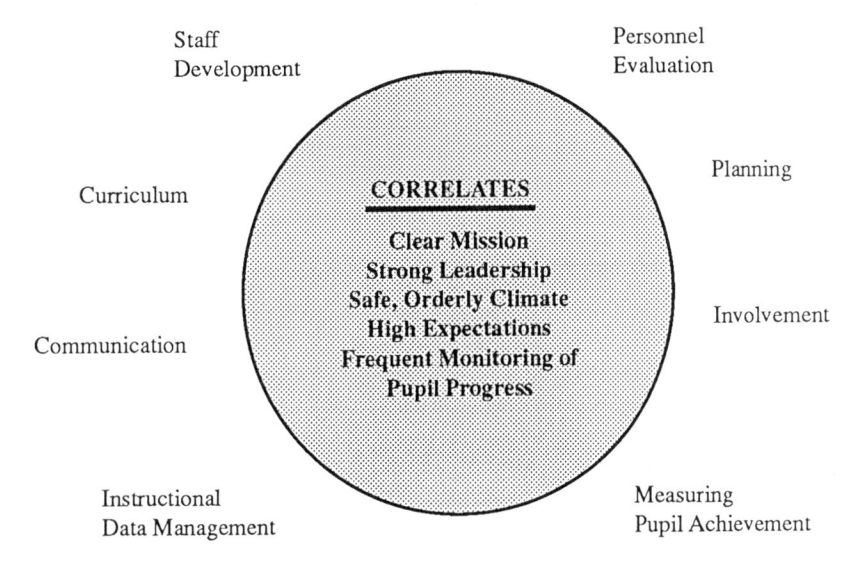

```
              Staff                        Personnel
              Development                  Evaluation

                                                      Planning
    Curriculum         CORRELATES
                       Clear Mission
                       Strong Leadership
                       Safe, Orderly Climate
                       High Expectations       Involvement
    Communication      Frequent Monitoring of
                       Pupil Progress


    Instructional                          Measuring
    Data Management                        Pupil Achievement
```

Figure 9. Correlates and Components of the Effective School process in Jackson, Mississippi

cess of the movement has been the involvement of all groups who have an interest in the schools either directly or indirectly: the school board, administration, teachers, parents, students, classified employees, businessmen, and other community members. Much planning has been and continues to be done. The curriculum has been restructured, tests have been written, pupil achievement has been measured, and data have been analyzed to determine district progress, and directions changed as needed. Both staff development and the personnel evaluation system have received increased attention. Communication continues to be of major importance as programs are implemented.

Community support reached a major milestone in 1986 when the Jackson Chamber of Commerce established an Education Foundation Trust Fund of one million dollars. School and community members raised approximately $250,000 in cash and have accepted about $400,000 in pledges to be received in 1990. The Chamber of Commerce has set an ultimate goal of $2 million. Because of the trust, more money was available to fund projects which supplement the curriculum. Interested teachers submitted grant proposals to a committee which selected 20 projects for funding. Grant winners were selected based on (1) rewarding academic achievement, (2) supplementing and enriching the curriculum, (3) affecting a large number of students, and (4) demonstrating measurable results.

Eight years have passed since the superintendent first asked the question, "Can all children learn?" and received the answer yes. Those who answered yes and those whose yes came with reservations have come to realize that though the journey toward equity and excellence has been long and at times difficult, the results have been well worth the effort expended. Ask anyone in the district now, "Can all children learn?" The answer will be even more resounding than before. "Yes! All children can learn! Just look at ours!"

Implementing Effective Schools Research in Spencerport, New York

Robert E. Sudlow
Assistant Superintendent for Instruction

Spencerport (New York) School District
Became involved in Effective Schools process in 1982–83

Community

Population
18,901 (1980 census)

Largely suburban. Suburb of Rochester. Employers in high technology factories and industries of the Rochester area include: Kodak, Xerox, Bausch & Lomb, and Taylor.

Almost all middle class. Six percent qualify for free-and-reduced price lunch. Median family income (1980 census) $27,135. Per capita income (1980 census) $12,643. Fifteen percent are poor.

School District

Enrollment
3,322

Ethnic Composition (percent)
African-American	2
Asian-American	2
Caucasian	95
Hispanic	1

Schools

Per Pupil Expenditure
1988–1989 $5,577

Percent bussed
95

Area (in square miles)
37.1

Elementary schools (K–6)	3
Middle Schools or Junior high schools	1
High school (10–12)	1

Number of Staff
Administrators	15
Certified teachers	211
Support staff	249

Student-Teacher Ratio
(Classroom Teacher—Total staff/student ratio is much lower)
Elementary	24:1
Junior high	23:1
High school	22:1

Percent college-bound
4 year college	50
2 year college	26
Other post-secondary	17
	93

Abstract

This long case study is printed in its entirety because it details extensive steps taken to plan and then implement the Effective Schools process in a suburban setting. Ronald Edmonds believed the Spencerport plan was an "outstanding" operational example of the research. The opening pages of the case study precisely define the phases and the pitfalls of the "start-up" of the Effective Schools process for school improvement. A flow chart shows the pre-planning or development phase of the program, and the implementation phase that had annual cycles.

Funding for the school improvement program is budgeted in a line item as a symbol of commitment to the Effective Schools process, as a management tool for planning, and as a recognition and incentive system for work well done.

The actual language from the district's master plan is detailed in this case study and integrated into the narrative describing the faculty's and principals' rationale for planning, goal-setting, and articulation of the schools' missions. The "excellence goal" and "annual school improvement goal" are fine examples of this explication.

Especially useful in this case is the detailed description of the motivating influence of the process of disaggregating data and reporting the analysis to all school personnel over the years of the project. It shows how this process is applied.

The development of curriculum and the staff development program are also highlights of the Spencerport case study. Although Spencerport took five years to complete a system-wide curriculum development process, it may under certain circumstances be accomplished more quickly. The same may be the case with preparing criterion-referenced tests for the district. Spencerport developed these processes themselves, so therefore proceeded slowly.

Practitioners like those in Spencerport are the hub of the Effective Schools process development efforts. Most of the systems used by schools and districts to support the school improvement and Effective Schools process were designed by school-site personnel working with central-office administrators, under the guidance of university and other consultants. The mode and collaboration of Effective Schools Research consultant/trainer with district and school personnel is a true partnership, as well described in this case study.

Overview

In 1982–83 the Spencerport Central School District decided to see if the Effective Schools Research could be used to help a good school system become better. The fact that a significant number of unrelated research studies discovered a common set of factors which were present in Effective Schools (Edmonds, 1979) was impressive. Although this research was primarily conducted—and first implemented—in urban minority elementary schools, the research held promise for helping a good school district become better.

Spencerport's More Effective Schools/Teaching Project is unique because Spencerport is significantly different from the locale in which the early Effective Schools Research was conducted and in which the early school improvement projects based upon the Effective Schools Research were implemented.

Early Projects	Spencerport
urban	suburban, and by some standards, rural
large minority population	5% minority
poor	middle class
large districts	small district (3,322 pupils in 1988–89)
project done in some individual elementary schools	district-wide K–12 project for all buildings

Spencerport's More Effective Schools/Teaching Project started to evolve during 1981 when Superintendent Joseph Clement, Jr., and Assistant Superintendent for Instruction Robert E. Sudlow studied the emerging Effective Schools Research. They were intrigued by the fact that numerous independent research studies conducted throughout the United States and in England reported similar findings, something rare in education. Further, these findings made sense to the practitioners in Spencerport. They agreed with the conclusions that learning is a function of the school and that "All children can learn." The correlates identified by the research seemed crucial, basic, noncontroversial elements of a good educational program. If they were not present in Spencerport's schools, they should be.

The Spencerport Central School District also was experiencing declining enrollment. Two schools had been closed and teachers with seven to ten years experience in the district were being laid off. Given an increasingly stable staff, Spencerport needed to infuse systematically new ideas and new research into the district. Spencerport professionals believed they had an obligation to consider significant new research hitherto unavailable to the profession. They also believed that examining this research would be an excellent vehicle for introducing new concepts and reexamining long-held beliefs.

After considerable investigation, the assistant superintendent for instruction contacted Ronald Edmonds and Lawrence Lezotte at the Institute for Research on Teaching located at Michigan State University. They decided to work with Spencerport because it was significantly different from the locales of the early Effective Schools projects.

During the fall and early winter of 1982–1983 the superintendent and assistant superintendent met with each building faculty to describe and discuss the Effective Schools Research. The videotape "Teacher and School Effectiveness" from the Association for Supervision and Curriculum Development (ASCD) was shown to each faculty, and later that fall to the board of education. At the same time the board received a summary of the research and a proposed plan of action.

In January of 1983 Edmonds and Lezotte met with the board of education to describe their research. That evening the board approved a recommendation to work with the Institute of Research on Teaching to learn more about effective teaching, effective administration, and effective schools. The administrative council, the curriculum council, and K–12 teacher leaders learned of the board's decision in early February in a memo which set forth highlights from the research and listed events planned for designing and implementing the project.

Later in February Edmonds and Lezotte held awareness sessions for the administrative council, the curriculum council, and the teachers' union executive committee. No administrator attended the meeting with the union. This was a crucial move because of the importance of the teachers' union in the social structure of the school system.

After the awareness sessions in March of 1983 Edmonds and Lezotte conducted an intensive two-day staff development program for the administrative council. And, a similar two-day program was held for the district-wide leadership planning team.

The district-wide leadership planning team consisted of two key teachers from each building and each building principal. Other members of the team were the district's testing expert, a representative from the teachers' association, and the assistant superintendent for instruction. The members of this group worked many hours to learn the research and to find ways to apply it to suburban Spencerport. From the beginning, this team exhibited considerable leadership

Schedule 1:	Awareness/Developmental Phase of the Project
Fall 1982	Pre-planning
Fall-winter 1982	Awareness Building Faculties Key Leadership Groups
Winter 1983	Inservice Leadership Planning Team
Spring 1983	Development of Master Plan
May 20, 1983	Awareness (Superintendent's Conference Day) Total K–12 Faculty
June 15, 1983	Approval by Superintendent
June 22, 1983	Approval by Board of

in inaugurating and conducting the project in each building.

The leadership planning team was charged with the task of preparing a master plan for school improvement in Spencerport based upon Effective Schools Research. The Team was given a firm deadline for sending a report to the superintendent. If the team had not been given this deadline, it might still be talking about the research, not implementing it. The team developed and unanimously approved a master plan that was sent to the superintendent in June 1983. The superintendent and the board approved the plan before the end of June (Sudlow, 1983). This planning process is detailed above.

Through the awareness and planning processes, the More Effective Schools/Teaching Project became an official, major thrust of the district. (see Schedule 1) With the board's approval of the plan, neither the superintendent nor anyone else had the authority to arbitrarily launch the district in a different direction. Hence the staff is protected from a sudden change and from the "faddism" that too often bedevils school districts.

When the plan was completed, Ronald Edmonds remarked that it was an "outstanding" operational statement of the research. Subsequently other school systems have developed master plans based upon the Spencerport model. This model is used by rural school districts (e.g., South Lewis, New York), other suburban school districts (e.g., Valley Central, Montgomery, New York), urban school districts (e.g., Cohoes, New York) and schools for the deaf (e.g., School for the Deaf, Rochester, New York).

One unique feature of the master plan is a statement of the basic assumptions (shown on p. 157) upon which the project rests. The process of writing and revising these assumptions significantly helped members of the leadership planning team to internalize the research. Ownership by the team members for the project increased as they debated and agreed upon the assumption as well as the other segments of the plan.

Another unique feature of the master plan was a statement of functions of the building planning team in each school:

Functions of Building Planning Teams

To develop a plan for the building based upon the needs assessment data. This plan shall emphasize strengths and areas of needed improvement.

To identify and agree upon the most important needs and subsequent objectives.

To share this plan of action with the total faculty for the purposes of study, discussion, and change before adopting a final plan of action by October 1.

To establish specific vehicles for both formal and informal ongoing communication with the faculty so that its deliberation are, and are perceived as, open.

To establish regular opportunities for input and review throughout the school year.

To meet periodically throughout the year to monitor and to facilitate the implementation of the plan.

To prepare a new plan for the second and future years based upon the annual evaluation of the building plan.

Building planning teams are small, only five to nine members, because in small groups everyone is likely to be an active participant. The members are the key leadership group of the school, not the grade-level chairpeople or the department chairpersons. The teams consist of the principal and teachers respected by their colleagues who are broadly representative of the faculty. (The principal personally must attend every meeting, on time, and leave at the end, because teachers often key on the behavior, not the words, of the principal.)

For the first year of the project, teacher members of the district-wide leadership planning team were ex-

Spencerport's Fifteen Assumptions About More Effective Schools/Teaching Projects

1. Virtually all students are educable when educability is defined as pupil acquisition of basic school skills.

2. Research concludes that school effects are more powerful than familial effects. This conclusion must not be taken to mean there is no familial effect in pupil acquisition of academic skills. In some families, background does not limit a student's ability to acquire basic school skills, but some families can enhance student achievement well beyond basic school skills.

3. The annual goal of education is to bring each student to at least the standard minimum academic performance for that grade level so that he or she can perform successfully in the next grade level. Further, the goal of education is to prepare students so that they can make as many choices as possible. Thus, upon graduation from high school all students should be able, as a result of their education, to choose whether or not to enter college, or to attend another form of post-high school education, or to obtain a job.

4. There is a positive correlation between academic student achievement and staff expectations.

5. An emphasis upon learning, upon academic achievement, is the prime purpose of public education.

6. Teachers and principals can and do make a key difference in the quality of education each child receives.

7. A school building is a complex social system with a set of norms, beliefs, and patterns of behavior which can facilitate or hinder learning.

8. Collaborative, cooperative, collegial, supportive, non-coercive planning, especially at the building level and accompanied by support from district office personnel is the key approach to improvement.

9. The building principal has a key role in establishing the climate of his or her building.

10. Change is a process, a series of related events, not one event.

11. Ideal change fosters ownership and commitment by all participants.

12. In many ways, the schools in this district are effective. The challenge is to make them more effective.

13. This project affects all school personnel.

14. Because the climate of a school is dependent upon all of its occupants, the individual school building as a whole is the strategic unit for planned change. To obtain change, attention must be paid to the culture of the schools; focusing on the behavior of individual teachers or students is not sufficient.

15. Focusing on Effective Schools Research may necessitate realignment of other priorities within the building.

pected to be on their building's planning team. They were expected to link the work of the district team to the newly formed building team. Other teachers were selected, depending upon the culture of the building, by election, by volunteering, or by selection. When teachers left teams, other teachers replaced them. Some teachers rejoined their teams after being absent for a year or two.

As the district-wide leadership planning team approached completing its work, it began to plan for operational implementation in each building. This started with a superintendent's conference day held on May 20, 1983 for all teachers and administrators. Ronald Edmonds provided a brief overview of the research. Teachers then completed the needs assessment instrument which the leadership planning team had selected,[1] and professors from Michigan State University described various aspects of effective teaching research.

Each building then selected teachers to be on its building planning team. At approximately the same time achievement tests, mandated New York State tests, and final exams were given. Because the school system had no socioeconomic status (SES) information for each child, the mother's level of education (Frederiksen and Edmonds, 1977) was obtained through the annual census mailed to each resident of the district. Research revealed that responses to the census card request were representative of the community (Sudlow, 1983a). The district proceeded with confidence to conduct the first disaggregated analysis of test data. During the summer of 1983 Edmonds and Lezotte analyzed the Connecticut School Effectiveness Questionnaire needs assessment data and prepared written profiles for each building.[2]

This completed the turnkey phase of implementing the project:

Turnkey Phase of the Project

May–June 1983	Formation of building planning teams
May–June 1983	Initial needs assessment: disaggregated analysis presence of correlates
Early summer 1983	Preparation of school profiles
Late summer 1983	Data analysis of building planning teams
Due by September 1	Preparation of draft plan by building planning teams

As mentioned above, when the project began Edmonds and Lezotte analyzed the data from the Connecticut Questionnaire and prepared a written profile of each school. The building planning teams used this document to prepare their draft plans of action for the 1983–84 school year. Additional staff development was needed to review the data and develop a plan. During the summer of 1984 Dr. Patrick Proctor from the Connecticut State Department of Education[3] trained each team regarding the processes to follow when analyzing needs assessment data and writing a plan. This was a most helpful workshop which many still regard as a highlight of the project.

The right side of Figure 1 presents the annual implementation cycle of building planning teams. The faithful implementation of these steps is the heartbeat of an Effective Schools project. Lawrence Lezotte once observed that "the good news about school improvement is that you can start it any time. The bad news is that once you start, you can't stop!" Figure 1 illustrates this statement.

One step in the annual implementation cycle is review and approval of building plans by the superintendent. If superintendents do exercise the option of disapproving a plan, they should disapprove building plans **only if** building planning teams commit one of the two types of errors teams may make in their initial years. One error is that the action plan is not related to the needs assessment data. For example, suppose that the needs assessment data reveal a major problem in arithmetic and the team proposes to install a content area reading program. Although content area reading is an excellent, valid program, it will not solve a major arithmetic problem. The second error occurs when the team proposes an action plan which "puts the monkey on someone else's back." For example, the school will become effective when the district forms a committee to study student retention policies.

A building planning team should not "place the monkey on someone else's back." How a staff chooses to use its time, money, and human and material resources will determine if a building becomes effective. This is because in the original research, Ef-

---

[1]. The leadership team examined four needs assessment instruments which measured the presence of the correlates and selected the Connecticut School Interview. Because secondary versions of this instrument did not exist, Edmonds and Lezotte helped the team to modify the elementary instrument so that it is appropriate for the junior and senior high school levels.

[2]. The profile for the Cosgrove Junior High School was the last paper Edmonds wrote before his untimely death on July 15, 1983.

[3]. Dr. Proctor currently is assistant superintendent for instruction, Windham Public Schools, Willimantic, Connecticut.

EFFECTIVE SCHOOLS PROJECT FLOWCHART

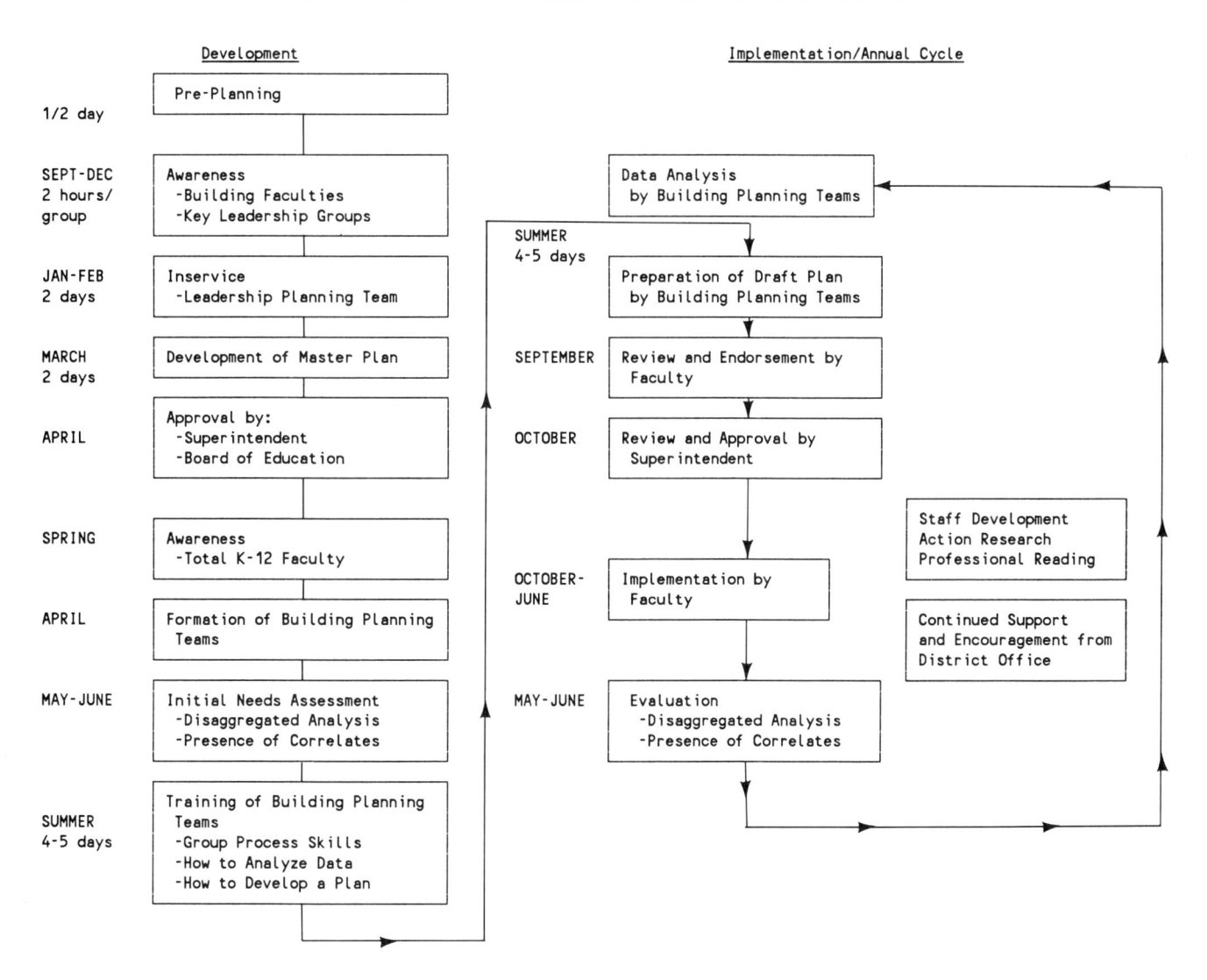

Development

1/2 day	Pre-Planning
SEPT-DEC, 2 hours/group	Awareness -Building Faculties -Key Leadership Groups
JAN-FEB, 2 days	Inservice -Leadership Planning Team
MARCH, 2 days	Development of Master Plan
APRIL	Approval by: -Superintendent -Board of Education
SPRING	Awareness -Total K-12 Faculty
APRIL	Formation of Building Planning Teams
MAY-JUNE	Initial Needs Assessment -Disaggregated Analysis -Presence of Correlates
SUMMER, 4-5 days	Training of Building Planning Teams -Group Process Skills -How to Analyze Data -How to Develop a Plan

Implementation/Annual Cycle

SUMMER, 4-5 days	Data Analysis by Building Planning Teams
	Preparation of Draft Plan by Building Planning Teams
SEPTEMBER	Review and Endorsement by Faculty
OCTOBER	Review and Approval by Superintendent
OCTOBER-JUNE	Implementation by Faculty
MAY-JUNE	Evaluation -Disaggregated Analysis -Presence of Correlates

Staff Development
Action Research
Professional Reading

Continued Support and Encouragement from District Office

Figure 1. Effective Schools Project Flowchart

fective Schools were found where learning was occurring and was independent of the students' socioeconomic class. Three blocks down the street, in the same neighborhood, ineffective schools were found. Because the types of children attending both schools were the same and because issues as per-pupil budget allocations and class size are district-wide, one concludes that although both buildings had the same types of resources, the same "inputs," the adults in building A organized and used their resources differently than did the adults in building B. Hence what a staff does with its resources determines if a building is, or will be, effective.

During the first two years of Spencerport's project several buildings made one of these types of error. When the superintendent rejected part of a plan or raised serious questions about it, there was initial resistance from some building planning team members. Fortunately, other members observed that issues were raised which the team had not considered. Thus, a superintendent's review of a building plan can help a building from inadvertently committing basic errors.

The overall process described above is the essence of a school improvement project based on Effective Schools Research. In summary it consists of:

- Creating extensive awareness.
- Having a representative group of teachers and administrators write a master plan for the district that is approved by the superintendent and board of education
- Administering a needs assessment instrument which measures the presence of the correlates
- Disaggregating student achievement data
- Having a building planning team that represents the faculty and administration. The team annually develops a proposed school improvement plan based upon the needs assessment data and works with colleagues to implement it
- Having faculty review and approve the proposed plan
- Evaluating the effects of the building's plan by re-administering the needs assessment instrument and by disaggregating spring testing data
- Preparing a new or continuing plan of school improvement based upon the spring evaluation data

If a school system includes all of the above in its project, then it is doing a school improvement project based upon the Effective Schools Research. If any one of the above is absent, then the school is conducting a generic school improvement project. These two types of projects are related, but different (Sudlow, 1984a). See Figure 1 for a flowchart of the overall process.

Needed Resources: Funding and Time

Spencerport is not a high wealth "silk stocking" district. Out of the 18 school districts in Monroe County, Spencerport ranked 14th in wealth per pupil and is 16th in expenditures per pupil. Spencerport is 25 percent below the state average in both wealth and expenditures per pupil. (see Table 1)

All of the funds to support the improvement process came out of the local budget. On the average Spencerport spent $20,000 to $25,000 to initiate and support the project. Funds are used for consultant services, clerical costs (part-time clerks to record data and data analysis at peak periods cost $5,000 to $6,000 annually), supplies, and travel. Nationally the median budget for Effective Schools projects is $5,000 per building (Miles, Farrar & Neufeld, 1983). Spencerport recommends this as a guideline for planning an annual budget for an Effective Schools project. (see Table 1)

Time is a symbol of importance and of support. If teachers and administrators are asked to do a project **in addition** to a full work load, that sends one message. If arrangements are made for the project to be a part of the regular work day, another message is sent.

During the developmental phase of the project, released time was provided for the awareness sessions with the curriculum council and the administrative council, and there were other incentives. The evening awareness session for the Teacher's Union Executive Committee occurred in a local restaurant with an excellent dinner paid for by the district. The extensive staff development sessions of the administrative council and the district-wide leadership planning team ran from 9:00 A.M. to 3:00 P.M. Released time was provided for the leadership planning teams to write, edit, and approve the master plan.

The building planning teams worked long and hard. Rather than espousing only one model to meet their time needs (for example, released time one afternoon a month), time was provided in a manner appropriate to the task. For example, full days and half days of released time were provided for specific projects. The school district rented meeting rooms and purchased excellent dinners in good hotels for late afternoon and evening meetings. For the first time in its history, the district authorized summer curriculum monies to support the work of building planning teams (both as groups and as individuals working on projects) during school vacations. Four half days of time were provided each summer for a building planning team to analyze the needs assessment data and write a draft plan. If the teams request additional days, they are provided. In addition, building planning teams met frequently throughout the year either just

Table 1
PER PUPIL - OPERATING EXPENDITURES

Year	State Average	Monroe County Average	Spencerport Actual	Spen. % Below County Average	Spencerport Rank in County
1982–83	N. A.	$ 3,243	$ 2,684	17.2	16/18
1986–87	N. A.	4,420	3,846	12.9	16/18

A district adopting the Spencerport model in 1988 could at a minimum expect to incur the following costs during the development phase of a project.

Planning—1 consultant day @ $500	$ 500
Awareness—0 to 2 consultant days @ $500	500
Training of district leadership team—4 consultant days @ $500	2,000
Training of building planning teams—4 to 5 days @ $500	2,000
Consultant travel expenses	Variable
Sending 5 or 6 key staff members to regional or national Effective Schools awareness conferences @ an estimated $500 each	3,000
Sending 10 to 20 teachers and principals to visit where the replicating district is located.	Variable

Additional part-time clerical help to
    disaggregate test data
    process needs assessment data
    help prepare annual evaluation report
	5,000

Released time during the school year for training of district leadership team. Costs depend upon local substitute teacher rates.	Variable
Summer curriculum pay for the building planning team for training and for developing a plan. Costs depend upon local contract.	Variable
Supplies	5,000

Costs of implementing building plans. This can be done by any one or a combination of the following:
    reallocating current summer curriculum funds
    reallocating current staff development funds
    reallocating current teacher conference funds
    (providing an allocation of $2,000–$4,000 to the buildings)
	2,000–4,000

ESTIMATED TOTAL	$20,000–22,000

before or just after school. Thus, time to operate the project came partly from the district and partly from the teachers.

Symbolic support and regular communication about the project has been and continues to be important. Annually the superintendent meets with each building planning team to ask: How are things going? What are you doing? What can I do to help you? Several times the board of education financed "thank you" receptions and dinners in local hotels. Twice the district sponsored state-wide conferences about the project and featured the work of building planning teams. It is rare for teachers to have the opportunity at state-wide conferences to describe what they do, their accomplishments, and their problems. Teachers who were involved in these conferences said that their participation was motivating and provided a feeling of accomplishment.

Evidence That the Schools Are Improving

Student Achievement

Because the Spencerport district-wide leadership planning team believed that the schools would not immediately achieve the project goal, the team wrote an annual school improvement goal.

Should a school building not be effective according to the project's goal, then the following criteria for school improvement will be used until a building becomes effective: (1) There shall be an annual increase in the proportion of students who demonstrate minimum academic mastery, and (2) There shall be an annual decrease in the proportion of youth demonstrating minimum academic mastery as a function of socioeconomic class.

While the district-wide leadership planning team was meeting and deliberating, Edmonds and Lezotte observed that in the early Effective Schools projects the achievement of all the children rose even though they concentrated primarily on the children just at or below minimum academic mastery (Edmonds and Lezotte, 1983). After considering the implications of this statement the team decided to write a concomitant goal addressing the achievement of children who normally receive excellent scores. Thus through the concomitant goal, the team made this a project for **all** students. The district could not be accused of improving the learning of students who normally fail at the expense of students who normally do well.

The concomitant goal, now called the "excellence goal," states:

The number of students with outstanding achievement will rise:

1. There shall be an annual evaluation of the percentage of students scoring in stanines seven, eight, and nine on the Stanford Achievement Test in Reading Comprehension and Total Mathematics or of the percentage of students scoring at or above 90 percent on a Regents examination.[4]
2. For those subjects in which a significant proportion of the students take a Regents exam, (1) There will be an annual increase in the percentage of students scoring 65 percent or higher, and (2) There will be an annual increase in the percentage of students taking the exam.

Many school districts which traditionally have good or excellent achievement doubt that an Effective Schools project will help them. The "excellence goal" certainly would challenge them. By all traditional criteria Spencerport was a good, respected school system. Spencerport wanted to use the Effective Schools Research to help a good school system become better. The "excellence goal" is an important part of the effort.

Spencerport did not want the starting of the Effective Schools project to give the impression to constituents (teachers, administrators, students, board of education, community) that the school system was ineffective, a reason many districts may not embark upon an Effective Schools project. This problem was solved by placing the word *More* in the project title: "More Effective Schools/Teaching Project."

Evaluation data for the project are presented annually in open session to the board of education. The first annual report on school improvement was presented in October 1984 (Sudlow, 1984b). For each building the report presents data using disaggregated analyses of student achievement that show how students are improving and the degree to which the correlates of an Effective School are present. A summary of the report is distributed to all employees, both professional and support staff. Each principal and each member of a building planning team receives all the data for his or her building.

The annual evaluation report is significant because it causes teachers and administrators to realize that the district is serious about the project. Further, it provides the board of education with evidence that the project is improving both the quantity and quality of student learning and that the climate of the schools is improving. As a result, board support for the project has continued. (See Table 2 for definitions.)

---

4. New York Regents Examinations are criterion-referenced tests developed annually by the State Education Department. They generally are considered appropriate for the average and above-average student, the college-bound student.

Table 2
Evidence of School Improvement

Evidence that the schools are improving as a result of the project needs to be measured against the project's goals. The master plan sets forth the following goals for each building in the district:

1. Ninety-five percent or greater of all the students at each grade level should demonstrate minimum academic mastery. Students who achieve minimum academic mastery have been prepared so that they will be predictably successful in the next grade in either their own school district or in any other school district throughout the nation. Minimum academic mastery is measured by performance on a standardized achievement test (preferably criterion-referenced, otherwise norm-referenced).
2. There shall be no significant difference in the proportion of youth failing to demonstrate minimum academic mastery as a function of socioeconomic class.
3. The above two conditions shall have been obtained for a minimum of three consecutive years.

This goal can be illustrated as follows:

	Low Socioeconomic Classes	Middle and Upper Socioeconomic Classes
At or above minimum academic mastery	$\geq 95\%$	$\geq 95\%$
Below minimum academic mastery	$\leq 5\%$	$\geq 5\%$

Two phrases, "minimum academic mastery" and "socioeconomic class," need to be defined to understand the project's goals. There are:

1. *Minimum Academic Mastery.* Students who achieve this standard will be predictably successful in the next grade either in this or in any other school district throughout the nation. Minimum academic mastery shall be measured by performance on a standardized achievement (norm- or criterion-referenced) test. The cutoff point between minimum and unsuccessful academic mastery shall be established in advance.
2. Socioeconomic class is determined by the number of years of formal education of the student's mother. If the level of the mother's formal education is not available, then the level of the father's formal education will be used. Should a child not be living with his or her parents, then the number of years of formal education of the surrogate female parent shall be used.

These definitions were made available to the field (Sudlow 1984a, 1985), and are used in at least two states, South Carolina (*School Effectiveness*, 1985) and New York (*New York State School Improvement Program Guidebook*, 1987).

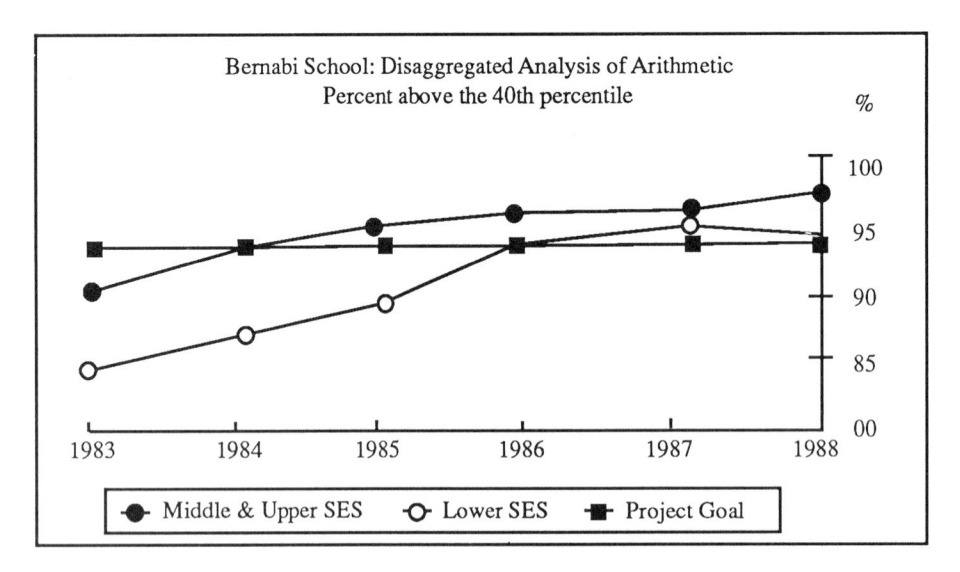

Figure 2. Bernabi School: Disaggregated Analysis of Arithmetic

Project Goal

When the Spencerport disaggregated analyses of student achievement were studied, two categories of effectiveness emerged based on Regents exams and the Stanford Achievement Test. They are:

1. *Effectiveness*—95 percent or greater of both the lower SES group and the middle and upper SES groups attain minimum academic mastery.
2. *Near Effectiveness*—90 percent or greater of both the lower SES group and the middle and upper SES groups attain minimum academic mastery.

The June 1988 data, for example, show the levels of achievement for Spencerport's schools and for how many years and are displayed in Table 3.

In Figure 2 the disaggregated analysis for Bernabi School arithmetic is presented. The project goal was that 95 percent of all students, regardless of socioeconomic status shall achieve minimum academic mastery. This is represented by the straight line. The proportion of middle and upper SES students who attain minimum academic mastery is represented by a solid circle. The data for the lower SES students is represented by an open circle.

There are many ways to measure achievement. Spencerport identified minimal academic mastery as scoring at or above the 40th percentile on the Stanford Achievement Test. The Stanford Achievement Test was selected on the basis of a three-year study to ascertain which achievement test best measured district curriculum. Of all the major norm-referenced tests, the Stanford to a substantial degree measures Spencerport's intended curriculum (Ferris, 1982).

Figure 2 represents the ideal, what should be. The trend lines for both SES groups are upward **and** the achievement gap between the two groups is steadily decreasing. Ninety-five percent, or greater, of both groups have scored at or above minimum academic mastery for the three most recent consecutive years, illustrating the classical definition of effectiveness.

A graph typical of an improving school (here Munn school was selected) appears below in Figure 3. In this figure there is an upward trend line for both the lower and the middle and upper SES groups. The achievement gap between the two groups has varied, but appears to be decreasing.

School Improvement Goal

The school improvement goal (interim project goal) which appears earlier calls, in part, for an annual increase in the proportion of students scoring above minimum academic mastery until 95 percent of all students (including the mildly handicapped, the learning disabled) score at or above minimum academic mastery. The effect of this goal upon student achievement in reading and mathematics is shown in the following tables.

Table 3
Effectiveness and Near Effectiveness Student Achievement by School

For Reading Achievement at various schools

1. Near Effectiveness   Bernabi (Grades 1–6), Stanford Achievement Test, 4 years

2. Effective   Wilson (Grades 10–12), Regents Competency Test, 5 years

For Mathematics Achievement

1. Near Effectiveness   Bernabi (Grades 1–6), Stanford Achievement Test, 2 years
   Munn (Grades 1–6), Stanford Achievement Test, 1 year
   Town Line (Grades 1–6), Stanford Achievement Test, 1 year
   Cosgrove (Grades 7–8), Stanford Achievement Test, 7th and 8th Math, 1 year
   Cosgrove, Math Regents Competency Test, 2 years
   Cosgrove, Math Regents Exam, 1 year

2. Effective   Bernabi, Stanford Achievement Test, 3 years
   Cosgrove, Math Regents Exam, 2 years

For Science Achievement

1. Near Effectiveness   Cosgrove, Earth Science Regents Exam, 3 years
   Wilson, Science Regents Exams, 2 years

2. Effective   Wilson, Science Regents Exam, 1 year

For Social Studies Achievement

1. Near Effectiveness   Wilson, Regents Exam, 4 years

For English Achievement

1. Near Effectiveness   Wilson, Regents Exam, 2 years

2. Effective   Wilson, Regents Exam, 2 years

For Writing Achievement

1. Effective   Cosgrove, Regents Competency Test, 2 years
   Wilson, Regents Competency Test, 5 years

Detailed data to support the above appear in the Fifth Annual Report (Sudlow, 1988a).

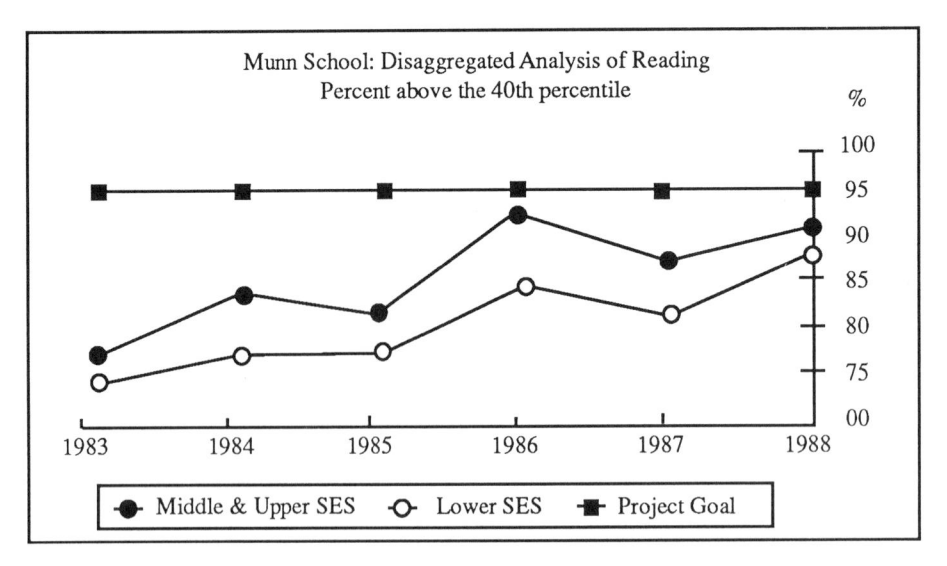

Figure 3. Munn School: Disaggregated Analysis of Reading

Table 4
Reading comprehension: Percent of students at or above the 40th percentile on the Stanford Achievement Test

School	82–83*	83–84	84–85	85–85	86–87	87–88
Bernabi (Grades 1–6)	87	90	91	92	93	95
Munn (Grades 1–6)	74	80	78	83	81	90
Town Line (Grades 1–6)	77	80	83	85	87	87
Cosgrove (Grades 7–8)	72	76	78	80	80	83

*Base line year

The tables show that Spencerport started with high proportions of the student body above minimum academic mastery and that these proportions improved, thus further substantiating the claim that the school improvement goal is being met.

Concomitant-Excellence Goal

By one stroke this goal made our project advantageous for all students because it connected the achievement of students who normally do well with those at risk. Briefly, it says that the proportion of students who attain scores indicative of excellence (i.e., stanines 7-8-9 or a grade of 90 percent or better on a Regents exam) will either remain the same or increase. It also calls for an annual increase in the proportion of students passing and taking Regents examinations. This standard is demonstrated also in the results of student scores on the Stanford Achievement Test. (See Tables 4, 5, 6)

Table 6 shows that Spencerport started with high proportions of the student body scoring in the top three stanines. Nevertheless, the proportion increases in ten of twelve instances. An analysis such as this, that is of the proportion of students who obtain excellent scores, is not one which school systems normally develop. When the school district prepared this analysis, both teachers and administrators were happily surprised at the number of students who did well. This motivated them to improve their efforts.

Table 5
Total Math: Percent of students at or above the 40th percentile on the Stanford Achievement Test

School	82–83*	83–84	84–85	85–86	86–87	87–88
Bernabi (Grades 1–6)	89	91	93	97	96	96
Munn (Grades 1–6)	86	84	88	90	89	93
Town Line (Grades 1–6)	83	88	87	88	89	92
Cosgrove (Grades 7–8)	81	85	86	86	92	92

Table 6
Percent of Students Scoring in Stanines 7–9 on the Stanford Achievement Test

	82–83*	83–84	84–85	85–86	86–87	87–88
Reading Comprehension						
School						
Bernabi (Grades 1–6)	47	47	49	47	49	56
Munn (Grades 1–6)	30	32	34	40	40	45
Town Line (Grades 1–6)	41	44	46	45	48	51
Cosgrove (Grades 7–8)	34	27	32	34	35	34
Total Mathematics						
School						
Bernabi (Grades 1–6)	55	57	62	68	74	72
Munn (Grades 1–6)	50	47	53	56	53	59
Town Line (Grades 1–6)	49	50	51	55	62	60
Cosgrove (Grades 7–8)	34	45	49	45	52	60
Subject						
Language (Grades 7–8)	31	35	35	39	40	34
Listening (Grades 7–8)	29	27	26	28	32	31
Science (Grade 8)	37	26	28	24	31	30
Soc. Studies (Grade 8)	33	37	38	33	37	41

*Base line year
For a frame of reference with which to interpret the above, nationally 23 percent of the students score in stanines 7–9 of the Stanford Achievement Test.

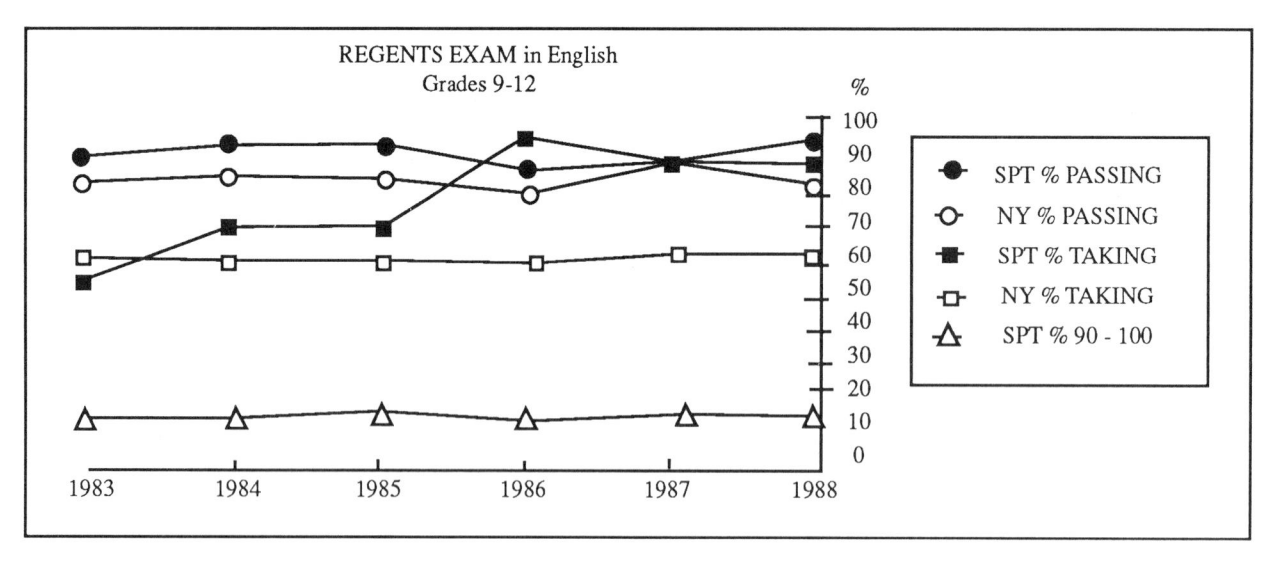

Figure 4. Regents Exam in English, Grades 9–12

The impact of the excellence goal upon the 9–12 instructional program can be seen in the graph in Figure 4, data on Regents Exam achievement in English.

In this graph Spencerport data for the percent passing and taking are represented by the filled symbols and New York State data are represented by the open symbols. The proportion of Spencerport students taking the comprehensive (i.e. it measures grades 9–11) eleventh grade Regents exam in English increased from 53 percent in 1983 to 86 percent in 1988. At the same time the percent passing dropped from the 95 percent range to 92 percent—which is equal to or better than the state average percent passing when only slightly over half of the students throughout the state take the exam. Further the proportion of students attaining excellent scores of 90 percent or higher increased from 7 percent in 1983 to 9 percent in 1988.

"This is proof that all kids can learn," one administrator commented while discussing the graph. Such a dramatic increase in the percent of students taking the course, being successful in it and successfully passing the state exam, could only occur as a result of teachers who, in private and in their classroom, have high expectations for success and then take action. It could not have occurred as a result of administrative intervention. In the past, administrative efforts to resolve problems with various Regents exams resulted in more students being successful, but these efforts did not increase the proportion of the student body taking the academically more challenging Regents level courses and passing the accompanying examinations.

Other Student Data

Ron Edmonds observed that a key gatekeeper course in most high schools is algebra. If a student takes it, then he or she is much more likely upon graduation to be able to choose whether or not to go on to further education or to enter the world of work. If, on the other hand, a student takes general math instead of algebra, his or her possibilities of being able to choose to go on to further education are greatly diminished. Hence a school should structure its instructional program so that all students should be able to take algebra and be successful in it (Edmonds, 1983).

As the Spencerport math teachers thought about this, they decided in the spring of 1987 that if they had the general math students for a little more time they could teach them algebra. The added time was found by using study hall periods opposite a Monday, Wednesday, and alternative Friday gym class. Instead of sitting in study halls, students gained ground in math by having it 7 1/2 periods a week. The impact of this upon the proportion of students taking Regents algebra appears in Figure 5.

Instruction was modified so that one half of the additional time was spent on the content and one half was spent on the affective domain—because these traditionally were the students who had been least successful in math and probably did not like it.

Many of these students were successful. End-of-the-year results on the Regents exam were:

A—7%   B—22%   C—26%   D—19%   F—26%

Four of the seven students who failed the Regents did so by only one to four points. These results are outstanding for students who previously were considered not capable of taking and passing the Regents algebra course. A related program with similar results also occurred in the ninth grade Regents earth science course (Sudlow and Werth, 1988).

As teachers' and administrators' expectations of what students could do increased, so too did their

REGENTS EXAM ALGEBRA
9th Grade

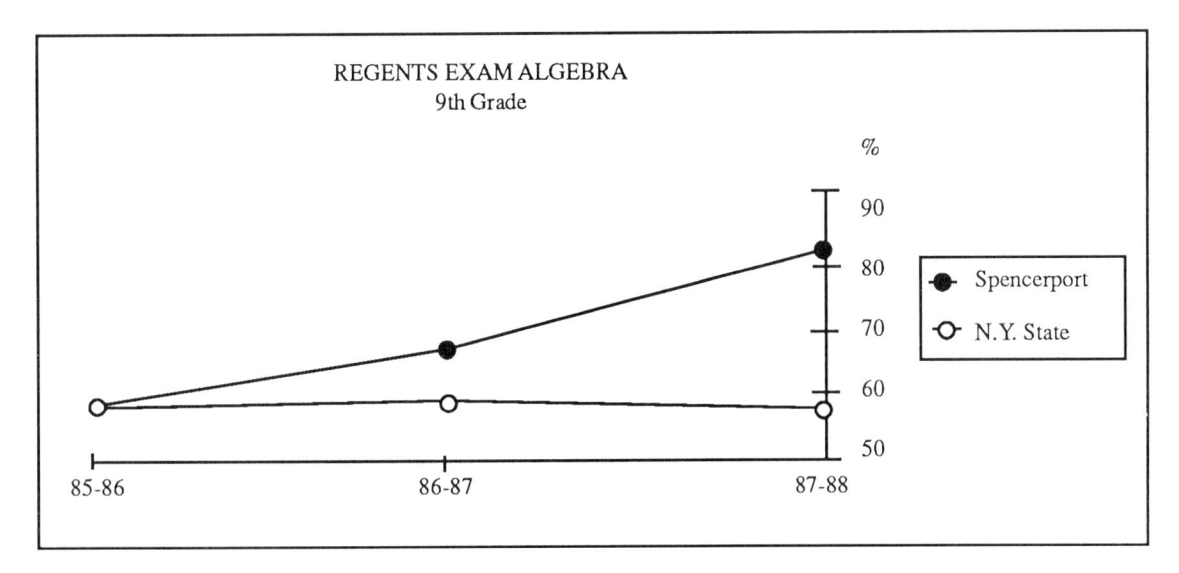

Figure 5. Regents Exam in Algebra, 9th Grade

level of aspiration. This resulted in far more students earning the academically demanding Regents diploma than ever before (Figure 6). When reading this graph, it is useful to know that in school districts serving the highest socioeconomic areas of the county, 65 to 70 percent of the students receive a Regents diploma.

Presence of the Correlates of Effective Schools

To ascertain the extent to which correlates of an Effective School are present in a building, a needs assessment survey based upon the Effective Schools Research was taken. The building planning team, composed of the principals plus a small group of respected, representative teachers, analyzed the data from the needs assessment instrument to determine priorities and to develop a proposed plan of action. This plan of action was presented to the faculty for approval.

The Connecticut School Effectiveness Questionnaire, an instrument developed by the Connecticut State Department of Education, was selected because it specifically ascertains the presence of the correlates of an Effective School. Validity was established through a review of the literature and a content validation study. Construct validity was established through multitrait-multimethod analysis (Villanova, 1984; Proctor and Villanova, 1984).

Because the interview was prepared solely for elementary schools, Spencerport modified it, under the direction of Edmonds and Lezotte, to be appropriate also at the junior and senior high school levels.

When Spencerport started its project, for all practical purposes the correlates used to describe Effective Schools were absent. The district is making substantial progress in manifesting the correlates of an Effective School. This is summarized in Table 7.

Personnel Data

If the data show that both the equity **and** quality of student achievement have improved, then what is the reaction, the opinion of the principals and teachers who daily work to implement building plans? During late 1987 and early 1988 an outside researcher interviewed each principal and representative members of each building planning team. Interviews were confidential. The interviewer reported:

As the interviewees talked about the project, many topics were mentioned by more than one person. For example, the project was credited with improving communication. They mentioned more communication between teachers, teachers and principals, and between staff in the schools and the central office. Several mentioned the project's healing effect on wounds from a strike in the mid-nineteen-seventies.

The project was also credited with encouraging collaboration. The feeling seemed to be that they were all together now and working on the same goals. Central office seemed to have demonstrated its long-term commitment to the project by providing the necessary resources and by allowing building autonomy within the district guidelines. Principals accepted criticism of their instructional leadership and had delegated some decisions to the building committees. Teachers expressed ownership in the project and satisfaction in being involved in the decision-making processes of the district. Some felt more professional because of the project activities.

Adult learning was mentioned frequently as a byproduct of the project. Two district staff development programs, "Elements of Instruction" and "TESA" (Teacher Expectations for Student Achievement) were named specifically, but also interviewees mentioned informal staff development through project activities. This learning was recognized as a necessary means to the desired end, an Effective School with ef-

172 Case Studies in Effective Schools Research

```
          PERCENT RECEIVING REGENTS DIPLOMAS
                     1983-88                              %

                                                          70

                                       ●──────●──────●
                                    ╱                    60
                                ●                            ● Spencerport
                     ○                                       ○ N.Y. State
          ●─────●────                                     50
          ○─────○         ○──────○──────○
                                                          40

                                                          00
          1983   1984   1985   1986   1987   1988
```

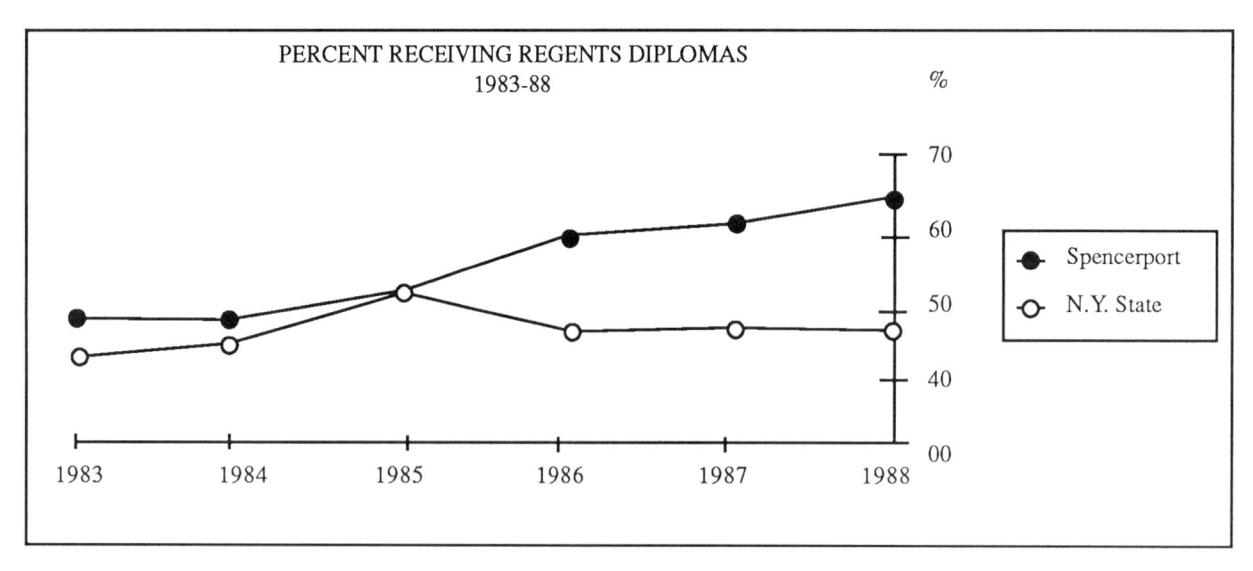

Figure 6. Percent Receiving Regents Diplomas, 1983–88

Table 7
Number of correlates in place in each school[a]

School:	Bernabi (K–6)	Munn (K–6)	Town Line (K–6)	Cosgrove (7–9)	Wilson (10–12)	Total	Possible[b]
May 1983*	1		2			3	35
May 1984	5	2	3			10	35
May 1985	5	3	5	2	3	18	35
May 1986	7	5	5	2	5	24	35
May 1987	7	5	7	7	4	30	35
May 1988	7	7	7	7	6	34	35

*Base line year
(a) A correlate is considered to be present when two-thirds of the faculty indicate on a needs assessment instrument that the characteristics which comprise the correlate are present in the building.
(b) Seven correlates per building times five buildings.

fective teachers. The adjectives fun, stimulating, and enjoyable were associated with project involvement. However, stress and accountability were also discussed. One interviewee was planning to retire early and another was planning to work longer, due to the project (Wooley, 1987).

During the spring of 1988 a free-lance writer also interviewed a large number of teachers and administrators to write a series of eight articles about the project. During the interviews she noticed several underlying themes regarding the project's impact. Her observations noted many patterns as follows:

When I began interviewing teachers for a series of Public Information articles on the More Effective Schools/Teaching Project in Spencerport, I at first regarded similarities of attitudes and responses as a vague coincidence. As I talked with a larger random sample of teachers from all five building in the district, it became obvious to me that what I was hearing clearly reflected the impact of the project at all levels, in many different areas.

No matter which correlate we were discussing, teachers used different words to describe similar feelings. The most overwhelming sentiment was that the project BREEDS COLLEGIALITY.

"It's like we all care about the same thing."

"It gave us a reason to sit down and talk about what we all care most about—doing our best with kids."

"It gives us a process for problem-solving that involves ownership and agreement."

Over and over again, teachers spoke favorably about how the committee work, the needs assessment, the focus on testing and curriculum, had forced them into a type of COMMUNICATION with their colleagues which they found both satisfying and stimulating.

Many referred to the fact that the way the project is organized to include EVERYONE in the district from the administration to the custodians, fostered a sense of real participation and OWNERSHIP. They felt their opinions mattered.

Several people I spoke with, most notably one principal, reflected on how many aspects of the project (e.g., ELEMENTS OF INSTRUCTION AND TESA) and re-kindled the kind of excitement and enthusiasm he had felt as a young teacher and had long since lost. And a general reference to a renewed feeling of PROFESSIONALISM was often repeated.

"The project has given teachers the opportunity to teach and the students the opportunity to learn."

"It has made it so we have a good feeling about coming to that door every morning."

"We just want to be able to teach what the kids need to know, share with out colleagues, and have a little fun along the way. Now we are doing that."

Part of their honesty revealed skepticism, past and present. Some teachers admitted that not every member of their faculty was involved in implementing, or necessarily even believed in, the project. Some admitted that it is possible for someone to not put forth the work and still reap the benefits of the changes that are occurring. But no one suggested that this was sufficient reason to abandon the project or coerce a colleague. There were also recurring statements that indicated that some teachers felt that some of the things that have been precipitated by the project would have happened eventually anyhow. They saw the project as a means of accelerating some things because their importance became clearly recognized.

Past skepticism was seen as a necessary part of the process. Few believed that the project would be able to deliver the kind of results it seemed to promise and are proud and happy to have been proven wrong. They referred often to initial FEARS about the project; the COMMITMENT of time and effort it would require, the hesitancy to CHANGE established patterns and practices and above all, the level of ACCOUNTABILITY that is so obvious, fine-tuned, and ongoing.

One day, as I explored the work of a correlate team with a teacher, I shared with her my overwhelming feeling that everything I was hearing had led me to believe that if one were to apply the process of the project to a marriage, a family, or a business—that too would become more successful. We both agree that what was being taught then, BY teachers and FOR students, was really a PLAN FOR LIFE!

Perhaps that is why the quality of life in Spencerport's school buildings seems so positive and productive today. There is something good happening there for everyone (Werth, 1988).

Influence of the Effective Schools Process Upon Program Components

Curriculum

"How can you do district-wide curriculum projects if the emphasis of an Effective Schools process is upon individual buildings?" is a frequently asked question. In 1981 Spencerport implemented a long-range plan for systematic curriculum study and renewal. This plan established district committees, processes, and timelines for the study and improvement of each curricular area. Consequently because of this plan and efforts which preceded it, prior to the start of Spencerport's More Effective Schools/Teaching Project there were district curriculum guides for each of the major curricular areas.

Since the project started, the timelines for the long range curriculum plan and the More Effective Schools/Teaching Project have run on parallel tracks. While buildings work on installing the correlates, each district subject-area curriculum planning committee reviews and revised the K–12 curriculum. Because the process calls for considerable systematic dialogue, feedback, and evaluation over an extended period of time between the curriculum planning committee and the faculties in each building, teacher implementation of revised curricula is a smooth, effective process. This process is summarized below.

Year 1—Program Presentation

The curriculum planning committees for subject areas make presentations to the administration council and to the board of education on the major historical movements in the subject areas both locally and nationally since 1945, how the current instructional program for the subject area is organized and taught, and the results of the current evaluation data.

The purpose of these presentations is not to say "These are our needs." The purpose of these presentations is to discuss with key audiences "What is (for example) mathematics education in Spencerport as viewed by mathematicians?" These teaching presentations serve as an extended anticipatory set for the extensive needs assessment work which will commence the next year. Another purpose is to provide (or require) the curriculum planning committees with the opportunity to become thoroughly acquainted with what is occurring in the district prior to embarking upon a needs assessment.

Year 2—Needs Assessment

A traditional needs assessment of the strengths and weaknesses of the curricular area is conducted. Recommendations for improvement emanate from this needs assessment.

During the summer following the needs assessment, a team of representative teachers from throughout the district meets to consider the results of the needs assessment, the latest changes in State Education Department syllabi, and current and emerging trends in their subject area. Using these data, the committee either develops a new curriculum guide for the district's teachers to use or revises an existing curriculum guide.

Year 3—Introduction to the Staff

Meetings are held with principals, faculties, and/or departments to review and discuss the content of the new curriculum guide. Staff development is designed to assist teachers in implementing the guide. Depending upon the complexity of the topics, a few short sessions or an extended year-long inservice for the new curriculum might be needed. Materials requisite to implementing the guide are identified and ordered.

If these steps are omitted, if a district moves immediately from curriculum writing to full implementation, massive indigestion can result. Teachers might well feel that something is being "shoved down their throats." This used to occur in Spencerport. With eagerness "to get on with it," "to see results," teachers and administrators skipped the orientation phase. The analysis of the symptoms caused by skipping the orientation phase led to the development of the long-range curriculum plan.

Year 4—Pilot Implementation

If the orientation phase requires only a short timeline, then pilot implementation can occur during year 4. After the introduction to the staff (Year 3) is completed, teachers use the curriculum guide in the classroom. At the same time they are asked to report periodically the strengths and, more importantly, the problems they encounter. No matter how good a curriculum guide is, it will have problems. If teachers know that the problems will be identified and resolved, then they are much more willing to work with a flawed document. Based upon the ongoing evaluation of the curriculum guide which occurred during the year, in the following summer the curriculum committee which wrote the guide meets to revise and improve it.

Year 5—Full Implementation

As can be seen, this curriculum timeline is long and slow because it includes a consensus-building process. Throughout the process it is common, and expected, for curriculum committee members to give progress reports at faculty and/or department meetings and to seek feedback from their colleagues. This organized dialogue and the provision of time for it to occur justifies the title of the long-range curriculum plan—Considered Action for Curriculum Improvement.

Staff Evaluation

The More Effective Schools/Teaching Project has had no impact upon teacher evaluation. Teacher evaluation procedures which existed prior to the project are in use today.

In contrast, the project has had a significant impact upon the evaluation of principals. Their job descriptions were revised to include a statement that they are responsible for their building becoming an Effective School and for having the correlates continually present in their school. For their annual self-evaluation, principals are required to emphasize the work their buildings have done to either install and maintain the presence of the correlates. This document then serves as the basis of the evaluation conference held with the superintendent and the assistant superintendent for instruction. This conference was moved from early June to mid-July so that current disaggregated data of student achievement and data on the presence of the correlates could be discussed. The superintendent's written evaluation presents correlate data and the disaggregated student achievement data. Appropriate comments are made in the narrative portion of the document. For some, this could be an intimidating process. Nonetheless, it does emphasize what the district values; **it is data driven, and the ground rules are known ahead of time.**

Impact on the Way Student Achievement Is Measured

Disaggregated Data

Immediately prior to the inauguration of the project, the district completed an extensive 3-year study of all the major standardized norm-referenced tests. For each level and for each sub-test of each test the extent to which that sub-test measured Spencerport's intended, written curriculum was determined. Based upon this study, the district concluded that the Stanford Achievement Test measured Spencerport's curriculum (Ferris, 1982). Consequently when the leadership planning team learned how to disaggregate data it had no qualms recommending disaggregating the norm-referenced Stanford Achievement data.

Annually a report is prepared for each building which contains detailed disaggregated data for each subject and/or grade level as well as summary data for the entire building. This report is sent to each building prior to the time the building planning team meets to prepare next year's plan. Because of this report, principals and teachers look at their building and what they do in new ways, raising questions which otherwise would not have been asked. The summary data in the disaggregated data report for each building serve as the basis for the annual district evaluation report.

Criterion-Referenced Tests

It is often said that: "What gets measured gets done" **or** "What gets measured gets learned." The best way to ascertain the degree of student learning is through criterion-referenced tests (CRT). When the More Effective Schools/Teaching Project started, the E. J. Wilson High School decided to use the New York State Education Department's Regents Examination and Regents Competency Tests to measure the attainment of both equity and minimum academic mastery. This meant, however, that for the large number of courses which did not end with either a Regents Exam or a Regents Competency Test, no testing device was available. Consequently, the building planning team for the high school decided to embark upon developing CRT's for all the other courses.

The 1983–84 year was devoted to studying the feasibility of this project and to developing plans for implementing it. The team decided to offer a course in June 1984 on how to write skill objectives. (Efforts to obtain consultants to teach the course at the time were unsuccessful.) Subsequently the high school reading teacher, James Dentinger, and a high school assistant principal, Edward Groszewski, organized and taught the course. One resource which was a great continuing help was the *Handbook of Formative and Summative Evaluation of Student Learning* (Bloom, 1979). Following this course, summer curriculum time was provided for writing skill objectives.

As teachers wrote their skill objectives and attempted to develop mid-term and final examinations based on them, it became clear that they needed instruction and/or review regarding the construction of test materials. Consequently a second course was organized to teach teachers what a test matrix is, how to construct one, how to apply various levels of Bloom's taxonomy, and how to incorporate curricular content to a test matrix. This course was first offered in the late spring of 1985. Once again summer curriculum time was provided to write CRT's.

During the 1985–86 school year each CRT that a teacher wrote was reviewed relative to how well it reflected the curriculum for the course, the extent to which the various levels of Bloom's taxonomy were used, and the extent to which the exam reflected its test matrix. Additional opportunities were provided for training in writing skill objectives and developing test matrices. At the end of the school year more summer curriculum time was provided.

At about the same time the New York State Education Department, as a part of the Board of Regents overall effort to improve education statewide (called the Regents Action Plan), decided to change the required syllabi for many courses. This meant that Spencerport teachers either had to write new CRT's and/or that the overall CRT project timeline had to be modified to reflect the scheduled state-wide implementation of the new syllabi.

Through the 1985–86 school year, faculty participation in this project was voluntary. Even so, a majority of the teachers took the proffered training, wrote skill objectives, test matrices, CRT's, and then reviewed them with the high school reading teacher. But as the 1986–87 school year commenced, the building planning team decided that to ensure consistent curriculum alignment it was necessary for all teachers to participate in the project. Consequently when the members of the building planning team met with the superintendent of schools, they asked him to issue a mandate that every teacher whose course did not end with either a Regents Exam or a Regents Competency Test must have his or her CRT's written by a certain date. (When have you ever heard of a group of teachers asking for a mandate from the superintendent? He responded in the affirmative—gladly.)

In addition to providing curriculum time to assist the teachers during the summer of 1985 and 1986, paid time during school year vacations was provided, thus breaking new ground for the district. During the summer of 1987 the high school prepared a CRT construction manual to assist teachers (Dentinger, 1987). It was being revised and expanded during the summer of 1988. By June 1987 CRT's were offered in all designated high school courses. The 1987–88 school year was devoted to further refining these tests. Disaggregated analyses of student achievement are computed from results of this testing. A similar project to develop CRTs for each subject area is underway at Cosgrove Junior High School.

Impact of the Project on Staff Development Programs

After a school begins an Effective Schools project, teachers ask, "What does this project mean to me?" "What can I do in the classroom to achieve the project's goals?" Sometimes they phrase their questions in terms of the correlates which describe an Effective School where **all** children learn. Teachers ask:

If **high expectations for success** of all students is a goal, what can I do in the classroom to achieve this?

If **instructional leadership** is a characteristic of an Effective School, how can I be more of an instructional leader in the classroom?

If **frequent monitoring of student progress** is a correlate of an Effective School, how can I more effectively diagnose students' work and evaluate curriculum?

Classroom teachers wonder how to translate the Effective Schools Research into practice. A staff development program based upon the effective teaching research helps answer their needs. Staff development is the "how to" of an Effective Schools project. It gives teachers a research foundation upon which to base their instructional decisions so that more effective teaching will occur. Effective teaching research shows teachers how their behavior enhances learning.

This type of staff development program differs from the all-too-common one-shot inservice days which often are of the "listen and then go back and do as I say" design. Oftentimes teachers attend these sessions with little idea of how or where it fits into their classroom, building, or district. These inservice sessions typically are short, not necessarily job-related, and do not contain a follow-up component (Seaburn and Sudlow, 1987, pp. 1–3).

Four major staff development programs were inaugurated by the district as a result of the project. They dealt with the Hunter model, teacher expectations, discipline, and the research on Effective Schools.

Elements of Instruction

This program, based on the Madeline Hunter model of the teacher as a decision-maker, is an intensive 5-day workshop for teachers and an intensive 11-day workshop for principals and supervisors. The administrators' workshop includes 6 days devoted to a model of clinical supervision which may be used to assist teachers in implementing various components of the elements of instruction.

The Elements of Instruction workshop reinforces and strengthens skills which teachers intuitively know are effective by giving them the research-based rationale for their behavior. It also emphasizes research regarding how children learn and translates this research into teaching practices. Extensive time is provided the practice the skills taught.

Ninety percent of the K–12 faculty have voluntarily taken this program. About half of this group have taken subsequent workshops designed to reinforce and strengthen skills they acquired (or reviewed) in Elements of Instruction.

TESA (Teacher Expectations and Student Achievement)

During a 7-session, once a month program, participants in TESA are taught to distribute fifteen specific supportive and motivating behaviors equitably among the students in a class. TESA helps to make teachers aware of the unconscious discriminatory interactions they exhibit between their perceived high achievers and their perceived low achievers. The rationale for TESA is that teachers can directly affect the quantity and quality of students' learning by the expectations they hold for pupil performance and how they manifest these expectations. Between sessions, teachers observe one another practicing the behaviors; then they discuss what they learned at the beginning of the next session. Fifty-nine percent of the K–12 faculty has participated in the TESA staff development program.

Assertive Discipline

The concepts of behavior modification and reinforcement techniques appropriate to the classroom and to the building are developed in this series of workshops. Two buildings, the Wilson High School and the Town Line Elementary School, have implemented this program. One building, the Bernabi Elementary School, has partially implemented it.

Effective Schools Research

An annual workshop is held for new building planning team members and for current members who wish to refresh their knowledge. The Elements of Instruction program was first taught by Ernest Stachowski, retired Director of Professional Development for Long Beach, California. His workshops were offered to all school districts in the Board of Cooperative Educational Services (BOCES).

As a part of this program, Dr. Stachowski offered a series of workshops to prepare teachers and administrators to become qualified Elements of Instruction trainers. Spencerport created the full-time position of Instructional Specialist for Staff Development and sent her, Mrs. Bonnie Seaburn, to these workshops. To become a qualified trainer she participated in over 50 days of formal training. In effect her first 6 months on the job was an in-house sabbatical, financed by the district, to become a qualified trainer.

This extensive training is essential for the quality and the success of an Elements trainer. Once Mrs. Seaburn completed this training she offered the basic elements course and elements follow-up courses. She also developed a long-range staff development plan which was reviewed by a representative group of teachers, the administrative council, and approved by the board of education (Seaburn and Sudlow, 1986). When Mrs. Seaburn left the staff development position to become an assistant principal at the high school, the district once again provided a 6-month in-house sabbatical for her successor, Mrs. Marjorie Perez, to maintain the quality of the program.

TESA workshops are led by the instructional specialist for staff development and other Spencerport teachers who attend to TESA trainer workshop offered through Phi Delta Kappa. The local trainers helped make the training work.

The cost for the staff development program essentially consists of the salary and fringe benefits of an experienced teacher. In addition, the 1988 district budget included approximately the following sums to support the programs;

Staff Development Budget

Inservice Training—Teachers	$14,500
Inservice Contractual	2,300
Inservice Supplies	2,500
	$19,300

In 1985 Spencerport received a "special commendation" from New York State's Commissioner of Education, Gordon M. Ambach, for its staff development program.

Other Developments Pertinent to the Project

At lunch one day Ron Edmonds said, "Spencerport is going to become famous." We thought, "You're crazy! We're a small school system in western New York unknown to the state, let alone the nation. All we want to do is to see if this research will help us." But Ron was right.

Three years into the project, after the basic homework was done, Spencerport sponsored the first State-wide Effective Schools Conference in New York State. Approximately 75 attended this well-received conference.

In February 1987 New York State's Assistant Commissioner of Education, Bruce H. Crowder, and his staff visited—and probed—the Spencerport district. They visited classrooms; they met with building planning teams; they did not talk with the district office. On the basis of this visit plus (no doubt) other data, Dr. Crowder organized a major state-wide awareness conference on Effective Schools Research and its implementation. The Commissioner of Education, Gordon Ambach, was the keynote speaker. A member of the New York State Board of Regents, the deputy commissioner, two assistant commissioners, key members of the New York State Education Department, and key educators from throughout the state were present. The Spencerport district was the only model featured at this 4-day conference. In July and December of 1986 and in July and November 1987, the department sponsored additional Effective Schools awareness conferences featuring the Spencerport model. Approximately 1,600 New York State educators attended these conferences. In addition, 250 completed one of two 5-day Effective Schools facilitators training workshops sponsored by the State Education Department. These workshops were designed to teach people how to implement the Effective Schools model. A survey in the spring of 1988 revealed that by the end of 1987–88, approximately 114 districts (out of 771) throughout the state have initiated an Effective Schools project. Further, implementation of the Effective Schools Research has become a major thrust of ten Boards of Cooperative Educational Services (BOCES) and for the five regional managers of the State Education Department's Effective Schools Consortia Network. The network has developed numerous publications and several Effective Schools needs assessment instruments and assists school districts embarking upon Effective Schools projects.

The New York State Education Department (SED) also reprinted and widely distributed Spencerport's Effective Schools resource notebook, *Sharing a Shared Vision of School Improvement*. Spencerport has been featured in Effective Schools conferences held in Pennsylvania, Michigan, Illinois, Wyoming, Arizona, Iowa, and New Jersey. Spencerport personnel have given invited presentations at annual conferences of the Association for Supervision and Curriculum Development, the American Association of School Administrators, and the National School Boards Association.

This extensive visibility has had a major impact on the district. So many come to visit the project that the district had to organize visitors' days. These visits make some feel like they are "living in a fishbowl."

In July 1987 Deputy Commissioner of Education Gerald Freeborne and Assistant Commissioner of Education Bruce Crowder invited Spencerport to apply to be validated by the State Education Department's Transferring Success Program. This program is the state version of the National Diffusion Network. Validation is a long, arduous, thorough, highly professional process. One out of every two applicants is not validated. Spencerport's project was validated in May 1988.

When Richard Egelston, on behalf of the department, presented a certificate to the board of education, he said that no applications "have been more complex than this and it (the Spencerport project) has become a very great priority in the SED office." He further noted that Spencerport's More Effective Schools/ Teaching Project is "one of the few projects I have encountered in all my years with the Department that backs with resources the issues it believes to be important . . . to break old habits with new learning and to translate educational research into tools for teaching in the classroom." Spencerport is the first school district in New York State to receive validation for a district-wide (K–12) project. All other projects the State Education Department has validated have been for specific areas of the program, such as middle school career education ("Spencerport Schools Get Project Award," 1988).

Problems Encountered

Resistance to a new program is common. "Is this another fad?" "Wait for a year or two and it will go away." "I am suspicious of anything which the district office initiates." Trust. Credibility. Apprehension of something new. These were key problems when the project started.

These problems were overcome in a number of ways. When the project was presented to the board of education for approval the board agreed that it would receive priority funding for the next three years. This sent a strong, clear signal to administrators and teachers. How many projects does a board fund so far in advance? Further, as staff needs for time and resources emerged, support was provided. An excellent staff development program to help teachers learn and implement new research supported by released time or paid summer inservice days also helped develop trust and credibility.

The Effective Schools process essentially asks teachers and principals to work together in a new way. They are asked to form a cohesive team that requires collegial problem-solving. They must work on key issues that affect the quality of education and life in the building. Central office administrators assumed that somewhere in their careers, teachers and administrators had acquired and mastered good group dynamics skills. This was not the case. Teams needlessly stumbled and were inefficient because they did not have these skills. But somehow they "muddled through." As the teams saw the process start to work, as they saw it gradually improve life in the building and student achievement, they were encouraged to use it even more.

When starting school improvement, building planning teams did not always know how to analyze the needs assessment data and develop a plan. This was solved in the second year of the project when Dr. Patrick Proctor from the Connecticut State Education Department taught the teams how to perform this task. The teams subsequently developed and refined this process even further.

About the third year into the project it was evident that many new building planning team members were unaware of the research. They possessed only surface awareness and knowledge. Consequently they were having problems developing and implementing meaningful projects. This problem was solved by annually conducting a "review of the research" workshop for new building planning team members and for current team members who wished to refresh their knowledge.

Advice for Schools Initiating School Improvement

The Spencerport case suggests several things: Go slowly, do thorough planning, and pay your dues up front. Hasty planning = rough implementation; conversely, extensive planning = smoother implementation. The flowchart and suggested timeline for a project (Figure 1) should be useful, but modified to meet local needs.

Many assume that because school improvement is school-based and that because school improvement occurs one school at a time, all action should be at the building level. Yet a building is a part of a larger complex social organization called a district which has its own unique ways of encouraging, discouraging, rewarding, punishing. If a project starts and lives only at the building level, its long-term, multi-year presence and success is far more likely to be dependent upon the stability and leadership of the principal; it is less likely to be institutionalized into the life of a school. Many such projects cease to function when the principal leaves.

It is commonly assumed that bottom-up planning by teachers is essential to start a project. Yet a recent summary of four large-scale multi-state school improvement studies reported that:

There is a great need for initiation, leadership, commitment, and management by top administrators. While belief that change would only "bubble up" from the bottom held sway for many years, recent studies find that central leadership can help and indeed may be critical. Without central leadership schools' efforts to change are less successful.

Teacher involvement in the specifics of planning and implementation is important, but teachers do not need to be directly involved in initiation.

Good programs are essential. Successful school improvement initiatives install proven programs that meet local needs. It is more important to use a validated program than to develop a new program (Anderson, 1987).

Other common findings of these research studies which are worthy of careful attention by those planning to initiate a school improvement program are:

Fidelity of implementation, especially for validated programs, is essential. Downsizing programs during implementation reduces the difficulty of change, but blunts the impact. All pieces of a program must be implemented if the program is to be effective. Pressure for fidelity, accompanied by assistance, is a powerful ingredient of a successful school improvement.

Mastering new practices takes time, but it is mastery that leads to commitment. Commitment builds gradually but solidifies at the end of the process, when teachers and administrators can use new techniques with relative ease and see their effects on students.

Change is usually an incremental process that is strengthened by initial and continuing success. These successes help develop and maintain commitment.

The most successful school improvement activities target core elements of education, improved student achievement, better curriculum, and greater instructional effectiveness. Activities on the periphery have less impact and generate less interest.

Whether improvements begin with a focus on individuals (training in effective instruction, for example) or school-wide improvements (creating the characteristics of Effective Schools, for example), when successfully implemented, they affect both individuals and schools (Anderson, 1987, pp. 80–81).

Based upon research, experience, and observations of other districts, Spencerport administrators and teachers **strongly** recommend that a school improvement process based upon the Effective Schools Research start with the formation of a district-wide leadership planning team composed of representatives from all key constituencies in the district. This team should receive, as a group, thorough training in the Effective Schools Research and various recommended procedures for implementing it. The team then should prepare a master plan to be submitted to the superintendent and to the board of education for formal approval.

Teachers are peers and colleagues. This, however, does not automatically mean that teachers and administrators possess small group dynamics skills such as consensus building, conflict resolution, and so forth. These skills are not a part of teacher preparation programs. If Spencerport were to begin again, the district would provide group process training for building planning teams. All of the teams successfully completed their work—but with more effort and more emotion than was needed. Indeed one team almost failed because its members, as a group, either did not possess or did not use small group process skills.

One type of training that was most helpful was a workshop on how to analyze data from a needs assessment instrument (which measures the presence of a correlate) and then develop a building plan based upon it. The first year the teams struggled because this was not done. This workshop was offered the second year of the project and many still regard it as a highlight.

Training workshops for facilitators for new building planning teams conducted by Spencerport personnel routinely offer several pieces of advice to consider in selecting projects for the first year of a project.

- Pick a project(s) which can be completed during the year and will have visible success. It can be as simple as painting the walls of the faculty room. As Americans we need to see in a reasonable period of time that something works, that the new building planning team has clout.
- Don't pick for the first year a project which is long, complex, and will require several years to complete, such as writing criterion-referenced tests for all the courses in the high school.
- Choose a project which is directly related to what the needs assessment data show. For example, if the data indicate a major problem with arithmetic, don't propose to solve it by installing content area reading. Because building planning team members have pet projects and because they are well respected by their colleagues, such jumps in logic do occur.
- Choose a project over which the building has control. For example, don't propose a project which requires the district office to form a district-wide committee. Inherent in the Effective Schools process is the basic assumption that each school has adequate time, money, materials, and human resources to become effective. It is how the adults in a school choose to use their resources that determines whether their school will or will not become effective.
- It is perfectly permissible to have a plan, that is, not to *do*, but to *study* and to *learn* what current research says about a topic and what the best practices are regarding the topic. The accumulated wisdom of the profession does not reside in any single school. Then, after the building planning team—or a subcommittee of the faculty—is knowledgeable about current research and excellent practices, develop an action plan based upon this knowledge. It is far more likely to be successful than one which is based upon the current conventional wisdom of the faculty.

Awareness usually occurs only when a project starts in earnest. Don't assume that a one-hour faculty meeting or a one-day conference is all that is needed to provide faculties with enough knowledge and understanding so that they can successfully plan, guide, and implement a project. Continuing awareness sessions should be organized and conducted by building planning teams. Procedures for orienting new teachers and administrators should be developed. Teach the research, in depth, to new building planning team members annually.

The many kinds of data generated in Effective Schools projects should not be used to compare one school to another. **The important issue** is whether or not the school is improving **over time** and moving in the direction of the desired goals set forth in the master plan for the district—**not** how does it stand in the American League batting averages compared to other schools.

Summary

The key features of Spencerport's More Effective Schools/Teaching Project are:

- A master plan. Included in the master plan are:

    A project goal that all students regardless of socioeconomic status shall achieve minimal academic mastery

    An annual school improvement goal

    An excellence goal for students who normally do well

- Annual disaggregated analysis of student achievement

    Use of a needs assessment instrument designed to ascertain the degree to which the correlates that describe an Effective School are present in each building

- Building planning teams in every school

    Annual review and prior approval by faculties of proposed action plans prepared by the building planning team

- An annual evaluation report detailing progress

- Comprehensive planning which flows from the literature on the change process (Huberman & Miles, 1984; Loucks-Horsley & Hergert, 1985; Hall & Hord, 1987; Hord, Rutherford, Hurling-Austin & Hall, 1987)

Spencerport recommends that all Effective Schools Research-based school improvement projects have **all** of the above components. About Spencerport's experience, Lezotte and Bancroft (1985) were able to write:

Spencerport's success illustrates that Effective Schools Research principles can be applied in a different context. . . . The program enables staff members and researchers to verify the Effective Schools Research model's versatility and adaptability to a broader variety of school types (Lezotte and Bancroft, 1985).

References

Anderson, Beverly, et al. (1987). State strategies to support local school improvement. *Knowledge: creation, diffusion, utilization.* 9(1). 42–86.

Bloom, Benjamin, Hastings, J. Thomas, & Madares, George F. (1971). *Handbook on formative and summative evaluation of student learning.* New York: MacGraw-Hill.

Dentinger, James. (1987). *A manual for the construction of domain referenced/criterion referenced tests.* Spencerport, N.Y.: Spencerport Central Schools.

Edmonds, Ronald. (1979). Effective schools for the urban poor. *Educational Leadership.* 37(1). 15–23.

Edmonds, Ronald. (1982a). On school improvement: A conversation with Ronald Edmonds. *Educational Leadership* 40. 15.

Edmonds, Ronald. (1982b). Programs of school improvement: An overview. *Educational Leadership.* December. 4–11.

Edmonds, Ronald. (1982c). *Programs for school improvement: An overview.* Unpublished paper. Michigan State University. Unpublished paper for presentation at the conference "The Implications of Research for Practice," Airlie House, Virginia. 20 pp.

Edmonds, Ronald. (1983). Presentation to the Administrative Council, Spencerport Central School District, February 22.

Edmonds, Ronald & Lezotte, Lawrence. (1983). Presentation to the Leadership Planning Team, Spencerport Central School District, March 16.

Educational Research Service, Inc. (1983). *Effective Schools: A summary of research.* Arlington, Va.: Educational Research Service, Inc.

Ferris, Frank. (1982). *Adoption of Stanford Achievement Test and the Otis-Lennon School Ability Test.* Spencerport, N.Y.: Spencerport Central Schools, xeroxed.

Frederiksen, John & Edmonds, Ronald. (about 1977) *Identification of instructionally effective and ineffective schools.* Cambridge, Mass.: Harvard University. Xeroxed, no date.

Hall, Gene E. & Hord, Shirley M. (1987). *Changes in schools: Facilitating the process.* Albany, N.Y.: State University of New York Press.

Hord, Shirley M., Rutherford, William L., Hurling-Austin, Leslie & Hall, Gene E. (1987). *Taking charge of change.* Alexandria, Va.: Association for Supervision and Curriculum Development.

Huberman, A. Michael & Miles, Matthew B. (1984). *Innovation up close: How school improvement works.* New York: Plenum Press.

Lezotte, Lawrence W. & Bancroft, Beverly A. (1985). Growing use of the Effective Schools model for school improvement. *Educational Leadership.* March. 23–27.

Loucks-Horsley, Susan & Hergert, Leslie F. (1985). *An action guide to school improvement.* Alexandria, Va.: Association for Supervision and Curriculum Development.

Miles, M. B., Farrar, E., & Neufeld, B. (1983). *The extent of adoption of Effective Schools programs.* Vol. II of Review of Effective Schools Programs prepared for the National Commission on Excellence in Education. Cambridge, Ma.: The Huron Institute.

New York State School Improvement Program Guidebook. (1987). Albany, N.Y.: Office of District Superintendents, New York State Education Department, Albany, N.Y. 3.

Proctor, C. Patrick & Villanova, Robert M. (1984). *Handbook for the use of the Connecticut School Effectiveness Interview and Questionnaire.* Hartford, Conn.: Connecticut State Department of Education.

School Effectiveness: The six indicators and student achievement. (1985). Columbia, S.C.: College of Education, University of South Carolina. 8.

Seaburn, Bonnie & Sudlow, Robert. (1986). *Staff development plan.* Spencerport, N.Y.: Spencerport Central Schools, xeroxed.

Seaburn, Bonnie & Sudlow, Robert. (1987). *Staff development implications of an Effective Schools project.* Spencerport, N.Y.: Spencerport Central Schools. ED 292-096.

Spencerport schools get project award. (1988). *Suburban News,* Spencerport, N.Y., July 12, p. 29A.

Sudlow, Robert E. (1983a). Disaggregated analysis. Spencerport, N.Y.: Spencerport Central Schools, Memo to Leadership Planning Team, June 17.

Sudlow, Robert E. (1983b). *Master Plan. More Effective Schools teaching project. Report of the Leadership Planning Team to the Superintendent of Schools.* Spencerport, N.Y.: Spencerport Central Schools, xeroxed. ED 273 025.

Sudlow, Robert E. (1984a). Conducting an Effective Schools program, *The Effective School Report,* 2, 9-10-11. ED 273–026.

Sudlow, Robert E. (1984b). *More Effective Schools/Teaching Project: First Annual Report.* Spencerport, N.Y.: Spencerport Central Schools, xeroxed.

Sudlow, Robert E. (1985). *What is an Effective School?* Spencerport, N.Y.: Spencerport Central Schools, xeroxed. ED 273 035.

Sudlow, Robert E. (1987). *More Effective Schools/Teaching Project: Fourth Annual Report.* Spencerport, N.Y.: Spencerport Central Schools, xeroxed.

Sudlow, Robert E. (1988a). *More Effective Schools/Teaching Project: Fifth Annual Report.* Spencerport, N.Y.: Spencerport Central Schools, xeroxed.

Sudlow, Robert E. (1988b). *Using a microcomputer to compute a disaggregated analysis.* Spencerport, N.Y.: Spencerport Central Schools, xeroxed.

Sudlow, Robert E. and Werth, Terry L. S. (1988). *Finding time to teach.* Spencerport, N.Y.: Spencerport Central Schools, xeroxed.

Villanova, Robert M. (1984). *A comparison of interview and questionnaire techniques used in the Connecticut School Effectiveness Project: A report of work in progress.* Paper presented at the Annual Meeting of the American Educational Research Association, New Orleans, Louisiana.

Werth, Terry L. S. (1988). *Teacher reactions to the More Effective Schools/Teaching Project.* Spencerport, N.Y.: Spencerport Central Schools, xeroxed.

Wooley, Sandra L. (1987). *The meaning of change to teachers: A case study of a district-wide Effective Schools project.* Syracuse, N.Y.: School of Education Syracuse University. Dissertation Proposal, xeroxed, pp. 9–10.

Middle Cities in Michigan

Lynn Benore
Project Coordinator
Middle Cities Education Association

Middle Cities in Michigan
Became involved in Effective Schools process in 1981

Community

Population
NA

Twenty-eight urban districts across Michigan; with large proportions of poor and/or minority students. Have enrollments ranging from 3,000 to 30,000 students. These districts serve a large proportion of compensatory-education and free-reduced lunch students. No complete actual figures on free lunch are available across all 28 districts; however of those reporting information, the range is 20 percent free lunch to in excess of 90 percent free lunch. 16,230 students qualify for free lunch; 7,083 students qualify for reduced lunch.

School District

Enrollment
300,000/28 districts

Ethnic Composition
Percent minority = 42.38
Range is 2.8 percent to 99.5 percent.

Per Pupil Expenditure
$2,715–$5,857
(Average is $3,568)

Area (in square miles)
NA

Schools
Elementary schools	404
Junior highs	77
High schools	57

Abstract

Formed in 1973, the Middle Cities Education Association (MCEA) comprises twenty-eight (1988–89) urban districts in the state of Michigan. MCEA members share educational concerns associated with urban areas "including ways to . . . educate the large proportion of poor and minority children in these districts."

This case study is particularly interesting because it demonstrates the need for flexibility in implementing the Effective Schools process, without losing programmatic emphasis on the fundamental components of the model (i.e., the disaggregation and faithful interpretation of data, and training for principals and teachers in skills of instructional leadership). Middle Cities trainers and facilitators of necessity allowed the districts to implement the evolving model of Effective Schools Research as the districts saw fit. In many cases during the early eighties the Effective Schools model for school improvement could not be accepted in its entirety because of local and state, political/social constraints. Disaggregation of data, the data gathering and interpretation process which drives the model, was not always done in all districts, nor was school-based management always implemented with enough training for members of the building teams. (The latter was true because the Effective Schools district model for school improvement was not developed well enough to demonstrate the importance of district involvement with the building teams.)

To counter some of these concerns, Middle Cities formed new staff development programs beginning in 1987 which culminated in a Professional Development Task Force (p. 18). These task forces deliberate on programs for training for school and teaching effectiveness, as well as on district and school policies and procedures to support school improvement efforts.

Brief Overview of the Programs

The Middle Cities Education Association (MCEA), a consortium of 28 urban districts in Michigan, was formed in 1973 as a non-profit corporation. The members have common educational concerns associated with urban areas, including ways to educate effectively the large proportion of poor and minority children in these districts. Middle Cities Education Association is affiliated with Michigan State University and its offices are located in the College of Education. Member districts include Flint, Battle Creek, Saginaw, Ypsilanti, Pontiac, Grand Rapids, Ann Arbor, Bay City, Lansing, Kalamazoo, and 18 other cities across Michigan. Collectively, these districts enroll over 300,000 students or about 18 percent of the K–12 population in Michigan.

The Middle Cities Education Association Effective Schools programs were initiated in June of 1981 when invited member district superintendents met with Ron Edmonds and Larry Lezotte for a two-day seminar to review the research on Effective Schools and consider possibilities for having MCEA districts serve as pilot sites to implement the research in Michigan. After that seminar planners developed a six-day workshop series in 1981–82 for five-person teams each consisting of the superintendent, assistant superintendent for instruction, director of evaluation, a principal, and a teacher. The workshop series was designed to initiate a pilot program in one school from each district. That program was an important step toward increasing the knowledge of the Effective Schools Research and planning process in member districts. Participants, however, perceived the need for more training on the meaning of the correlates, particularly the correlate of the principal's role as instructional leader.

To respond to this need, C. Robert Muth, executive director of MCEA, and Lynn Benore, an MCEA staff member, developed proposals based on Effective Schools Research and effective teaching research to enhance elementary principals' leadership skills. The W. K. Kellogg Foundation funded the development of a three-year program (September 1983 to September 1986) for all elementary principals from six MCEA districts and three small non-MCEA districts near Battle Creek. Due to financial limitations, one-third of the principals were to take part in the program for three years (Group I) and the rest of the principals were to begin in 1984, the second year of the project (Group II Principals). The U.S. Department of Education gave a similar grant from the Fund for the Improvement of Post-Secondary Education (FIPSE). This program covered two years (1983–1985) and included one-fourth of the elementary principals from 17 MCEA districts. All of those principals were in that program the entire two years. In all, approximately 150 principals and 150 lead teachers took part in these intensive programs.

The first year of both projects was devoted to training in the essential elements of effective instruction (Madeline Hunter model) so that principals could acquire stronger instructional skills. Although background on Effective Schools Research concepts and the school improvement planning process were introduced in the first year, major emphasis on development of the school plan did not come until the second year. Therefore only one year was available to FIPSE project principals and to Kellogg Group II principals to learn about and write school plans based upon Effective Schools Research.

At the conclusion of the elementary project, member districts asked to have MCEA assistance in moving the school improvement program to the secondary level, and again with W. K. Kellogg Foundation (in 1987) and FIPSE (in 1985) funded MCEA proposals for this training. The focus of the training changed from developing instructional leadership skills of principals to developing the capacity of building-based teams to lead programs of school improvement based upon Effective Schools Research. As a result, the secondary programs included training of 5- to 10-person teams from 26 secondary schools in the FIPSE project and 15 secondary schools in the W. K. Kellogg project. The training of these teams is taking place over a three-year period.

Though MCEA received outside funding to initiate both the elementary and secondary project, the in-kind contributions of member districts have met or exceeded that external funding. External sources funded a full-time project coordinator, consultants/presenters, and costs for training materials. Districts that have participated in the programs have been required to pay for all other project costs such as overnight charges, meals, and travel costs for participants; released time; and related in-district support to accomplish project goals (i.e. providing assistance to teams with data collection and analysis, in-district in-service costs for school staffs, allocation of time for district staff members to coordinate the program). In the case of the FIPSE Secondary School Improvement Project each district was also required to pay a substantial registration fee yearly to cover costs of programming not covered by external funding.

The purpose of outside funding has been to get the Effective Schools program underway in each of the MCEA districts, with the expectation that districts would develop ways to continue to support the effort in the future. Because of the scope of the projects, covering 26 districts, the level and kinds of internal support have varied, but all districts have continued to support the programs to some degree once external funds were terminated. In some cases the support has included the reallocation of at least one central office staff member's time to focus on Effective Schools Research implementation in the district. Some districts have a separate evaluation department that is responsible for analyzing and providing schools with disaggregated student achievement data, some assist in administering and scoring of faculty needs assessments. The Middle Cities organization is currently emphasizing a greater district role in the improvement process, including assisting member districts in development of district-wide plans if they are not currently in place.

Evidence of Improvement

Since 1981, MCEA has developed a series of four multi-year training programs for member districts. The two elementary programs ended in 1985 (FIPSE) and 1986 (Kellogg), while the secondary programs are still in process. The most extensive evaluation was conducted through the Kellogg elementary school principals' improvement program. Most of the evidence cited in this section comes from that program.

Achievement: An Analysis of Achievement Data in MCA/Kellogg Project Schools (Group I)

The achievement test results reported here are based upon school summary data for the Michigan Educational Assessment Program (MEAP) Test in schools that were participants in the MCA/Kellogg project between 1983 and 1986 (Kellogg I schools). The results reported are for the fourth grade at 21 schools. (It should be noted that the three non-public schools were not included in the analysis because they do not administer the MEAP test. Four other public schools that participated in the Group I sessions do not have a fourth grade. During the project, one school with a fourth grade reorganized and incorporated two other schools' classes, so that school was not included.) The results compare fall 1983 data (prior to the project) with fall 1986 data (at the conclusion of the project). Results are reported by the percentage of students in the fourth quartile, which is defined by the State of Michigan as the mastery level. The analysis of data is reported in three ways:

1. Identification of groups of schools that demonstrated improvement and identification of groups that declined.

2. An analysis of the differences between the State of Michigan average scores and the average scores of Kellogg I schools.
3. A disaggregated analysis based upon the categories of free/reduced and paid lunch students for the years 1983 and 1986 in eleven schools.

In the first analysis, schools were categorized by whether they demonstrated growth in percent of students in the fourth quartile between 1983 and 1986. Those results are as follows:

- Thirteen buildings improved in both reading and math.
- Three buildings improved in reading **or** math, with no change in the other area.
- One building improved in reading or math and declined in the other area.
- Four buildings declined in either reading or math, or both areas.

In the second analysis the average change in the percent of students in the fourth quartile for the State of Michigan was compared to that of the 21 Kellogg schools a weighted proportion of students demonstrating mastery was calculated. To arrive at that average the number of students in each school taking the test was multiplied by the percent that attained mastery (fourth quartile); those figures were summed across schools then divided by the total number of students that took the test in those 21 schools.

Traditionally, urban schools (Middle Cities Education Association districts) have fallen below the state average for both reading and math at fourth grade level. However, between 1983 and 1986 that gap has been narrowed by 43 percent in reading and 5 percent in math for these project schools. While the average percentage of students attaining mastery state-wide has risen between 1983 and 1986, the average gain for these Kellogg project schools has been greater than that of the state. In 1983 there was a 5.8 percent gap on the reading test between the State of Michigan average and the 21 project schools; by 1986 that gap was 3.3 percent. In math the gap had been lessening each year, going from 4.4 percent in 1983 to 3.3 percent in 1985, but moving back to 4.2 percent in 1986. The actual results are as shown on the next page. (Table 1)

In the third analysis, fourth-grade MEAP results for Kellogg I schools were also disaggregated by free/paid lunch for 11 of 21 schools for which MCEA staff had completed pupil-by-pupil data from fall 1983 through fall 1986. Ten other schools either did not have available all individual pupil test results for the four years or were lacking complete free lunch information for those years. The disaggregated analysis of MEAP data for those eleven schools with complete

Table 1
Reading (Percent Mastery Students in Fourth Quartile)

State		Kellogg I Schools	GAP
1983	75.9%	70.1%	−5.8%
1984	77.7%	73.0%	−4.7%
1985	79.3%	75.1%	−4.2%
1986	80.3%	77.0%	−3.3%

Math (Percent Mastery)

State		Kellogg I Schools	GAP
1983	80.5%	76.1%	−4.4%
1984	82.6%	78.3%	−4.3%
1985	83.6%	80.3%	−3.3%
1986	85.0%	80.8%	−4.2%

Table 2
Disaggregated Analysis of Fourth Grade MEAP Scores 1983–1986
11 of 21 Kellogg I Schools

	Reading Free	Paid	Math Free	Paid
		1983		1983
4th Q	66.5%	75.7%	4th Q 69.6%	78.4%
1st Q	6.4%	5.1%	1st Q 5.2%	2.0%
		1986		1986
4th Q	70.7%	87.4%	4th Q 78.2%	86.2%
1st Q	4.3%	2.1%	1st Q 1.4%	0.4%

data reveals that the percent of free lunch students and the percent of non-free lunch students achieving mastery (defined as those in the 4th quartile) rose in both reading and math at those 11 schools between 1983 and 1986. The number of students in the lowest category of achievement (1st quartile) fell significantly for both free and non-free lunch students. The table above indicates the degree of change for the 11 schools in the 4th quartile, and the change in percent of students in the 1st quartile, or lowest level of achievement, between 1983 and 1986. (Table 2)

Connecticut School Effectiveness Questionnaire

Early in the first year (1983–84) of the W. K. Kellogg Elementary Project each principal was required to conduct a building-wide needs assessment to determine the extent to which the seven correlates of Effective Schools already existed, as perceived by the building staff. They used the *Connecticut School Effectiveness Questionnaire,* a 73-item questionnaire that was administered to all teachers and other instructional support staff. These questionnaires were computer-scored at Michigan State University and returned to the building administrators. With few excep-

Table 3
Kellogg 1 Schools: Connecticut Quex

Correlate	1983	1986	Change
Safe & orderly environment	3.9	4.0	+0.1
Clear school mission	3.4	3.8	+0.4
Instructional leadership	3.2	3.5	+0.3
High expectations	3.4	3.8	+0.4
Time on task	3.6	3.7	+0.1
Frequent monitor of pupils	3.7	3.9	+0.2
Home-school relations	3.4	3.6	+0.2

tions the schools complied with the administration of the *Connecticut School Effectiveness Questionnaire* at the start of the project.

The original project design also required all buildings to readminister the *Connecticut School Effectiveness Questionnaire* at the conclusion of the project, but during the course of the program it became evident this would not be appropriate for all schools. Some schools had not had an opportunity to implement fully the programs they had planned as of spring 1986 when the project ended. In several cases changes in principals created concern about administering a needs assessment when the new principal had not yet had time to make a difference. Thus, all schools were asked to either readminister the *Connecticut School Effectiveness Questionnaire* in spring of 1986 or to provide a written rationale indicating why it would not be appropriate at that time and to tell when it would be readministered. By the fall of 1986 project staff received results on the readministration of the *Connecticut School Effectiveness Questionnaire* from 19 of 29 schools in Group I of the Kellogg elementary program. The pre-project and post-project analysis is reported here. (Table 3)

The analysis of the Group I schools includes 15 of the 19 schools that readministered the *Connecticut School Effectiveness Questionnaire* in spring 1986. Four schools were not included in the analysis because they used different instruments originally or because they used a form of the *Connecticut School Effectiveness Questionnaire* different from the rest of the group. The teaching and instructional support staffs in 15 schools perceived positive changes in all seven correlate areas. The results are reported on a five-point Likert scale, with one (1) indicating little or no presence of a factor and five (5) indicating a high level of that correlate.

The areas of high expectations, clear school mission, and principal's instructional leadership demonstrated the most gains during the life of the project but gains were registered in all seven areas.

Progress on School Improvement Plans

One goal of all four funded projects was completion of a school improvement plan based on the Effective Schools and effective teaching research and during the projects participants learned about phases in its development. MCEA project staff requested participants to send parts of their plan to Middle Cities as it was completed.

As of June 30, 1986, the project staff received complete school improvement plans from 21 of the 29 buildings in Group I (principals in the program three years) of the Kellogg elementary schools project. The project received completed plans from 26 of the 48 buildings in Group II (principals in the program for two years) of that project. Most other buildings in both groups I and II sent the project staff data in one or more of the four categories in which we requested information: improvement team members, missions statement, disaggregated analysis of achievement, school plan. Those data reflected their involvement in the process as of the conclusion of the project. Three buildings in Group I and nine buildings in Group II did not send any data. Of those 12 non-respondents, one principal was newly assigned to a building in 1985–86 and in four other buildings the principals were retiring in June of 1986, which may indicate problems with level of commitment to the program.

In some instances the project staff was aware that data existed at the building, but that it was not sent to MCEA. For example, one school district runs a disaggregated analysis achievement for each of its schools. But not every school forwarded that analysis to the Middle Cities office.

Considering the time restrictions and work involved, variations in district and school environments, and the degree of individual motivation and commitment, the MCEA was satisfied with the response to the Kellogg elementary improvement project. Seventy-six percent of Group I principals and 54 percent of Group II principals sent completed school improvement plans. Only 15 percent of the schools in the project did not submit planning data.

Evidence of District Initiatives

Over the past seven years more emphasis has been placed on improving the instructional programs and student outcomes in most member districts. When many districts hire new teachers and principals, interviews now focus primarily on candidates' ability to successfully respond to questions of an instructional nature with special attention given to research on effective teaching and Effective Schools. Candidates for principal in particular are expected to demonstrate knowledge of Effective Schools and teaching research and to understand the impact of long-range planning on student achievement.

Boards of education in several districts are aware of the role of the instructional leader and some now emphasize those skills when interviewing candidates for superintendent. Some of the districts routinely have Effective Schools/school improvement agenda items at board meetings, including review of student data and presentations by school teams on their goals and written plans.

Though time constraints continue to be present, several districts have provided significant released time to improvement teams, especially in the initial planning stages. Some high schools in current MCEA projects have given one or two team members an additional planning period to coordinate the Effective Schools program. Already available staff development days are being used more frequently for activities associated with school improvement plans instead of the more traditional "one-shot" presentation on a variety of topics. Most buildings have also incorporated items related to the Effective Schools planning process into their regular staff meetings. Some districts have sponsored multi-day instructional skills training programs for teachers and administrators, often during the school day, or with stipends outside of school hours. Even in districts that offered intensive staff development opportunities after school or during the summer without stipends, the cost of the program itself was borne by the district.

Several districts now routinely have central office personnel disaggregate norm-referenced test and Michigan Educational Assessment Program test data for all schools in the district. More districts are moving in that direction. Assessment personnel work with individual schools to interpret results and use the data in planning. Most districts or schools use either free/reduced lunch versus paid categories or mother's level of education as indicators for social status. Some also disaggregate data based on race and/or gender. Some school personnel have expressed a need for their districts to more clearly define the curriculum and to set guidelines for mastery; in the absence of such district coordination, schools frequently have attempted to accomplish this in isolation.

Most MCEA districts have demonstrated a stronger emphasis on staff development directly as a result of our projects. Virtually all districts have conducted programs of effective instruction for their administrative and teaching staffs, which require a significant increase in the amount of time devoted to staff development. Several districts have made a substantial commitment to having staff members become instructional skills trainers, and some have changed the roles of some participants to include staff development responsibilities. Some districts have created new positions for directors of staff development and/or directors of school improvement. Some districts have created special funds schools can use to work with staff in writing and implementing their improvement plans. At least one district requires that all requests for staff development time or funds be linked directly to the school's written improvement plan. (See "Interviews with District Superintendents," page 190.)

Changes in MCEA Practices

Changes in Student Assessment Practices in MCEA

As a result of participation in Middle Cities Effective Schools programs, districts are more aware of the need to monitor more closely the progress of each student through analyzing disaggregated student outcomes data and by developing criterion-referenced assessments. This is particularly critical at the secondary level where appropriate measurement of student outcomes is weak. Inadequate student outcome data makes it difficult for districts to accurately determine the priorities for improvement and then select strategies designed to strengthen outcomes. Without a range of data, disaggregated by specific subgroups of the student population, schools do not have a clear indicator of how well they are accomplishing their agreed-upon mission. To address this need MCEA has sponsored a series of workshops on development of criterion-referenced assessments presented by Dr. Marc Becker, director of research and evaluation and evaluation at the Glendale (Arizona) Union High School District.

Several districts currently have limited criterion-referenced measures in one or two subject areas at the secondary level and are working on expanding the scope of those assessments both in terms of content areas covered and frequency of assessment. The directors of research and evaluation from Middle Cities districts meet monthly and have discussed development of a bank to be accessed by member districts. In the current secondary school improvement projects some individual schools have begun the process of determining student outcomes of greatest importance

Significant Changes: Interviews with District Superintendents
W. K. Kellogg Elementary Principals' Leadership Project

In the fall of 1986, at the conclusion of the W. K. Kellogg Elementary Principals' Leadership Project, Robert Muth, the former executive director of MCEA, and Muskegon Heights Superintendent John Sydnor, interviewed each district's superintendent to determine changes which resulted from involvement in the project. Included here are excerpts from six of these interviews.

What do you believe was the most significant behavioral change resulting from the principals' and teachers' participation?

The general responses of the most observable change was the increasing amount of time spent on school improvement discussions and planning with the building staffs. The most observable informal change was the ability of the principals to discuss instructional change and instructional planning in their conversations with each other and with the total administrative staff of the school district.

There also seemed to be an increasing willingness on the part of the principals to request and urge additional staff training.

At the building level the most significant total staff change was the cooperative work effort in developing the school mission and the school improvement plans.

Was there a significant degree of change (increase) in the district's monetary commitment to professional development?

The responses to this question were extremely encouraging to the interviewers. Every participating district had made contributions to a broadened professional development program. To most, this involved extending the training of effective teaching to many additional members of the teaching staff and to bringing in consultants for training in such programs as TESA (Teacher Expectations and Student Achievement) and Assertive Discipline. The direct monetary contributions from the districts ranged from $10,000 from the smallest district to $50,000–$60,000 in the larger districts. This cost did not include the indirect costs of teacher participation such as stipends for summer or weekend training. The managerial and fiscal support given to expanded professional development is a very concrete measure of the value of the project.

In addition to the fiscal support for expanded programming, the districts, of course, contributed substantially in substitute pay, travel, lodging, and meals for the participants in the project training. There is no doubt that districts made a greater contribution to professional development through this project than was anticipated when they began their participation and, in some cases, probably greater than they ever contemplated could be possible.

Have goals been established for improving student achievement?

Although all superintendents indicated their personal goals for improving student achievement, only one district was able to cite specific goals and measurable objectives for improving student achievement. In discussing the responses to the question, the interviewers were of the belief that until computerized data management systems were more readily available, student achievement goals would be more general than specific. But there was no doubt that improved student achievement was a primary school management goal. All school districts do spend considerable time in the analysis of the MEAP test data, including an item analysis which identifies areas of needed instructional emphasis.

and considering ways to develop criterion-referenced measures within the school when their districts are not yet prepared to do that district-wide. MCEA sees the development of such assessments as a priority in its future professional development activities.

Changes in Professional Development Programs

As an organization, MCEA has significantly changed its approach to staff development as a result of its involvement in programs of school improvement based upon Effective Schools Research. The central thrust of professional development in MCEA since 1981 has been implementation of the Effective Schools Research model at the elementary, secondary, and district levels. MCEA projects have evolved from programs intended to improve individual performance (i.e., teacher effectiveness training for individual teachers and instructional leadership training for principals) to programs intended to improve organizational functioning. MCEA now works primarily with building-based and district improvement teams to assist them in moving through the steps in the school improvement process and to help them promote collegiality and communication throughout the school and district organization.

In addition to offering long-term programs on the Effective Schools improvement process, MCEA provides related programs for training in areas such as implementing the research on teacher effectiveness, developing criterion-referenced assessments, and using the research on effective staff development. For example, superintendents and other central office personnel from member districts met in two-day seminars in the summers of 1985 and 1986 as well as five days of training during the 1985–86 school year to learn more about specific steps in the school improvement process, long-range strategic planning, how to implement a program of instructional skills training, and the requirements of effective staff development program design, implementation, and evaluation.

As a result of these school improvement projects, the Middle Cities Education Association initiated during the 1986–87 school year a Professional Development Task Force which has become an ongoing part of the organization. Middle Cities has 14 task forces that are made up of central office administrators who meet monthly in key educational areas such as the Instructional Task Force (directors of instruction or curriculum), Personnel Task Force (directors of personnel), and Research and Evaluation Task Force. An important issue the Professional Development Task Force has considered is the design and implementation of appropriate policies and programs for staff development based upon the research.

An advisory committee on MCEA professional development activities, made up of directors of professional development and assistant superintendents for instruction, has strongly recommended that the focus of MCEA programs continue to be on implementation of Effective Schools Research and/or programs directly related to the research that enhance districts' capacities to deliver appropriate educational strategies within their improvement plans. These include cooperative learning, TESA, organizational change and development, team-building, criterion-referenced assessment, goal setting.

Components of the Effective Schools Planning Process In MCEA

The major emphasis of Middle Cities in the Effective Schools Planning Process since 1981 has been to assist individual buildings in developing long-range plans. The planning process has consisted of the following steps:

1. gain an overview of the Effective Schools program for building administrators
2. select school teams
3. provide inservice to teams on the effective schools research and planning process
4. develop school mission
5. select student outcomes that measure progress toward the mission
6. gather and analyze student outcomes data
7. administer and analyze the faculty needs assessment and archival information
8. select priorities for improvement goals based upon the needs assessment and student data
9. write the three- to five-year improvement plans
10. implement and evaluate.

Within each project there have been district requirements for general support to the project schools, chiefly in the forms of financial and time commitments, as well as a commitment by each district to continue adequate financial support to the buildings once the projects have been completed. MCEA's newest project, the W. K. Kellogg Secondary School Improvement Project, gives strongest emphasis yet to assisting district improvement teams.

Through the Instructional Task Force, Professional Development Task Force, Evaluation Task Force, and periodic meetings with all MCEA superintendents, the MCEA staff has over the past seven years reviewed the improvement process followed by the school teams and has made central office administrators aware of specific forms of district support important to success. These meetings have included discussions of the need for curriculum alignment and criterion-referenced assessment in each local district, the need for adequate district-supported staff development programs designed to enhance the improvement process in the schools, the need to collect and disaggregate student outcomes data district-wide, and the need to provide better services to the school in terms of data analysis and uses of that data to improve the school's instructional delivery.

Though many districts have improved their support to the school-based teams in one or more of the areas described above, only a few of the districts have developed district-level teams and a district plan of improvement based upon Effective Schools Research. Through its professional development division MCEA is presently considering a comprehensive training model for district teams in writing long-range district improvement plans that support and complement the individual building plans.

Problems/Issues/Concerns

Though the Middle Cities Education Association, which serves 28 urban districts, must handle a variety of issues in different districts, common areas of concern are detailed here. These are areas to be addressed during the process.

A major concern has been with a philosophical commitment to district support of programs once project funds were concluded, particularly in districts without district-wide plans. MCEA has been successful in getting commitment to Effective Schools Research implementation from most districts in part due to the ongoing communication of the MCEA office with the superintendents, including several multi-day workshops beginning in 1981, and interviews conducted with each superintendent during the project. Although MCEA has not progressed as far as it would have liked in promoting a **district** as well as building planning processes for members, the superintendents and boards have actively encouraged the association to continue working with individual buildings and to move from the elementary to the secondary school level.

Strong indications of district commitment to continuation of programs at the school level can be seen in the secondary school improvement projects. As the FIPSE Secondary School Improvement Project was originally funded it allowed for eight districts to be a part of the program. MCEA superintendents asked the project staff to find a way for 19 districts to participate, even though that required a substantial yearly registration charge. Both the Kellogg and FIPSE Improvement Projects require attendance of building teams in a workshop series during a three-year period, which is a substantial increase in district financial commitment over previous projects in which only principals were asked to participate.

A second concern is district financial planning to continue programs, particularly when so many districts are in urban areas with limited resources and high unemployment. Many districts have had severe budget cuts, and are presently facing even more, but in several districts there has been an emphasis on continuing to make Effective Schools programs a financial priority. For example, one superintendent recently said that maintenance of highly professional personnel with time to work collaboratively on approaches to improve pupil performance is at the heart of the school organization, and that core value will be protected even though budget reductions may be needed in the system. Districts have looked carefully at available resources to determine ways to more effectively use funds to promote and maintain school improvement, though most need even more assistance in lining up budget allocation priorities with instructional priorities related to Effective Schools.

A third concern surfaced when MCEA began working at the secondary schools level. Project consultants, staff members, and some superintendents anticipated a high degree of reluctance or skepticism on the part of secondary school faculty because most existing research was conducted at elementary level. Also, the more departmentalized, autonomous nature of secondary schools makes collaboration for change more difficult. This concern was not as critical as first anticipated, due in part to the involvement of all school team members throughout the training. Most teams were receptive to learning about the research. Skepticism on the part of some members at the beginning of the project lessened considerably as the team progressed through the program. Secondary school teams found it to be particularly helpful to share progress and problem-solving strategies with other urban districts.

Not yet met is an overall need for better team communication with the rest of the faculty as well as their involvement. The size, organization, and culture of most secondary schools makes such involvement difficult, and consequently, the reluctance of other staff members to commit to the program may result in part from a lack of understanding of the change to be accomplished. Faculty members who have not had the opportunities that teams have had to thoroughly learn about the Effective Schools Research need to learn about the improvement process.

Conclusions and Recommendations

Over the seven years that Middle Cities Education Association has sponsored school improvement programs based upon Effective Schools Research, MCEA has modified several aspects of the training. This section briefly highlights key areas of modification as well as suggestions for those who are initiating programs. Those highlights and suggestions include:

- Plan for **inservice follow-up** before the program begins. Assigning well-qualified facilitators to each school and/or district team is important to successful follow-through on concepts and activities presented at workshops. Facilitators should schedule regular visits to the school teams.
- **Set clear program goals** and expectations of participants at the beginning of the project or program so that everyone knows for what they are "signing on."
- Provide **a high quality orientation** to building and district leaders to lay out the premises of the Effective Schools Research and the steps in the planning process. Leaders must understand the "big picture" and the beliefs upon which the model is based. Leaders should also be guided on appropriate selection criteria for school improvement teams because the membership of those teams is critical in accomplishing the planning tasks and in getting the rest of the faculty to buy in to the program.
- Conduct **most training with the entire team** to ensure adequate communication and understanding of key concepts and planning activities. Working with principals in isolation puts a tremendous burden on people who are already overloaded; the involvement of the entire team in the training sends the clear message that all of the faculty shares responsibility for improvement as well as creates the opportunity for principals to learn how to involved other faculty members in shared decision-making.
- **Assign a team member to serve as "point" person** whose major responsibilities include making sure the whole team is knowledgeable and **uses** information in specific areas. Key planning and research areas needing a point person are: gathering and analyzing student outcomes, organizational change research, and research on effective staff development.
- Educators, especially those at the secondary level, need intensive **training** and support to develop and effectively **monitor student outcomes** data.
- Beware of the tendency for teams to focus on "doing something about the correlates" without ever **paying attention to student outcomes**. The correlates are only a vehicle toward the real goal of improved student performance; they should be viewed as inputs or strategies to help reach the **goal of improved student outcomes.**
- To avoid having correlate improvement become the major goal, **gather and analyze the student outcomes** data prior to administering the correlate assessment. **State all long-range improvement goals in terms of student performance indicators.** The correlate assessment may then be used to develop strategies to move you toward your improved student performance goals.
- A critical part of the early planning for schools and districts should include **reassessing current time commitments** and priorities so that time is made for school improvement activities. The district organizational patterns should be looked at closely early in the process so that time is used in the most focused and effective manner, and to ensure that the time used for school improvement programs is built into the organizational calendar, and is not viewed as an "add on" or voluntary.
- School improvement teams need to **select at least one short-term goal** that can be accomplish even before the plan is written. This gives them the chance to work cohesively and to demonstrate quickly to the rest of the faculty that changes can be accomplished. When teams wait until the entire plan is written before implementing any aspects of it, they often become frustrated and their peers question the purpose of the team.
- Make available **scheduled opportunities** throughout the year for all school teams from a district to meet with each other to share concerns and progress. The superintendent and district team should also meet with the teams several times to enhance communication and demonstrate support.
- In projects such as the MCEA-sponsored programs that involve several districts, teams from various districts **meet regularly** together to share progress and learn from each other.
- Though effective-teaching training models are important in building instructional leadership skills, **start the program with a framework of Effective Schools Research.** After the SI team has written the improvement plan, effective-instruction training can be added as a strategy within the plan. Attempting to introduce Effective Schools and effective-teaching research simultaneously proved confusing and too overwhelming a task for most participants in earlier projects.

References

Anderson, Beverly, et al. (1987). State strategies to support local school improvement. *Knowledge: creation, diffusion, utilization.* 9(1). 42–86.

Bloom, Benjamin, Hastings, J. Thomas, & Madares, George F. (1971). *Handbook on formative and summative evaluation of student learning.* New York: McGraw-Hill.

Dentinger, James. (1987). *A manual for the construction of domain referenced/criterion referenced tests.* Spencerport, N.Y.: Spencerport Central Schools.

Edmonds, Ronald. (1979). Effective schools for the urban poor. *Educational Leadership.* 37(1). 15–23.

Edmonds, Ronald. (1982a). On school improvement: A conversation with Ronald Edmonds. *Educational Leadership* 40. 15.

Edmonds, Ronald R. (1982b). Programs of school improvement: An overview. *Educational Leadership.* December. 4–11.

Edmonds, Ronald R. (1982c). *Programs of school improvement: An overview.* Unpublished paper. Michigan State University. Unpublished paper for presentation at the conference "The Implications of Research for Practice," Airlie House, Virginia. 20 pp.

Edmonds, Ronald R. (1983). Presentation to the Administrative Council, Spencerport Central School District, February 22.

Edmonds, Ronald & Lezotte, Lawrence. (1983). Presentation to the Leadership Planning Team, Spencerport Central School District, March 16.

Educational Research Service, Inc. (1983). *Effective Schools: A summary of research.* Arlington, Va.: Educational Research Service, Inc.

Ferris, Frank. (1982). *Adoption of Stanford Achievement Test and the Otis-Lennon School Ability Test.* Spencerport, N.Y.: Spencerport Central Schools, photocopied.

Frederiksen, John & Edmonds, Ronald. (about 1977) *Identification of instructionally effective and ineffective schools.* Cambridge, Mass.: Harvard University. Photocopied, no date.

Hall, Gene E. & Hord, Shirley M. (1987). *Changes in schools: Facilitating the process.* Albany, N.Y.: State University of New York Press.

Hord, Shirley M., Rutherford, William L., Hurling-Austin, Leslie & Hall, Gene E. (1987). *Taking charge of change.* Alexandria, Va.: Association for Supervision and Curriculum Development.

Huberman, A. Michael & Miles, Matthew B. (1984). *Innovation up close: How school improvement works.* New York: Plenum Press.

Lezotte, Lawrence W. & Bancroft, Beverly A. (1985). Growing use of the Effective Schools model for school improvement. *Educational Leadership.* March. 23–27.

Loucks-Horsley, Susan & Hergert, Leslie F. (1985). *An action guide to school improvement.* Alexandria, Va.: Association for Supervision and Curriculum Development.

Miles, M. B., Farrar, E., & Neufeld, B. (1983). *The extent of adoption of Effective Schools programs.* Vol. II of Review of Effective Schools Programs prepared for the National Commission on Excellence in Education. Cambridge, Ma.: The Huron Institute.

New York State School Improvement Program Guidebook. (1987). Albany, N.Y.: Office of District Superintendents, New York State Education Department, Albany, N.Y. 3.

Proctor, C. Patrick & Villanova, Robert M. (1984). *Handbook for the use of the Connecticut School Effectiveness Interview and Questionnaire.* Hartford, Conn.: Connecticut State Department of Education.

School Effectiveness: The six indicators and student achievement. (1985). Columbia, S.C.: College of Education, University of South Carolina. 8.

Seaburn, Bonnie & Sudlow, Robert. (1987). *Staff development plan.* Spencerport, N.Y.: Spencerport Central Schools, photocopied.

Seaburn, Bonnie & Sudlow, Robert. (1987). *Staff development implications of an Effective Schools project.* Spencerport, N.Y.: Spencerport Central Schools. ED 292-096.

Spencerport schools get project award. (1988). *Suburban News,* Spencerport, N.Y., July 12, p. 29A.

Sudlow, Robert E. (1983a). Disaggregated analysis. Spencerport, N.Y.: Spencerport Central Schools, Memo to Leadership Planning Team, June 17.

Sudlow, Robert E. (1983b). *Master Plan. More Effective Schools teaching project. Report of the Leadership Planning Team to the Superintendent of Schools.* Spencerport, N.Y.: Spencerport Central Schools, photocopied. ED 273 025.

Sudlow, Robert E. (1984a). Conducting an Effective Schools program, *The Effective School Report,* 2, 9-10-11. ED 273-026.

Sudlow, Robert E. (1984b). *More Effective Schools/Teaching Project: First Annual Report.* Spencerport, N.Y.: Spencerport Central Schools, photocopied.

Sudlow, Robert E. (1985). *What is an Effective School?* Spencerport, N.Y.: Spencerport Central Schools, photocopied. ED 273 035.

Sudlow, Robert E. (1987). *More Effective Schools/Teaching Project: Fourth Annual Report.* Spencerport, N.Y.: Spencerport Central Schools, photocopied.

Sudlow, Robert E. (1988a). *More Effective Schools/Teaching Project: Fifth Annual Report.* Spencerport, N.Y.: Spencerport Central Schools, photocopied.

Sudlow, Robert E. (1988b). *Using a microcomputer to compute a disaggregated analysis.* Spencerport, N.Y.: Spencerport Central Schools, photocopied.

Sudlow, Robert E. and Werth, Terry L. S. (1988). *Finding time to teach.* Spencerport, N.Y.: Spencerport Central Schools, photocopied.

Villanova, Robert M. (1984). *A comparison of interview and questionnaire techniques used in the Connecticut School Effectiveness Project: A report of work in progress.* Paper presented at the Annual Meeting of the American Educational Research Association, New Orleans, Louisiana.

Werth, Terry L. S. (1988). *Teacher reactions to the More Effective Schools/Teaching Project.* Spencerport, N.Y.: Spencerport Central Schools, photocopied.

Wooley, Sandra L. (1987). *The meaning of change to teachers: A case study of a district-wide Effective Schools project.* Syracuse, N.Y.: School of Education, Syracuse University. Dissertation Proposal, photocopied, pp. 9–10.

Lessons Learned

Lawrence W. Lezotte, Ph.D.

Lessons Learned

Lawrence W. Lezotte

In the preceding chapters the reader was presented with series of "portraits" of local schools as they have implemented and continue to implement programs of school improvement based on the Effective Schools Research. Each of the districts portrayed in the case studies was asked to organize their story from an outline that was provided. (See *Appendix A & B*.)

The outline was not designed to constrain the authors, rather it was intended to direct the authors to those questions most frequently asked by both researchers and other practitioners. The outline also allowed us to "look across the cases" for the lessons that have been learned through those experiences. These case studies have retained the authors' styles and tell the stories as they were perceived to have occurred by those directly involved. They represent portraits of improvement from the view of the practitioners who daily faced the challenges of school improvement. The case studies are truly examples of work in progress and therefore any lessons learned might be thought of as "craft knowledge" about the school change process.

The good news seems to be that certain identifiable trends appear and, for the most part, these trends tend to parallel the findings reported in the school-change literature (See the *Introduction*). While the trends are not exhaustive they do allow others to have greater confidence in the Effective Schools Research, to proceed with programs of school improvement based on it, and most importantly, to increase their sense of efficacy about successfully planning and implementing their own program of school improvement based on the research.

Perhaps the proper context for describing the trends that emerge in the cases is to point out that in each case study, certain Effective Schools concepts provided the underlying structure for the school improvement process. The themes tend to be those most frequently associated with the Effective Schools Research. They include a focus on quality and equity, on seeking observable or measurable results, on the school site as the critical unit for the ongoing change process, on the empowerment of school-based professionals for the purpose of taking charge of change, and on data-driven monitoring and analysis of current organizational functions. The reader should also notice that no two schools or districts addressed these themes in precisely the same way. In other words, there are many variations on these themes, and it is through the local process of adaptation that each district and individual school develops the ownership and commitment necessary to initiate and sustain this long-term and incremental process.

What are the lessons to be learned from the analysis of the case studies?

Lesson 1. Planning and implementing programs of school improvement does not follow a recipe or formula.

Local schools or districts that may contemplate using the ESR framework to guide this school process must recognize that the ESR framework is neither a "project" nor a "program." Rather, it is better viewed as a *process,* a way of thinking about and looking at our schools as changing and changeable organizations. This means that it cannot simply be implemented as a "pre-packaged program" as has been so often alleged by many of the critics of the Effective Schools process.

Lesson 2. School improvements based on Effective Schools Research has been successfully demonstrated in a variety of organizational settings.

One of the more powerful statements that can be made about the ESR framework after one reads the case studies is the generalizability of the ESR framework. In the early years, a common criticism of the Effective Schools Research was that it was conducted mainly in urban elementary settings serving concentrated populations of poor and economically disadvantaged minority students. This led many of the critics to conclude that the process of school improvement based on the research would only be possible in those settings. These case studies clear away that erroneous notion. Some cases talk about large school districts that are urban, often poor and minority, and others describe suburban, almost rural, non-disadvantaged districts. The cases described programs that have worked in lower as well as higher achieving districts. They speak about successful change in elementary, middle, and high school settings. They speak about all regions of the country: North, South, East, and West. It would be hard to imagine after reading these case studies, districts where the ESR framework would not be relevant.

Lesson 3. The participating districts have outcome evidence to substantiate their claims that their schools and the district are improving.

In soliciting the case study materials each author was expected to provide evidence that students were, in fact, the beneficiaries of the school improvement effort and not merely the teachers or administrators. Like the model itself, the evidence of results comes in many forms. Some districts have relied heavily on standardized, norm-referenced measures of student achievement, at the same time acknowledging the limitations of such measures. Others have focused on state-wide, criterion-referenced measures because of political considerations and because the districts could align their instructional programs to these measurements more easily. Some districts found it more desirable to develop their own curriculum-based, criterion-referenced measurement system to augment the other systems already in place. However, all districts measured student performance.

Measurement issues are of major concern in education in the United States today. The Effective Schools-based districts seem to be a little ahead of some in coming to terms with the complexity of the issue. These case studies illustrate that those educators recognize the power that is conveyed in the concept "what gets measured gets done" in a complex organization. These districts are well aware of the limitations of measuring only basic and lower-level skills. They are addressing this concern by facing head-on the development of higher-level teaching and seeking additional assessment strategies.

The case studies describe districts and schools that have the courage to "confront" the measurement issues. They are striving to instill in their districts the following tenet: for schools to become effective and remain so, teachers must believe in their head, heart, and "gut" that if they teach the intended curriculum and the students learn it, the students will do well on the measures of achievement. Teachers in most schools today do not share this belief, and as a result, institutional anxiety is severe and pervasive. The schools that are implementing the Effective Schools framework are a bit closer to it and are therefore leading the nation.

More than anything else the Effective Schools framework requires schools and districts to assume ownership of student achievement and the problems that go with it. The case studies describe a set of districts which have stopped blaming low achievement on the low achiever. The empowerment that serves to sustain the Effective Schools process often comes when the participating schools see that they can achieve greater success for more of their students if they are committed to doing so.

Lesson 4. While school improvement occurs school-by-school and one school at a time, support from a central office (that itself is restructured toward school improvement) significantly increases the likelihood of sustained positive change.

In varying ways, each case study verifies Ronald Edmonds' belief that when it comes to school improvement, there are no unimportant adults in the organization. Early attempts to bypass the central office and local board of education proved to be an unintended mistake. These cases illustrate the power of *total organizational alignment* toward the overall organizational mission of teaching for learning for all. Probably the single most revealing indicator of total integration of the organization for school improvement is the level of direct and active involvement evidenced by the superintendent. A second powerful indicator relates to school board and community involvement. The extent to which policies, resources, and program evaluation discussions begin to focus on the issue of more effective schools and school improvement indicates how soon the culture of the organization will begin to shift toward the aims and purposes stated in that mission.

Additionally, the cases suggest the need to decentralize decision-making and move closer to a site-based management model. The evidence indicates that this management strategy will serve the interests of school improvement if, and only if, principals and school-based collaborative groups of teachers are properly trained to function in this manner. As suggested by the cases, the cost of successfully implementing this process is not excessive. However, all available staff development resources need to be harnessed and channeled to assure maximum impact.

Lesson 5. Ultimately, personnel evaluation systems must be aligned with the values of the school improvement program and they should be growth-oriented.

Several case studies show that changes in the way central office, principals, and even the superintendent were evaluated called into play the values inherent in the Effective Schools process. For obvious reasons, one cannot expect people to take risks and behave differently if old systems and outdated criteria are used to evaluate staff and administrators. Perhaps the place to begin this alignment process is to alter the basis on which the superintendent is evaluated by the board of education. In several cases, it was clear to all that superintendents had deliberately "put themselves on the line" on behalf of school improvement. When this happens everyone in the organization realizes that school improvement is "real." As more superintendents are hired to lead school improvement and as more are let go because they cannot lead school improvement, a whole new set of norms, beliefs, and expectations will develop.

Lesson 6. Teacher improvement can work if the mission is clear and if time and other resources are available to support school-based planning and training processes.

The most frequent concern expressed by teachers is the lack of time available for school improvement. In the case studies, the issue of time was always in the background. The best results were realized when the board of education made the hard decision to allocate resources to support school-based planning and staff development time. When one tries to alter the actions and behaviors of an organization as complex as a school, allocating resources for retraining becomes essential to program success. The case studies reflect the lesson we all need to learn from our private sector colleagues: improvement and change are not free; maintaining the status quo is free because the forces of institutional inertia will tend to have us repeat past behaviors. Change is deliberate, technical, and consumes time and other resources. On the other hand, no school district reported spending more than one percent of its resources on the improvement process—a real bargain indeed.

Lesson 7. Perceptional surveys of the characteristics of Effective Schools when coupled with other indicators of strengths and weaknesses provide a valid basis for school-based planning and school improvement.

When the faculty of a school has been appropriately oriented regarding Effective Schools research and when they understand how school-based data are to be used to promote improvement, they seem able and willing to provide honest assessment of the school's strengths and weaknesses. Each of the case studies used some type of data-gathering instruments to inform the building level planning process. While the surveys were similar, each district tended to "fine-tune" an instrument to its own context. Again, this process tends to increase understanding and commitment to the results which flow from its use.

Two points should be stressed. First, the particular survey and other data-gathering strategies should remain true to the Effective Schools Research and not simply represent the beliefs of someone in the research office. Second, the data should not be used in a mechanical way, rather these survey data need to provide the basis for both reflection and sustained discourse before conclusions are drawn.

Lesson 8. Schools and districts need to explore more and better ways of bringing research into the school-based discourse on school improvement.

In the case studies, the participating districts were challenged to be creative in thinking about efficient and effective ways of informing school-based practitioners of their research findings. One limitation of the school-based model is that school improvement teams often have difficulty looking beyond their own experiences in formulating an action strategy to respond to an identified need. Though collective experience is often powerful enough to solve the local problems of a school, new ideas from research should be an integral part of the discussion process. Make no mistake, research does not improve schools—people do. At the same time those people have an obligation to themselves as professionals to review continually research and practice related to what works in teaching their students.

Lesson 9. School improvement is a complex and ongoing process that requires patience and persistence.

The case studies indicate that there are few, if any, quick fixes when it comes to enduring school change. Staff members need to be mentally prepared for the "long haul," otherwise they will become discouraged quickly. A strategy that seems to help involves celebrating small successes at both the school and district levels. People need to realize that progress is being made even though larger, longer-term goals may still be some distance away. In education, we often do not recognize the impact that celebrations can have in sustaining the effort and to maintaining the focus around the core values associated with school improvement.

Lesson 10. The Effective Schools process works best when schools and districts disaggregate and publicly display their student performance data.

These districts emphasized repeatedly the need for disaggregating measured or observed student outcome data. This process differs from place to place, but when it is done and discussed it forces institutional attention to be directed toward the issues of equity. Publication of outcomes makes it difficult to ignore the mission of teaching for learning for all.

We are learning more about the processes of working efficiently and effectively with student performance data. As we gain more experience we will be able to streamline the procedures by taking full advantage of computer technologies that are already available.

The key to the success of this analysis process is to choose performance indicators (See Appendix) that accurately reflect the core values of the organization. Too often, data are extensively analyzed because they are available, not because they are "carriers of the values" of the schools. It would be better to focus on fewer and even less refined measurements if the ones selected are closer to the vital signs—values—of the organization's culture.

Summary

These ten lessons are illustrated across the case studies. The National Center for Effective Schools Research and Development has as one of its goals not only to continue to monitor programs in these districts, but also to add new districts to the "data base" for our applied research on planned change. As more is learned, we believe we can make a significant contribution to school improvement by helping others to apply this knowledge to their own processes of school improvement based on the Effective Schools Research process.

Glossary

Accountability: The shared responsibility of the educational community (district and schools) to teach all children and be held to specific valid and reliable measures and standards of student performance outcomes. If all students are to succeed at the next level of study, they must be required to obtain certain knowledge and skills, agreed upon by teachers and administrators, and supported by parents and citizens. The locus of responsibility for successful academic achievement of all students is with the teacher. The principal and district need to support the classroom teacher in his or her efforts and they all should be held accountable for results.

Active learning time, time-on-task, engaged time, allocated time: These terms refer to time spent by students in classrooms interacting with each other and/or their teacher in didactic activity. The following figure illustrates the relationship of these concepts:

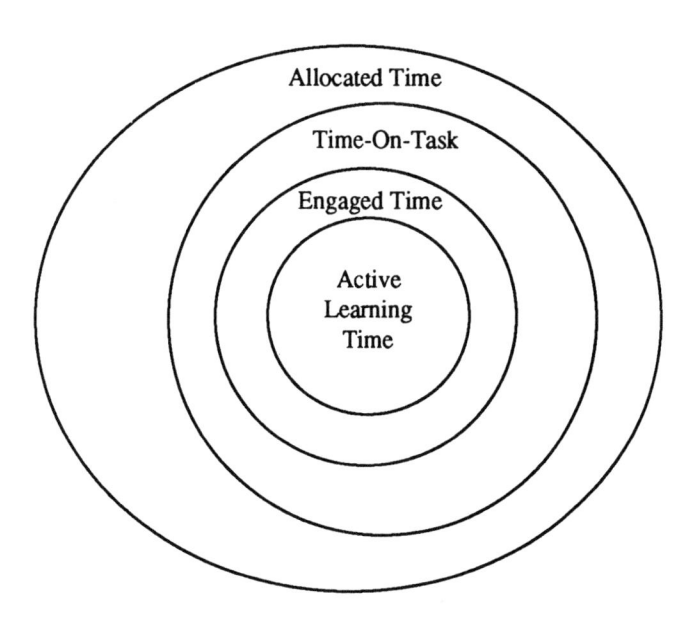

After Harnischfeger and Wiley, 1981 and Berliner, 1984.
© National Center for Effective Schools Research and Development and Barbara O. Taylor, Ph.D.

Allocated time is that time scheduled each day for a learning unit or activity. **Time-on-task** is that amount of time students are actually working on or thinking about the subject matter and the understanding it may require. In the graph, allocated time and time-on-task are shown not to be directly proportional at all times. This is because teacher variables and student variables interact to preclude a relationship which is always symmetrical. The same asymmetrical relationship is obviously the case for allocated time and time-on-task, and a greater discrepancy in proportion can be present. **Engaged time** is the period of time where student concentration is intense and the possibility for learning and acquisition of skills is greatest. **Active learning time** is that portion of time when actual learning and/or acquisition of knowledge and practice of skills is taking place.

Assertive discipline: A discipline plan that requires students to match their behavior to a set of rules predetermined by the school faculty and individual teacher and posted in the classroom. The process provides due process as well as emphasizing the importance of reinforcement of acceptable behavior. (see Lee Canter, *Educational Leadership,* October 1988.)

At-risk students: Students who, often because of a disadvantaged (i.e. multi-problem family, poverty, child abuse, drug abuse) background, tend to fall behind in basic skills and studies, and have a high probability of dropping out of school by ninth or tenth grade. Often defined by educators to include those students who are two years behind in reading by the sixth grade (Kyle, 1985), and/or who have high absentee rates and low grades in second, third, and fourth grade (Hess, et al., 1989). The later attributes together (low grades plus absenteeism) predict with .90 accuracy that the student will drop-out in high-school.

Baseline data: "Pre-test" or pre-intervention data: Outcome measurements gathered at the beginning of the school improvement process against which future outcome data can be compared. Also used in Effective Schools planning at school and district level.

Bloom's Taxonomy: Benjamin S. Bloom's two-volume *Taxonomy of Educational Objectives* (McKay, 1974) was designed to 1) describe thinking skills from lower level comprehension or recall to higher level thinking skills of analysis, synthesis, and evaluation, and 2) describe affective educational objectives. This was the first time an educational researcher had made a comprehensive taxonomy of educational objectives, and these two volumes are now classics and universally referred to.

California Achievement Test (CAT): This test, the Stanford Achievement Test, and the Iowa Test of Basic Skills are the three most widely used standardized, norm-referenced achievement tests for assessing student performance in the United States.

Comprehensive assessment: A complete evaluation or appraisal of educational outcomes of teaching-learning criteria, program criteria, or policy criteria. Used to determine the state of educational quality and equity in these categories in order to make decisions at the classroom, school, or district level. The criteria and standards (level of accomplishment in each criterion) should be agreed upon by teachers and administrators before the comprehensive assessment takes place.

Comprehensive Test of Basic Skills (CTBS): A standardized norm-referenced achievement test given in elementary and secondary schools.

Cooperative Learning: A cooperative learning group usually consists of two to five students who work together for a common purpose—to complete a task and to include every member of the heterogeneous group. This program was authored by David W. Johnson and Roger T. Johnson and is taught in staff development programs.

Correlate assessment: Perception data usually provided from questionnaires/interviews that describe the relative presence of the seven school characteristics found in highly effective schools. Data from these assessments are used as an information base for determining how to improve the quality and equity of student outcomes.

Correlates: School characteristics that researchers have found to be present in schools that effectively teach all children. These characteristics become part of the language for carrying on the discourse of school improvement and include: clear and focused mission, strong instructional leadership, positive learning climate, high expectations for success, opportunity to learn and time on task, frequent monitoring of student performances, and positive home/school relations.

Criterion-referenced test/Curricular-based testing; Criterion-referenced tests are designed to assess whether a student has mastered the taught subject matter that is specified in the written curriculum.

Culture: The behavioral norms, organizational structures, beliefs, shared values, and attitudes of a school or district which distinguishes it. The culture defines "the way to do things around here." Effective Schools are characterized by cohesive cultural norms with the central belief that schools can create the conditions which promote learning of the intended curriculum by all students.

Curriculum alignment: Through this process the written curriculum is matched to the taught-and-tested teaching objectives in a school, school district, or state.

Data-driven decisions: A key premise of the Effective Schools framework which focuses on the use of student outcome data and correlate assessment data to drive decisions related to improvement activities.

Disaggregation: A term used by researchers of Effective Schools to describe the process for analyzing outcome data by student subgroups within a school or district (e.g., gender, socioeconomic status, race-ethnicity) to determine the school's effectiveness in serving all children.

Empowerment: The investment of authority, responsibility, information and knowledge to the most appropriate and effective level of decision-making. To accomplish empowerment, district and school professionals must be provided programs of skill development, time, and materials to do the job well (Kanter, R. M., 1983) (Pink, 1990, in press).

Equity: The degree of fairness of the educational program in providing learning opportunities to all students, and making available and accessible the intended curriculum to all students. Equity is measured by the disaggregated distribution of student achievement scores on tests, preferably criterion-referenced tests, as well as on other student outcome measures such as attendance, tardiness, suspensions, and discipline infractions.

Equal opportunity to learn flows from these process concepts and from the content of the curriculum, and includes those alterable variables in classroom teaching which determine the requisite information and skills acquired by students to achieve mastery at successive levels of education (Carroll, 1963; Bloom, 1968, 1984; Harnischfeger and Wiley, 1981).

Frequent monitoring: The frequent assessment of student academic performance through the design and use of a timely and accurate student monitoring system to aid teachers in planning for remedial, accelerated, and enriched instruction.

Gates-MacGinitie Reading Test: Individual or small group reading achievement test commonly administered in elementary and middle schools.

High expectations: The organizational structures of the school and the attitudes and behaviors of the staff that reflect a belief that all children can learn and that the staff has the capacity to teach all children.

Instructional leadership: Leadership which gives direction, emphasis, and support to the school's instructional program and inspires others to work within the school's central "teaching for learning for all" mission. Instructional leaders are often teachers, support staff, and central office staff as well as principals.

Instructional Theory Into Practice (ITIP): Training which provides teachers and administrators the opportunity to review and apply researched effective instructional techniques within their classrooms and schools.

Iowa Test of Basic Skills: (Similar to the Comprehensive Test of Basic Skills). See California Achievement Test (CAT).

J-Curve: A mathematical expression of achievement that illustrates that most students can learn most things, most of the time. Unlike the traditional bell shaped curve, the J-curve shows gradations of student achievement, including failure, as "normal and acceptable," and targets areas of re-teaching for mastery.

Mastery learning: A model of learning in which all but a very few students are expected to achieve over time the mastery of predetermined subject matter and skills.

Measured student outcomes: The learning behaviors and skills of students which are taught as the intended curriculum and occur as a result of the instructional process. Different assessment processes are used, including testing, to discover the extent of change (short-term or long-term) of learning behaviors of each student.

Metropolitan Achievement Test: (Similar to Comprehensive Test of Basic Skills)

Mission: A charge to a school or district. A statement of what the school/district is striving to become, written in measurable, observable terms which can be operationalized for planning, implementation, and evaluation purposes.

Restructuring: Reforming the interrelationships of an organization to achieve a stated goal. A strategy used to analyze and redesign the current organization, its systems, roles, and reporting relationships in order to achieve desired student outcomes. In the classroom a teacher **restructures** the teaching-learning process by using a variety of teaching strategies and materials, and by reallocating time in order to facilitate learning for all students.

School-based management, site-based management, or site-based improvement: All are terms which describe the governance process and procedures which make day-to-day decision-making at the school building level work. School-based management (SBM) is a form of district organization and management in which the school and its community system is the key unit for day-to-day decision making and for school change and improvement. The SBM decisions are made collaboratively with faculty contribution, and the working structure of the school council or committee is decided upon by the principal and faculty, often with representation from citizens and parents.

School community relations: The dedication of school personnel to communicate with and involve parents and the community in roles that materially affect the school's ability to teach all children.

School improvement process: A long-term, outcomes driven and collegial process designed to create cultural and structural changes within the school that lead to student success. This process is usually led by a school improvement team which analyzes data and develops and implements an improvement plan.

School improvement team: A cross-section of personnel within the school that has been empowered to lead the improvement process and to work collaboratively with the entire staff to improve the conditions that contribute to student success. Part of the school-based management process, it often includes parent and citizen representatives.

School learning climate: The attitudes and practices within a school that affect the overall satisfaction and productivity of students and staff. A positive school climate evolves from a commonly agreed upon school mission and is characterized as safe, orderly, and business-like, conducive to learning and free from emotional and physical harm.

Socioeconomic status (SES): The socioeconomic status or background from which a child comes may serve to stereotype the school's expectations for learning by that child, and therefore the child may not perform to his/her potential. In these cases the school must have a way to track outcome data of student performance which identifies children from low SES backgrounds. Also the school must identify students who may lack educational resources in their homes. Ronald Edmonds' early research identified several variables which are a school's best indicators of SES. The two most common ones used are the mother's educational level (Has she graduated from high school?) and eligibility for free and reduced lunch. SES is a key variable used for disaggregating student achievement data.

TESA: Teacher Expectations Student Achievement: A training program to help educators to become aware of the research on how teacher expectations affect student achievement, and to develop pedagogical skills to increase teacher effectiveness in the classroom.

Time-on-task: See **Active learning time.**

Writing across the curricular program: A holistic approach to teaching writing through the context of each subject matter in the curriculum.

Writing to Read (IBM): A computer program set up in a learning computer lab or classroom that allows elementary students to develop writing skills in conjunction with a total language arts approach. Students work individually and in small groups.

References for the Glossary

Berliner, David. *Using What We Know about Teaching*. (Alexandria, VA: Association for Supervision and Curriculum Development, 1984).

Bloom, Benjamin. "Learning for Mastery," in *Evaluation Comment*, 1968, volume one, number 2, pp. 1–12 (UCLA–CSEIP).

Bloom, Benjamin. *A Taxonomy of Educational Objectives*. (New York: McKay, 1974).

Bloom, Benjamin. "The Search for Methods of Group Instruction as Effective as One-to-One Tutoring," in *Educational Leadership*, volume 41, number 8, pp. 4–18 (Association for Supervision and Curriculum Development, Alexandria, VA).

Canter, Lee. "Let the Educator Beware: A Response to Gerwin and Mendler," in *Educational Leadership*, volume 46, number 2, pp. 71–73 (Association for Supervision and Curriculum Development, Alexandria, VA).

Carroll, John. "A Model for School Learning," in *Teacher's College Record*, 1963, volume 64, pp. 723–733.

Harnischfeger, Annagret, and Wiley, David E. "Origins of Active Learning Time." (Evanston, Illinois: M–L Group for Policy Studies in Education, October, 1981). (Photocopied.)

Hess, Alfred; Lyons, Arthur; Corsino, Lou; and Wells, Emily. *Against the Odds: Early Identification of Drop-Outs*. (Chicago Panel on Public School Policy and Finance, June, 1989).

Kanter, Rosabeth Moss. *The Change Masters*. (University of Chicago Press, 1983) Chapter 7.

Kyle, Charles. Quoted in *Drop-outs in Chicago Public Schools*. (Chicago Panel on Public School Policy and Finance, 1985).

Pink, William. "Staff Development for Urban School Improvement: Lessons Learned from Two Case Studies," in *School Effectiveness and Improvement: an International Journal* (Creemers, Burt and Reynolds, David, editors. The Netherlands, Volume 1, in press in 1990).

Appendix: A

NATIONAL CENTER FOR EFFECTIVE SCHOOLS
RESEARCH AND DEVELOPMENT
2199 Jolly Road, Suite 160
Okemos, Michigan 48864
(517) 349-8841

March 28, 1988

Dear Colleague:

As you probably know, we have been busy developing the new national Center for Effective Schools Research and Development. We are pleased to report that the Center is now in operation and has three major program thrusts: research and development, training and technical assistance, and networking and conferencing. The purpose of this letter is to invite you and your colleagues to participate in one of our exciting programs.

A priority project of the Center is a monograph which contains descriptions of programs such as yours, where the effective schools process has worked. We plan to publish such a monograph by approximately September, 1988. We are hoping you can help us in this endeavor.

We would like to invite you and your colleagues to tell your story and celebrate your success. Many school district staffs around the country will not only be stimulated by your success, but also will benefit greatly by using your expertise to guide them through the complex processes associated with a planned change program.

Attached is a brief outline of the proposed monograph. We have set July 1, 1988 as the deadline for receiving your chapters. If you are unable to contribute to this monograph effort, please inform us in writing.

The monograph will be available from the Center at cost of production. If any profit is realized, it will be used by the Center to support future publication. In return for your assistance, we are offering you or your designee an honorarium of $500 for the manuscript, **or** fifty copies of the finished monograph for you to distribute. If neither of these options seem appropriate, please tell us in what alternative way we may recognize your efforts.

We sincerely hope you will be able to accept this invitation. Other schools and various research projects will benefit greatly from the lessons this monograph can teach all of us. Most importantly, we believe that with your contributions, we will illustrate that more children are being better served as a result of the effective schools program.

Respectfully,

Lawrence W. Lezotte, PhD
Director

Beverly A. Bancroft, PhD
Associate Director

BAB/mja
Enclosures

Appendix: B

Successful Effective Schools Research and School

Improvement Plans

Triumphs of
Leadership and Empowerment

National Center for Effective Schools
Research and Development
1988

The Proposed Monograph will be organized as follows:*

The **Preface** will create the purpose and context for the monograph contents. It will highlight featured case studies as examples of programs of school improvement based on the Effective Schools Research (ESR) which have, over time, evidenced successful results. These results have indicated measurable progress for growing numbers of public school students from all subsets of the school population.

Chapter One will be an overview of Effective Schools Research and an analysis of how the Framework is applied to programs of school improvement. It will be written by Dr. L. W. Lezotte and Dr. B. A. Bancroft.

Chapters Two through Thirteen will be individual case summaries written by program participants. The descriptions will generally follow the attached outline. The exact number of chapters will depend on the responses of school staffs who wish to contribute. Case summaries are to be limited to 25 pages. They should cover such questions as "How have the implementations and changes occurred?," "How have these changes affected the progress of students and the culture of the school?"

Chapter Fourteen will be a summary entitled, "Reflections and Implications." It will outline the question "What has been learned so far from these successful programs of school improvement?"

---

*Editor's Note: This is the original plan for organization. The present editors changed the format slightly once the case studies had been analyzed in order to clarify and compare the findings of the study.

Suggested Outline for Case Summaries
(each should be 25 pages or *less*, double spaced)

Title: Please include the name of the school district in the title or sub-title.

Authors: Please give complete credit for authorship of this case summary to key program personnel who contributed expertise and commitment to the program. This kind of credit can be included inside the case study.

1. *Brief Overview of the Effective Schools Program*

    A. What are the demographic characteristics of the district?
    B. What was the motivation for launching the program?
    C. When was it launched?
    D. Who were the key leaders?
    E. In general terms, what has been the level of funding needed to sustain the effort?
    F. How has the program been supported financially, symbolically, and with professional time, over its history?
    G. What has been, and is now, the source of funding for the program, both internal or external? (If not described before, please describe here.)

2. *What evidence does the district have that the schools are improving?*

    A. Measured Student Outcomes
        1. Norm Referenced Assessments
        2. Criterion Referenced Assessments
        3. Other Student Data (i.e. attendance rates, grades, percentage graduating, etc.)
    B. What documented changes are noted in the strength and presence of the Correlates of Effective Schools?
    C. What other organizational or personnel-related data suggest that the schools have improved? Use tables, charts, graphs or short descriptions to portray the findings.

3. How has the Effective School Process influenced the following program components?

   A. the curriculum
   B. program implementation
   C. program evaluation
   D. staff evaluation
   E. position descriptions
   F. community attitudes
   G. service and funding agencies
   H. recognition of the instructional process
   I. other areas not included here

4. How does the Effective Schools Process affect the way student achievement is measured?

   A. disaggregated data
   B. development of curriculum-based testing
   C. development of criterion-referenced tests

5. If professional and general staff development programs have changed or been modified as a result of the Effective Schools thrust, describe why and/or how.

6. Describe the components of the Effective Schools Planning Process.

   A. Is there a district-level coordinating team?
   B. What has been the involvement of the Superintendent, Teachers, Board, Central Office Administrators, and Parent or Student Groups in the program?
   C. Do individual schools have school-based teams? Do they develop individual school long-range plans?

7. How has the personnel evaluation system changed as a result of the Effective Schools Program?

8. What has developed in relation to the Effective Schools Process and not mentioned above, that might bear upon the following?

   A. policies
   B. procedures
   C. practices
   D. other

9. *What problems, issues, or concerns did your program encounter and how were they overcome?*

   A. external mandates
   B. community changes
   C. budget cuts
   D. other factors

10. *If your school district had it to do over again, knowing what you now know, what might you do differently? In other words, what advise might you give other schools just initiating school improvement?*

11. *Summary*

Note: The manuscript received will be adjusted to assure readers a similar format for the case summaries. The reworked draft will be forwarded to your authors for editing and approval.

Appendix: C

Some Performance Indicators used by Effective Schools Districts:

Standardized Norm-referenced Achievement Test Scores (disaggregated)

State-wide Criterion-referenced Test Scores

District-made Criterion-referenced Test Scores

Teacher-made (district or school-wide) Criterion-referenced Test Scores

Advanced Placement (high schools)

Student Promotion/Retention Data (disaggregated)

Student Discipline Infractions

Student Suspension/Expulsion Rates (disaggregated)

Vandalism Reports

Drug and Alcohol Abuse

Student Attendance

Student Tardiness

Staff Absenteeism

Staff Efficacy/Organizational Health/School Climate

Staff Perceptions of School Improvement Accomplishments (including Correlate Assessments)

Student Drop-out Rates (high schools)

Graduating Students' Attitudes

Student Employment Data (while attending high school and after high school)

Post-secondary Student Matriculation Data

Career Objectives

Physical Fitness of Students, Staff

Extracurricular Activities, Student Participation

Student Self-Esteem

Quality and Quantity of Student Homework

Parental Involvement

Supporting/Empowering Organizational Structures in Place and Functioning:

    Student Monitoring System
    Staff Development System
    Curricular Development System
    Discipline System